ANIMATION
AND 3D MODELING ON THE MAC

don and melora foley

Peachpit Press

Animation and 3D Modeling on the Mac
Don and Melora Foley

Peachpit Press
2414 Sixth Street
Berkeley, CA 94710
510/548-4393
510/548-5991 (fax)

Find us on the World Wide Web at:
http://www.peachpit.com

Peachpit Press is a division of Addison-Wesley Publishing Company.

Cover design by Don Foley
Set in Helvetica Condensed Light
Imagesetting by Advanced Laser Graphics, Washington, D.C.

ISBN 0-201-88420-8

9 8 7 6 5 4 3 2 1

Manufactured in Hong Kong by Everbest Printing Company

*for Savannah and Virginia,
the most animated
characters we know.*

TABLE OF CONTENTS

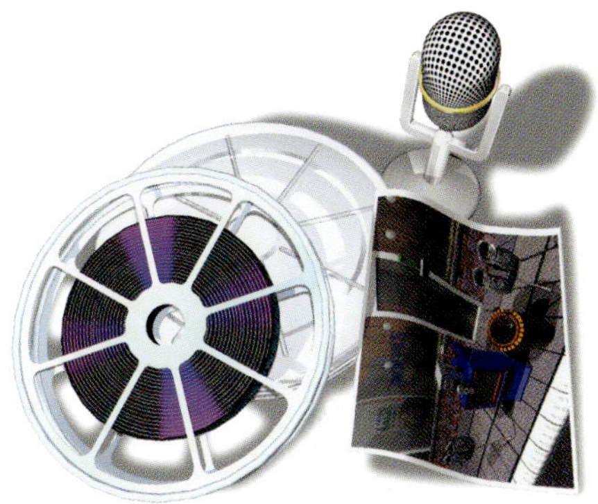

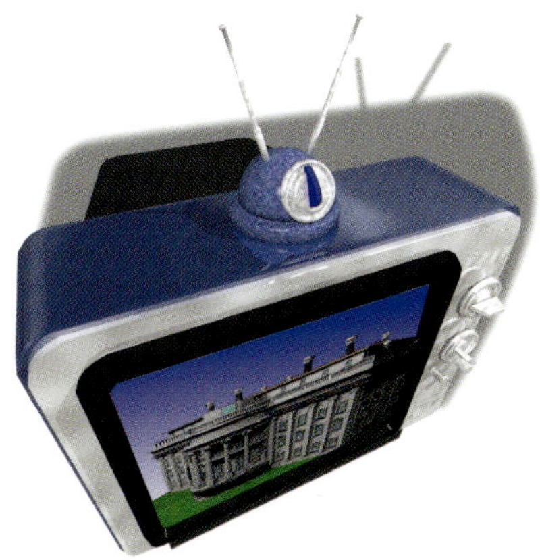

PREPARING IMAGES FOR PRINT
BACK OF THE BOOK STUFF

ACKNOWLEDGMENTS

Creating a book like this would have been impossible if not for companies that make high-end 3D animation effects possible for individuals and companies with low-end budgets. Most of the software packages explored in this book can be purchased for less than $1,000, many for less than $500. By comparison, the next step up from a Macintosh-based system is a Silicon Graphics workstation with 3D software packages costing $30,000. Therefore, we would like to thank Adobe (Photoshop, Illustrator, Premiere), Alias (Sketch!), form•Z (auto•des•sys), Macromedia (MacroModel, Three-D, Director, Swivel 3D Pro), Ray Dream (Designer, JAG II), Specular (Infini-D), Strata (StrataVision 3D, StrataVirtual 3D StudioPro) and VIDI (Presenter Pro) for their help and guidance in putting this book together.

We would also like to thank our friend and associate Dale Glasgow for clearing a path to our publisher's agent and Graphic-sha, who signed off on the book concept and gave us the freedom and time needed to complete this project.

Directly or indirectly many people have served as teachers or mentors guiding us to the point we are now. Without their unknowing help, this book would not exist. They are: Dee Lucas, John Allen, John O'Conner, Jeff Tudeen, Rob Oglesby, Howard Finberg, George Rorick, Bill Baker, Dennis Haas, Hugh Cunningham, Jean Chance, Alan Weinstein, Jan Belcher and the late Harry Stapler. Much of this book was created while our childcare assistants played with and otherwise entertained our children downstairs.

And of course, our parents for giving birth to and raising us in the first place.

INTRODUCTION

Photos this page courtesy of The MITRE Corporation Archives.

In the early 1950s, MIT's Whirlwind project computer filled an entire room. The photo (above) shows Whirlwind team members behind the supercomputer control center that had less computing power than the Mac sitting on your desk. This project was groundbreaking for the field of computer animation.

Writing and illustrating a 3D animation book presents certain challenges. The bulk of the material deals with 3D objects in motion. While books tend to be flat and static when providing insights into the dynamic world of computer modeling and animation, they do have the advantage of providing crisp resolution and instant information access.

To that end, we have developed a format that will guide the new user through the often confusing world of 3D animation. Building animations tends to be a hodgepodge of programs, images, concepts and theories, so we have built this book in tight, modular packages that offer basic concepts as well as advanced tips.

Example: Reviewing the Photoshop pages will help you establish textures to use with procedures in the "Tiled Texture" section. Later, you might use those textures on a lathe shape as described in "Lathed Objects."

Building and animating models tends to be a very nonlinear, free-for-all process. With that in mind, this book is designed so each section stands well on its own so that the user can skip through it as needed.

Determining the intended readership was also a challenge. While many animators use

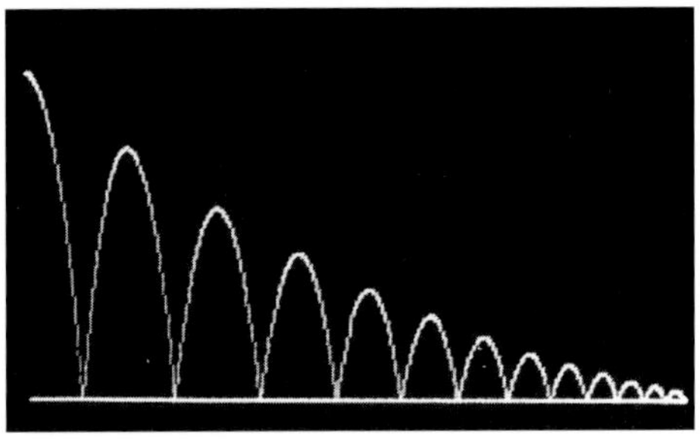

Bouncing ball! This was one of the first computer animations, thanks to the computer shown at top. This image was produced by the MIT team in 1951.

WHAT YOU NEED TO KNOW TO USE THIS BOOK

In many instances, this book is program generic. The reason for this is that many concepts cross software borders when dealing with 3D animation. Example: All modeling programs support lathed objects. The programs may implement the creation of a lathed object in different ways, but the basic concept and results are identical.

To make optimum use of this book, you need to have a fundamental understanding of your software package. Completing the program tutorial is the best way to learn the basics.

To dive into the tips and techniques presented in this book you must be able to:

- Create and edit a simple form.
- Navigate in your 3D world.
- Edit and apply surface textures.
- Use either your built-in animation sequence creation tools or a separate animation program.
- Render an image from a model.

The more you understand your program, the more you will get from this book.

The fun in building models and creating animations is experimenting and pushing the programs to their limits. No matter which modeling and animation package you choose, you are most likely going to be frustrated and overwhelmed at first. That is OK. It is even expected.

Only by understanding your program can you give yourself the freedom to fly. Read the software manual.

the programs mentioned in this book, the range of the projects they work on is fantastic and very specialized. Animators use these software tools to illustrate a variety of things – such as medical procedures, sales presentations, training tapes, games, architectural designs and industrial applications. The ever-improving quality of the software combined with the affordability and speed of personal computers has made 3D animation available across the board, from the hobbyist to the professional commercial animator.

In the first years of computer animation the scientists, not artists, dominated the field. They used the power of Crays and VAX's to help illustrate scientific calculations. In the early 1980s, the film industry began to cut its teeth on feature computer animation with movies like *TRON*–a box-office failure–and *The Last Starfighter*–a marginal box-office success. Still, these animations required a huge amount of computational power that was only available by tapping into the room-sized, supercomputers of that time.

Over the years, products from hardware and software companies like Silicon Graphics and Pixar made industrial and broadcast animation affordable, but it was the personal computer revolution that made animation available to the masses.

Early Macintoshes with CPUs running at 8mhz could not cope with the pace of 3D rendering, and early attempts at animation were reminiscent of flipbooks that students drew in high school art classes. As the Macintosh evolved, so did its processing capabilities and the addition of floating-point processors (FPUs) allowed the Mac to handle the math-intensive 3D rendering calculations. (FPUs are also known as "math processors" or "math chips.") Software developers quickly created packages to take advantage of the increased speed of the Mac. The Quadra line of computers with 33mhz CPUs, in combination with software and hardware network rendering schemes that shared the rendering load made serious animations possible.

The PowerPC line of computers with speedy processors that seem designed to be the workhorses in 3D animation has brought Macintosh animation to a new level. A single workstation has the power to render full frames of animation at three to four times the speed of the older systems. At the same time, the animation software tools have improved.

The competition among 3D software vendors has added a host of features and special effects with each upgrade. Tools once available only on high-end animation systems, such as Boolean operations and metaballs, are now available in inexpensive 3D modeling and animation packages. (Boolean operations take objects and use the information from one object to add to or subtract from another object, resulting in a single new shape. Metaballs merge spherical shapes to create organic objects.)

Working in 3D space opens up a whole new world for artists. In traditional mediums, such as oil or acrylic painting, the artist struggles over details that we take for granted in life, like shadows and light sources. In a painting, if the shadows do not fall properly or the lighting elements do not collaborate, the scene looks amiss.

In 3D work, the artist positions the lights wherever they serve the best purpose. Shadows, shading and highlights are left for the computer to figure out. The artist still should be concerned with the impact of the lights but the actual imaging of these elements is largely automatic.

Creating the images takes a grand departure from the norm as well. An artistic eye is still vital to the final image but the image is no longer drawn as much as it is constructed. Beams on bridges, hubs on wheels and wings on planes are actually built in a virtual workshop with an extensive array of tools. The construction methods often demand a set of skills more attuned to the construction of a parade float with all the jury-rigging involved than it does the talents of a traditionally trained artist.

An animator's key resource for drawing is the imagination. Many of the elements that end up in an animation previously existed nowhere else other than the animator's imagination. An exciting facet of 3D imaging is the ability to completely re-create in full detail the images from the mind's eye.

Imagine describing to a friend an object you saw in a dream. No matter how exact your description, the image in your friend's mind is sure to be different from yours.

However, if you use 3D modeling software to re-create your dream, you can rebuild the scene in its most finite detail. When you show the final product to your friends it will become part of their memory. In this action you have accomplished what was impossible a few years ago. Actually, you have used the 3D software to download an image from your mind and transfer it to another.

This capacity to re-create the existing world and completely invent worlds that do not exist has many possible applications and many possible 3D images.

The ability to educate by helping the student to visualize what may only be theory is one of computer animation's strongest applications. Product marketing and package visualization is another. For fine artists, it represents an exciting, visually stimulating toolbox. In the medical field, computer animation represents a wonderful training and educational experience. For industry, it means being able to build a machine or a whole industrial complex without ever lifting a wrench.

This entire book was created by tapping into a small portion of the power that computer aided visualization (CAV) offers. Except where otherwise noted, all the images in this book have been created by the authors, using the same hardware, software and techniques described throughout.

All of the images in this book are digital and were created using Macintosh hardware and software, with the exception of a few scanned and PhotoCD images. The 3D images were created with Infini-D, StudioPro, Ray Dream Designer, MacroModel, Swivel 3D Pro, Presenter Professional and form•Z. They were rendered at 300 dots per inch (dpi) resolution using each program's on-board rendering engine. Texture and background images were drawn with Photoshop, Illustrator or a combination of the two. Illustrator was also used extensively to create outlines for shapes.

The images were created and rendered on a Macintosh Quadra 950 with a PowerPC upgrade board, 40mb RAM, 700mb of hard disk space, a CD-ROM drive, and 44mb and 270mb SyQuest removable drives. The system has 16" and 13" color monitors, as well as a video encoder.

Rendered images were converted in Photoshop from RGB to CMYK, saved as Encapsulated PostScript documents and imported into QuarkXPress. Finished pages and images were compressed with DiskDoubler and sent to the imagesetter on 270mb removable cartridges. The images were reproduced on a 2,400 lines per inch (lpi) imagesetter.

Other than the "3D Showcase" art, the images and examples were created solely for this book. Most of the images were modeled in less than an hour, with rendering times varying between 20 minutes to 24 hours.

Fonts used throughout include Helvetica Ultra Compressed for the headlines and Helvetica Condensed Light for the body copy. Tekton was used for the workspace grid copy. Although using a condensed sans serif typeface breaks all traditional typographical design considerations, the condensed typeface takes up less room, and there is more space for the images and tips.

IN THE BEGINNING...

Everyone is a beginner at one time. If you are new to the 3D world, do not get frustrated. The index that follows outlines some shortcuts through this book to help you get set up and on the road to 3D animation and modeling.

THE SOFTWARE YOU NEED TO CREATE AN ANIMATION

Choose one of the following programs from each category to meet your needs:

1) A 3D modeling program is a must. This book will guide you through the complex world of 3D animation, but it will not replace your manual for precise operations. An integrated modeling-animating-rendering program, such as StudioPro is recommended, although stand-alone programs offer their own benefits.

2) For photorealistic images you will also need a bitmap-based image editing program. While Photoshop is recommended, any bitmap editing program can be used.

3) Many animators use a PostScript-based drawing program such as Illustrator or FreeHand to create both textures and shapes. If you have these on hand you will want to tap into their strengths; if not, you might consider buying one. Several modeling programs import PICT objects, so QuickDraw-based programs such as MacDraw or Canvas might be right for you.

4) While your rendered output might serve your purposes, for more sophisticated productions you might consider an editing program. Your choice will depend on your output needs, whether your animation is for broadcast, game creation or maybe a kiosk display.

The "Assembling Your Toolbox" chart on pages 38-39 will help you decide. Chapter 5 on "Editing" will also serve as a guide.

IT IS ONLY LIKE THIS IN YOUR MIND. One of the most incredible aspects of 3D animation is the ability for you to see an image in your mind's eye and accurately re-create that image using relatively inexpensive off-the-shelf software.

WELCOME TO THE OTHER WORLD

Imagine a three-dimensional photocopy machine that can take elements in the world–real or imagined–replicate them in its own digital environment and allow you to control these elements.

This machine is your Macintosh computer. And the power to create and control these elements is yours.

Since its beginning, the Macintosh computer has been an industry standard in the graphic arts field, attracting thousands of converts from more traditional platforms. The ability to create and edit designs on the fly and to take projects from concept to completion on a relatively fun, graphically-based platform was the key to the Macintosh's success in the graphic arts business.

Three-dimensional programs now take this visually stimulating platform to a higher level.

PARTS AND PIECES

Breaking through the initial barrier from 2D to 3D drawing programs can be a little intimidating and incredibly frustrating. Since artists drew on cave walls, we have been trying to replicate the world on a two-dimensional plane. You would think that trying to replicate a 3D world with 3D tools would be a simple matter. Well, it is not; just ask any sculptor.

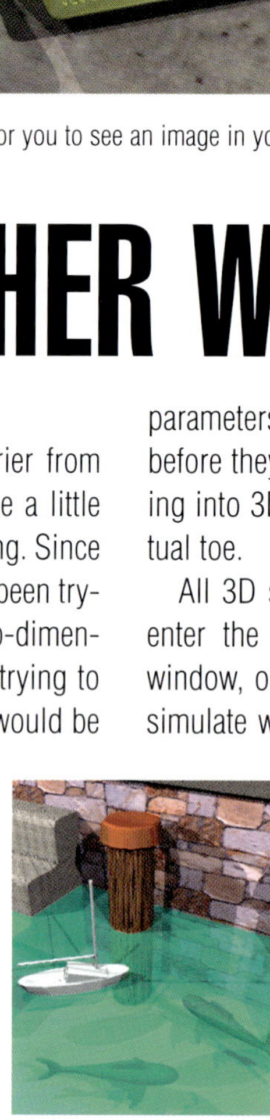

To create a model of an element from the real 3D world and translate it to a digital 3D world, you have to push and pull it though a 2D filter–your computer screen. Modeling and animation software does its best in presenting you with the tools you need to enter this arena, but the operators need to understand the parameters of the digital 3D environment before they go stumbling about in it, bumping into 3D furniture and stubbing their virtual toe.

All 3D software programs allow users to enter the artificial environment through a window, or several windows, that can either simulate working views, or "camera" views, which will be the focal point of their finished product. The user is given complete control over the lighting, camera angles, position of the elements and even in some cases, fog.

The subject matter of these stage settings are models. Models can be as simple as a single sphere that replicates a planet or dozens of objects, both simple and complicat-

3D modeling and animation in one fell swoop

Creating animations is a multistep process; here are the basic steps:

1 It all starts from the concept. Storyboarding helps create cohesive concepts.

2 The heart of the process is building the shapes with the tools available.

3 Creating surface colors, textures and treatments brings the shapes to life.

4 Adjusting lights, backgrounds and camera angles helps create the environment.

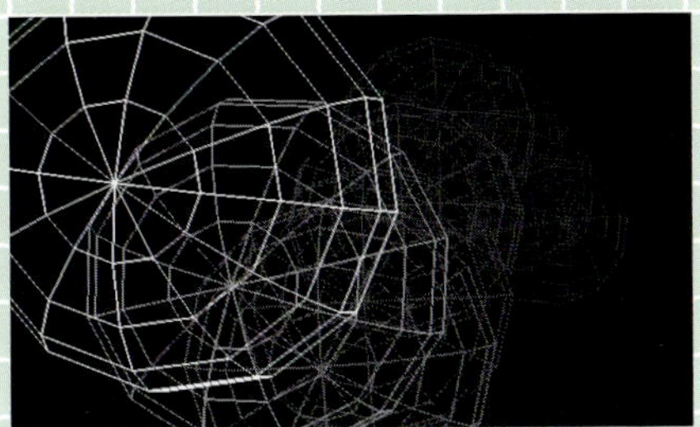

5 Adjusting object's position and direction within a timeline choreographs the action.

6 Rendering the animation and editing it together completes the process.

ed, that make up a more sophisticated object like a camera. Then, all adjoining pieces are linked together–like your foot is linked to your ankle, which is linked to your shin, which is linked to your knee, and so forth.

Links can be dynamic so that the object can pivot freely, or they can be constrained so that the direction of the pivot can be controlled. For instance, your elbow is constrained so it cannot bend backwards.

By themselves, the shapes, usually edited in a bareboned, wireframe mode for quick editing and placement, are uninteresting forms until textures, colors and surface treatments are applied.

Surface editing of the models is where the objects really take on a life of their own. A cube might become a brick wall, a tennis court, a 747 cockpit display panel or a glass pane.

With the lights set, the camera positioned and the objects in place, your next step is to choreograph the entire projection. The ele-

SETTING THE STAGE The imagined 3D digital world (above left) is put together one piece at a time. Each can, cup, book and photograph is crafted using tools not too different from what you would use in the real world. Cylinders are lathed; holes are cut; wallpaper is pasted–all in metaphors similar to a weekend home-improvement project. The stage is set up just like a photo studio (above right). The lights (in yellow) are positioned and adjusted in intensity and focus. The camera (in red) is moved into place and assigned a focal length.

ments on stage can be moved, rotated or scaled in sequence with a timeline. One ball can bounce across the set or everything on the stage can become animated.

Different motions can be timed to occur at different times: The door knob turns in the first second, the door swings open in the next second, the skeleton falls out of the closet in the last second.

When the elements are all done, you direct the computer to render the animation one frame at a time. Settings for the rendering can either make everything look photo-realistic, clean and polished or rough-hewn wireframes. The higher the quality, the longer it takes your computer to compute your scene.

Once rendered, you take the resulting files, usually in PICT or QuickTime format and edit them in separate editing software applications to create and combine animations, composite them with other images, and to add special effects or sound.

The final product can be transferred real-time to videotape or played back frame by frame. The digital file can become part of an interactive kiosk presentation or part of a video game. The choice is yours, because the world you created is yours. The only limitation is your imagination.

NONLINEAR THINKING

Do not get too caught up in doing things step-by-step, however. Although you can establish a set process for creating animations, you can also set up an amazingly non-linear procedure. Your work will often mimic objects and scenes in the real world. The procedures you follow to create images will be as dynamic as the world in which you exist. Since you are the "most-high" ruler of your computer world, the rules you follow are the rules you create.

The bonus of being the rulemaker is that you can let your creativity be your guide and not be restricted by media limitations or the size of your canvas. The drawback is that everything you create will be a product of your own mind and you will have few guidelines to help you with the task at hand.

Learning to think in 3D means either figuring out how to re-create the world around you in the computer modeling environment

RE-THINKING PRIORITIES

Creating 3D computer animations opens up the design process to a nonlinear approach. In traditional problem solving, each step follows a set pathway; each step builds on the next. In 3D animation, it is possible, and sometimes desirable, to work backwards. Example: In building a scene you might create a shape; use that shape to create a model; then create a texture to apply to the model. On the other hand, you might create a shape, use that as a template to create a texture and then make the model. Or, you might make a model for the sole purpose of creating an image that you would then use as a texture.

LINEAR THINKING

A linear approach is a good building block to understanding the process involved in creating 3D images and animations.

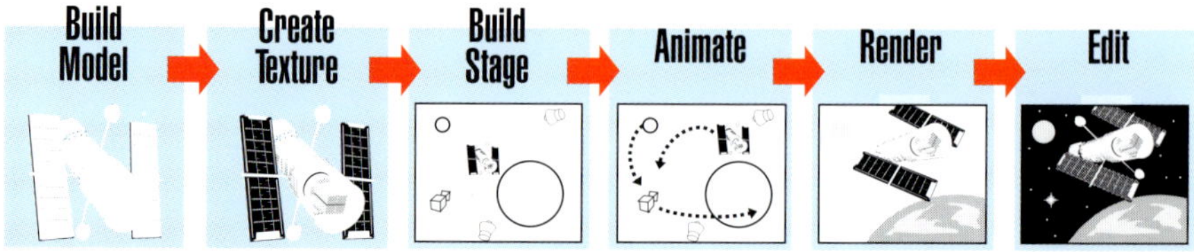

NONLINEAR THINKING

As your modeling and animation skills improve, you will find that everything fits together in a nonlinear flow. All the animation elements can fit together in a rather unstructured order. The ability to break free from a rigid sequence will allow the animator freedom to let imagination be the guide, not the process.

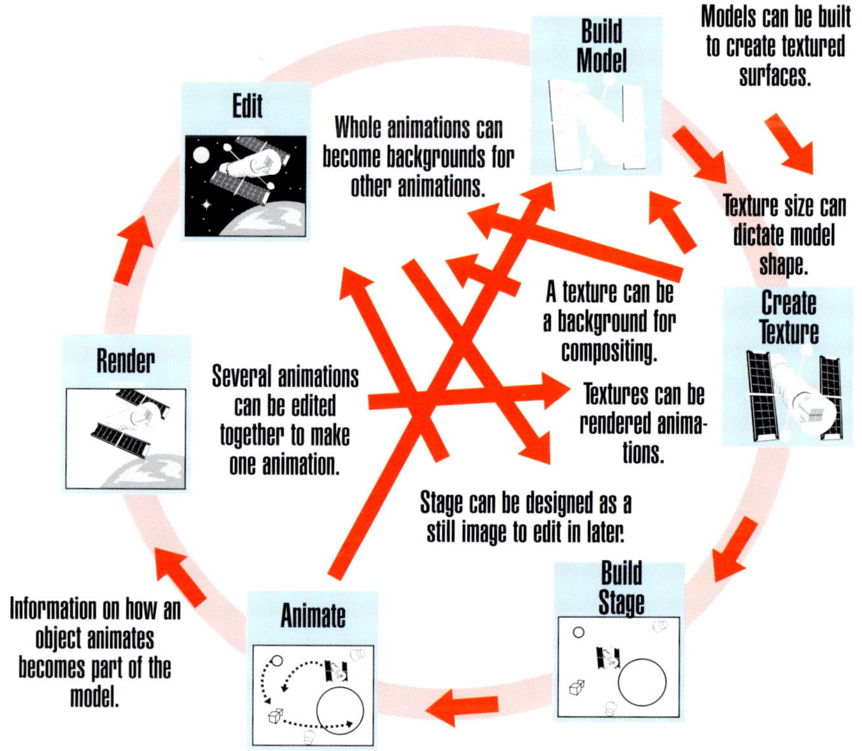

or learning to alter the world in your own fashion. Toying with real world images is often the best way to get an understanding of how to create images before attempting a more daunting challenge, like breathing life into imaginary spaceships and dinosaurs. It is best to learn to walk before you run.

Following the linear step-by-step process forms a good foundation for beginning an animation. If you are using an integrated animation package, half the work is already done for you when it comes to figuring out where to begin. Programs like StrataVision 3D, Infini-D and Swivel 3D offer a tight modular environment where you can model, create textures, animate and render without ever leaving the program. Exterior work in programs such as Premiere and Photoshop can augment the final product.

NEW DIMENSION

One of the first struggles with the transition to working in 3D is dealing with the new freedoms afforded you by the addition of the Z-plane.

In 2D drawing programs, all of the points of an object can be plotted on a flat X,Y-coordinate system. When you draw an image in a 2D program you usually do not even think about the X,Y-plane. In 3D modeling and animation, paying attention to your coordinates becomes all-important because of the added Z-axis which gives you depth.

Your design considerations are no longer limited to a simple world where an object can move up or down, side by side or rotate on one axis. In the 3D world, movement along the Z-axis allows the object to move closer to you or farther away–it gives you depth. Rotation is now possible on two additional axes. The ability to work and move in these new directions makes 3D modeling and animation dynamic–and challenging.

The key to overcoming this first roadblock is to familiarize yourself with as much of the new environment as possible. First, create simple shapes and learn how to change their orientation or attitude. Then experiment moving around in your new world. Most programs use the camera as your view to the world. Other programs give you a screen that represents a "world view" and allow you to create cameras that can also serve as viewing worlds.

READ THE MANUAL!

Macintosh users are known for their "I-do-not-need-to-read-the-manual" mentality. The ability to get right to work with unknown software is certainly one of the Macintosh's strengths. Disavowing the need for manuals is not usually arrogance on the part of the Mac user. It is the pleasant result of an easy-to-use, well-designed, consistent, graphic interface.

With 3D software, the rules change. **READ** the manual. Even if you are proficient with one 3D software package, chances are implementation of navigation and form creation with another 3D program will be radically different than what you are used to. As a side note, to those used to software upgrades, the old days when programs barely changed are gone. So save yourself the aggravation and read the manual when you get a 3D upgrade.

LEARNING CURVE

Compared to 2D software, there is a steep curve for learning and actually understanding the complexities of 3D software. Even packages that tout the ease of transition between 2D and 3D require a serious shift in the thinking process. The best suggestion is to complete the tutorial for the software. Although tutorial files are usually the first place Mac users turn when looking to free up disk space, it would be a mistake not to take advantage of these files.

Tutorials are usually geared to introduce the new user to the devices used for navigation, form creation and surface textures. Working in 3D is different from anything you have done before. Having someone, even a tutorial, walk you through each process step-by-step is a sure way to get the new procedures locked into your memory.

Several packages ship with a video tape that walks you through the tutorial. Any aid to getting you started is a positive step in the right direction. it is too easy to put the manuals back in the box with the best intention of getting back to it after the first trying sessions. After you finish the tutorial, then you can run wild and explore, but at least you will know what you are doing.

With your new freedoms, objects can get lost or be put into the wrong space very easily. One of the best ways to deal with this is to always build your scenes with the lens or view set at orthographic (see "Working in Orthographic," page 47.) This mode loses all perspective which allows you to position

XYZ and YOU

3D modeling uses an X,Y,Z-coordinate system to aid users in locating their position in the computer world, as well as the orientation of the modes in the scene.

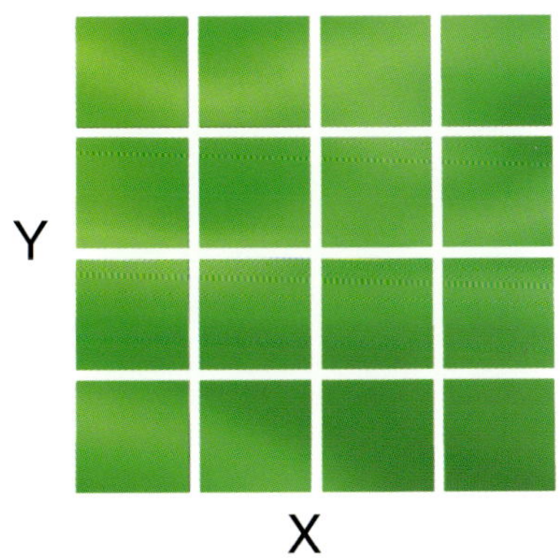

1) In 2D programs, the drawing coordinates are based on an X,Y-system. Every image can be plotted within this range. Positioning is limited to up, down, right and left.

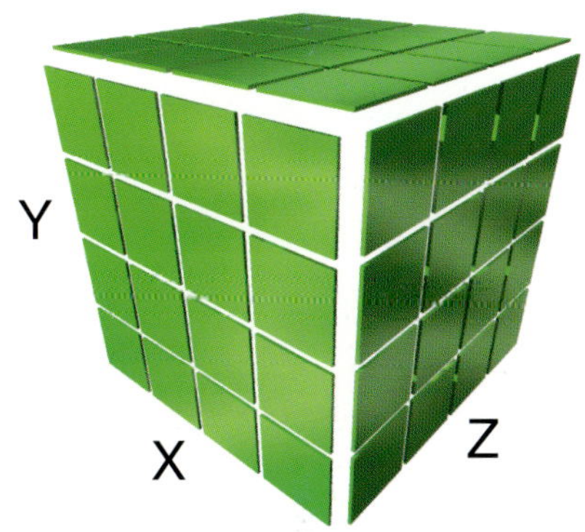

2) 3D programs add the Z-dimension, which is depth. Freed from the bounds of the two dimensions, objects can exist anywhere: close, far, up, down, right or left.

3) The orientation of objects in 2D is simple. Since objects can only rotate on one axis, rotation can be controlled by adjusting the degrees of rotation.

4) An infinite number of orientation movements are available in 3D. An object can pivot in two new directions. A combination of the three directions gives a full range of motion.

elements with regard to their true scale, and not what your perceived scale might be because of a perspective setting.

By working with a single window interface that allows you to jump between Top, Bottom, Right and Left views or a multiple window system that allows you to see several of these windows at one time, you can take advantage of orthographic editing. When your final scene is built, switch your camera or main view back to a normal view or a wider-angle lens setting. Failure to work in the orthographic mode when you start out modeling will result in much undue frustration as you try to position elements that look fine from one working view, but when you change the camera position or the viewing plane, things do not fit together.

ANIMATOR'S 10 COMMANDMENTS

1. **SAVE OFTEN.** And make occasional back-ups. Although 3D software has become much more stable over the years, most still ship with "known" bugs.
2. **NAME ALL YOUR OBJECTS.** Even a simple object can be a bear to find or select if it is lost in a complex model. Make this step a habit early on.
3. **LINK AS YOU GO.** As you put together a model, habitually link or group the objects that belong together. Constraining movements of pivoting objects is also a good thing to do as you work. Even if you do not think you will need to pivot the object you are working on, it will save a great deal of time later should you change your mind.
4. **COLOR ELEMENTS AS YOU GO.** Even the best-intentioned animator who plans to adjust all the colors and textures after the shapes are built will find a few objects shaded with default color in the final render. (Naming, linking, constraining and applying textures may seem tedious, especially for the smaller parts of a model, but failure to do so will make life much harder on you if you try to do it as an afterthought.)
5. **WORK IN SCALE.** Do not try to fool the camera by making things larger or smaller in comparison to other objects by moving them closer or farther away. You will be setting yourself up for trouble as the animation takes life. Establish a scale in your scene and maintain that scale with every new element you introduce.
6. **MAINTAIN A MAXIMUM 1:1 RATIO WITH TEXTURE MAPS.** Avoid pixelation by making sure that any bitmap in your scene holds the image resolution appropriate for your output.
7. **USE EASE-IN, EASE-OUT A LOT.** Almost all things in the real world accelerate and decelerate when in motion.
8. **ANTI-ALIAS AT ALL POSSIBLE TIMES.** Nothing makes a computer animation look more third-rate than jagged edges.
9. **NAME ALL YOUR ASSOCIATE FILES SIMILARLY.** Establish a naming format that works for you (file name.pict, file name.pics, file name.qt) to help organize the dozens of files you will create while making an animation.
10. **BUILD IN ORTHOGRAPHIC MODE.** Losing perspective will help you have a more realistic feel for how elements work together in both space and scale.

1. 3D SHOWCASE

3D SHOWCASE

In the three-dimensional illustration world, computer software is like a tube of paint in the traditional world. You may have all the supplies you need to create, but unless you put some talent behind the brush, you just end up with a blob of paint on the canvas. While these artists' mastery of the image has been aided by computer software, their visions are purely their own.

These images were created on the Mac, using the same software products mentioned in this book. The programs used to create these files are listed with each image, with the exception of Photoshop–which was used in almost every instance to create textures or composite the final scene. While most of the images are still frames, nothing stops the artist from flying the camera through the scene or adding motion and life to any of the elements–these images all exist in 3D worlds.

The modelers and animators featured here come from a cross-section of the 3D world. Most of the artists are freelance modelers and animators. Information on how to contact them can be found in Appendix D.

CASTLE–Chuck Carter modeled and rendered with StudioPro. (Top)

LIGHTHOUSE–Peta Allen modeled and rendered with Alias Sketch! (Above left)

MAZE RUNNERS–Peta Allen modeled and rendered with Alias Sketch! (Above right)

FILMSTRIP: WATERS–Randy Cates modeled and rendered with Infini-D; edited with After Effects.

VOYAGES—Joseph Kelter modeled, rendered and composited with Infini-D, Fractal Designs Painter and Specular Collage. (Top)

MAGIC—John Findley modeled and rendered with StudioPro. Texture maps done with Photoshop, Kai's Power Tools and Pixar 128. (Left)

ROBBY—Keith Carter modeled with Infini-D; rendered with BackBurner. (Above)

NEW WORLD—Joseph Kelter modeled and rendered with Ray Dream Designer; composited with Specular Collage, Fractal Designs Painter and Illustrator. (Above)

TEREZIN CHILDREN—David Teich modeled with form•Z, Cybermesh and Mr. Font; rendered with Electric Image. (Left)

FILMSTRIP: HIGH TECH PIONEERS— Chris Bernardi modeled with Infini-D; rendered with BackBurner.

COLORMAX—Gregory Chambers modeled and rendered with StudioPro. (Above)

FORTUNE TELLER—John Findley modeled and rendered with StudioPro. Texture maps created with Kai's Power Tools and Pixar 128. (Top)

ZEPLIN—Tim Landry modeled and rendered with Infini-D. (Above)

T-REX BATTLE—Ken Bryan modeled with form•Z; rendered with Electric Image. (Left)

CANYON—Chuck Carter modeled and rendered with KPT Bryce. (Far left)

GRASS ISLAND—Chuck Carter modeled and rendered with KPT Bryce. (Left)

MUSEUM—John Findley modeled and rendered with StudioPro. Texture maps created with Kai's Power Tools and Pixar 128. (Above)

PALACE & ADDIE—Tim Landry modeled and rendered with Infini-D. (Above)

FILMSTRIP: JO JO'S KINGDOM—Tim Landry modeled and rendered with Infini-D. Interactive movie compiled in Director.

RAPTOR—Ken Bryan modeled with form•Z; rendered with StudioPro. (Above)

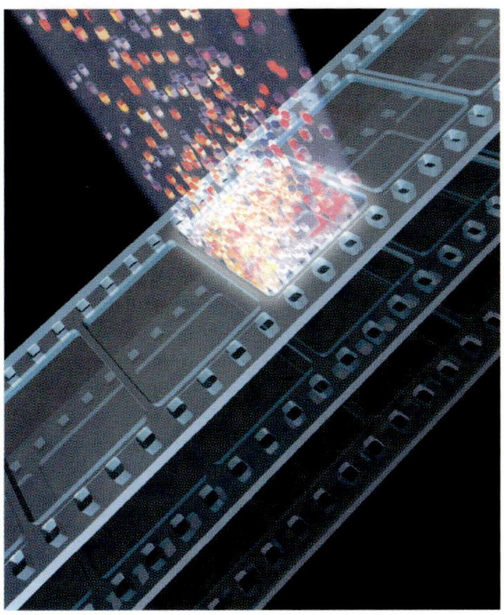

ZEPLIN SERIES—Tim Landry modeled and rendered with Infini-D. (Above)

CALLIGRAPHER—Ken Bryan modeled with form•Z; rendered with StudioPro. (Upper left)

MOTION PIXELS—Tim Landry modeled and rendered with Infini-D. (Left)

TIME—Joseph Kelter modeled with Infini-D, Alias Sketch!, Fractal Designs Painter, Specular Collage; rendered with Infini-D. (Above)

HELIX AND SILI—Peta Allen modeled and rendered with Electric Image. (Right)

FILMSTRIP: RETAIL—Randy Cates modeled and rendered with Infini-D; edited with After Effects.

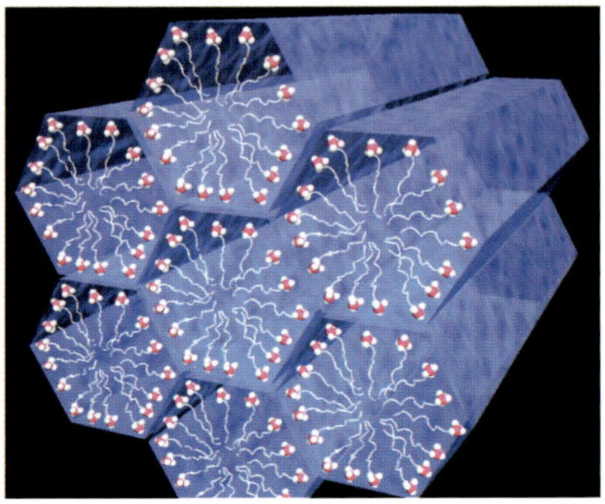

KBCI—Chris Bernardi modeled with Infini-D; rendered with Electric Image. (Left)

TEMPEST—Kevin Abbott modeled with StudioPro and Cybermesh; rendered with StudioPro. (Below left)

ROBOT YM-3—Keith Carter modeled with Infini-D; rendered with BackBurner. (Below)

SUNRISE IN SPACE—Bill Baker modeled with Infini-D; rendered with BackBurner. (Bottom)

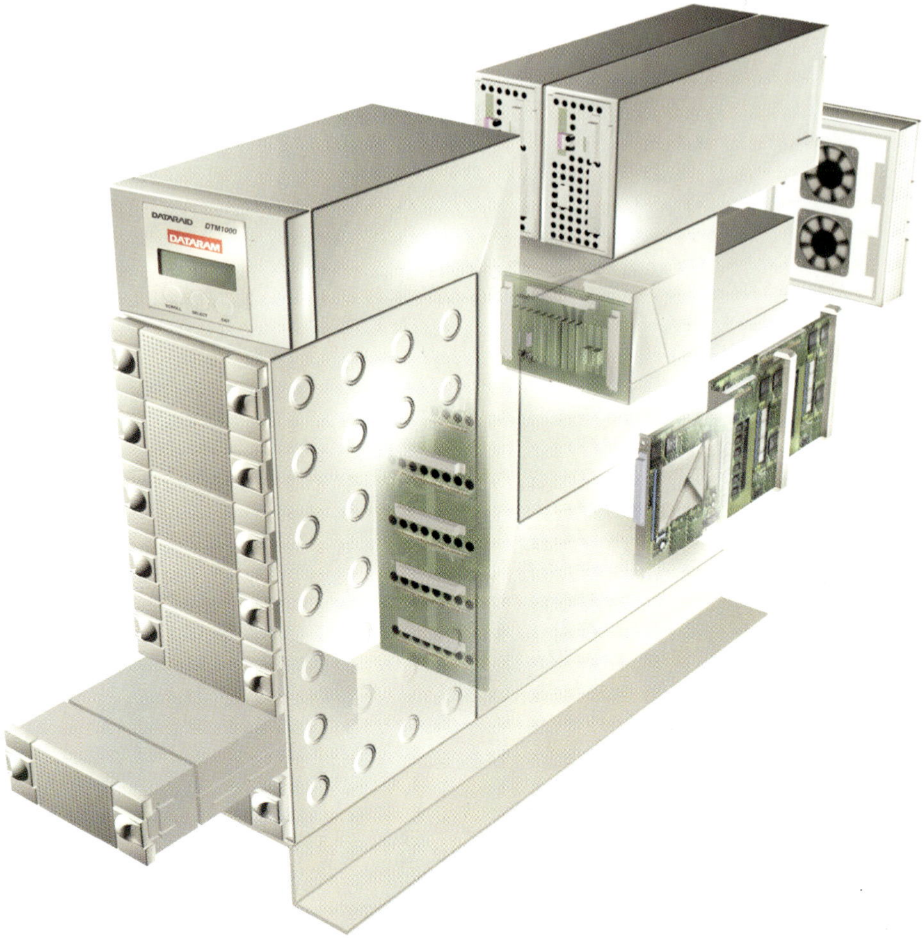

TECH ILLUSTRATION—David Teich modeled with form•Z; rendered with Electric Image. (Top)

ANNUAL—Chris Bernardi modeled with Infini-D; rendered with Electric Image; composited with Collage. (Above)

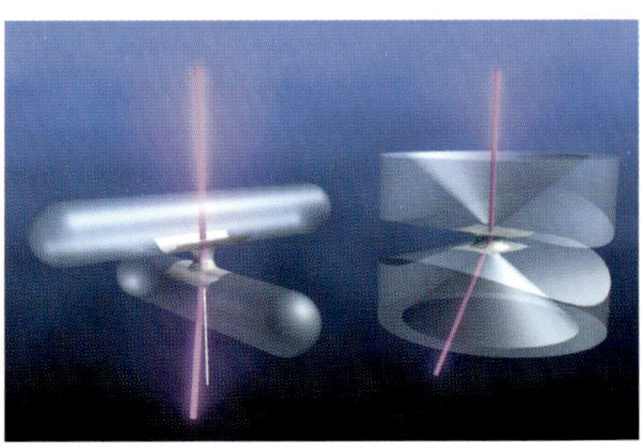

DEVICES—Peta Allen modeled and rendered with Alias Sketch! (Right)

FILMSTRIP: MDI—Chris Bernardi modeled with Infini-D; rendered with Electric Image.

CHERNOBYL—Chuck Carter modeled and rendered with StudioPro. (Upper left)

BRIDGE DIVERS—Bill Baker modeled with Infini-D; rendered with BackBurner. (Top)

CHEMISTRY—Bill Baker modeled with Infini-D; rendered with BackBurner. (Above)

BIOSCULPTURE—Will Morse modeled and rendered with custom modelers he wrote. The RIB files were imported to Showplace and rendered with MacRenderMan. (Above)

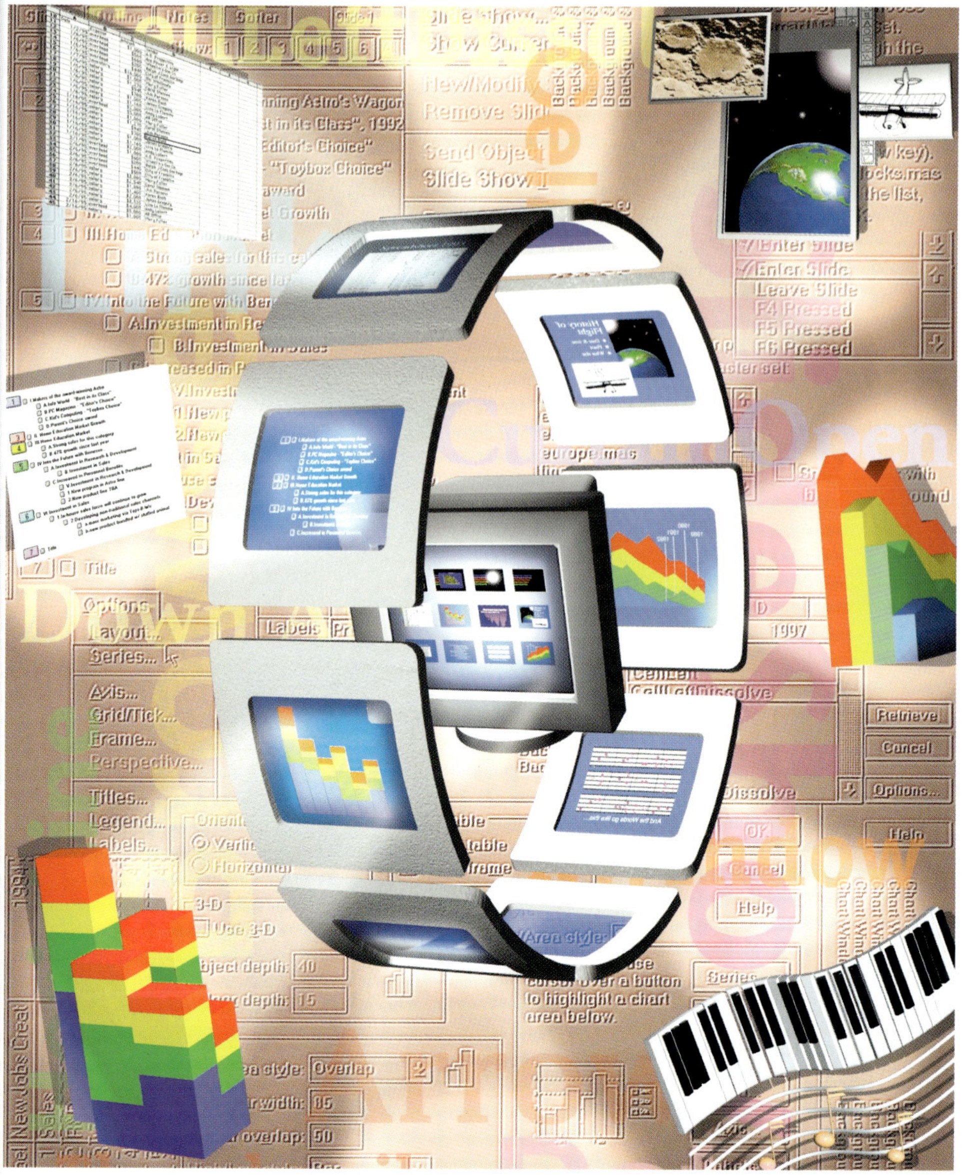

SLIDE WHEEL—David Teich modeled with form•Z; rendered with Electric Image. (Top)

HAMLET—Kevin Abbott modeled and rendered with StudioPro. (Above)

FILMSTRIP: MILLENNIUM—Randy Cates modeled and rendered with Infini-D; edited with After Effects.

MYST SCENES—Chuck Carter modeled and rendered with StudioPro. (Above)

STILL LIFE—Tim Landry modeled and rendered with Infini-D. (Top left)

MEDIEVAL WORKSHOP—Bryan Leister modeled and rendered with Alias Sketch! (Middle left)

ROBOTS AT SUNSET—David Teich modeled with form•Z; rendered with Electric Image. Landscape created with KPT Bryce. (Lower left)

BIG BROTHER/SISTER—Chris Bernardi modeled with Infini-D; rendered with Electric Image. (Top)

MOTH—Bryan Leister modeled and rendered with Alias Sketch! (Above middle)

BAYOU BOAT—Chris Bernardi modeled with Infini-D; rendered with Electric Image. (Above left)

PENNY TRAIN—Chuck Carter modeled and rendered with Infini-D. (Above right)

FILMSTRIP: DOMEVISION—Randy Cates modeled and rendered with Infini-D; edited in After Effects.

2. TOOLS OF THE TRADE

THE CPU: UNDER THE HOOD

The CPU can mean two things: the central processing unit–the little chip that runs your computer; or the main box into which you plug in your monitors, keyboard, CD-ROM and so forth. For our purposes, we will look at the CPU as the entire box.

Mac CPUs come in a variety of capabilities, most of which are suited for 3D modeling and animation. Since each user will have different needs, specific questions need to be addressed to match the right CPU up with the right use. These questions include:

- Does your CPU have a floating-point processor (FPU)? Right off the bat you can rule out any model that does not. Most modeling software and some imaging software require an FPU.
- Is it expandable? Unless your animation needs will always remain minimal, avoid CPUs with only one NuBus slot (or none at all). By the same token, five slots might be more than you really need *unless* you are planning to use your setup as a rendering powerhouse with additional co-processor boards.
- How much RAM can it hold? Determine your RAM needs (see chart on p. 33) before you buy your CPU so you will not underpower yourself too early in the game. Leave room for growth. Not too long ago 4mb of RAM was considered a lot.
- Does the CPU provide adequate video support? Some models, for instance, cannot drive a 16" monitor in 24-bit mode. If this is the case, you will have to use a NuBus slot with an additional video board–which is an added purchase.
- Is it fast enough? If you know your 3D needs will be minimal, and you are not an

NUBUS CARDS
These internally mounted cards can either provide self-contained improvement, such as acceleration, or provide a link for external devices, such as video cards. As a rule, the more NuBus slots you have in your computer, the better the outlook for growth and expansion. Even if you do not need the slots for a NuBus card now, the chances are you will need them eventually.

FLOATING-POINT PROCESSOR
3D rendering is a serious math-crunching process and you will need a Mac with an FPU (see page 29). Most modeling programs will not even load without the presence of an FPU.

CENTRAL PROCESSING UNIT
This is the brain of the computer. In general terms, the higher the megahertz (mhz) rating of the CPU, the faster the computer. Older Macs with 68000 series CPUs can handle modeling fine, but complex modeling and rendering is what the PowerPC line of Macs do best.

VIDEO SUPPORT
Depending on your final product, your video needs may be simple and satisfied with built-in video boards, or they may be sophisticated and require several boards to handle video compression as well as encoding to broadcast standard formats. Video RAM regulates the size of the screen your video support can display; some models use CPU RAM to support video.

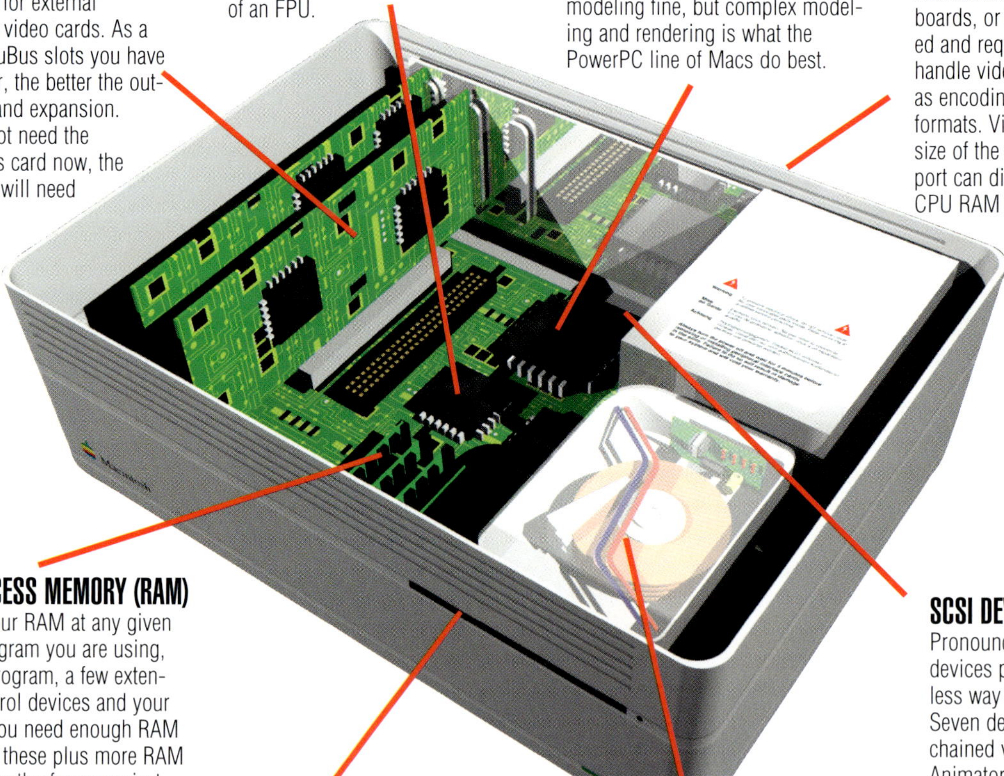

RANDOM ACCESS MEMORY (RAM)
Loaded into your RAM at any given time is the program you are using, your system program, a few extensions and control devices and your project data. You need enough RAM to juggle all of these plus more RAM to allow for growth of your project and maybe a second or third program. If your model has a PICT file mapped to the surface, the data for this file will be loaded as well. Animation is RAM intensive, so buy as much as you can afford. The results will be:

– A faster working environment, since you can run more programs at the same time;

– The ability to create and edit complex models and animations; and

– Fewer system errors when your computer chokes.

FLOPPY DRIVES
On becoming an animator, your days of using floppy drives for storage are pretty much over. They will still serve the purpose of loading new software, until that ritual is replaced by CD-ROM installers. Most of the files you will work with will exceed the capacity of floppies. A single frame of a 24-bit, full-screen animation will fit nicely on one floppy. A 10-second animation might have 300 frames.

HARD DRIVE
Too much hard drive space does not exist. 3D animations are disk hogs. To create even simple animations you will need hundreds of megabytes of free space. Your final file may only be 10mb, but to get there you might need 100mb of space to create the work files. The speed of your drive will also come into play if you are planning to play your animations straight to your screen.

SCSI DEVICES
Pronounced "scuzzy," SCSI devices provide a quick and painless way to expand your Mac. Seven devices can be daisy-chained via SCSI cables. Animators will often fill every slot on the chain with the tools available. These might include digitizing scanners, extra hard drives, CD-ROM drives and removable media drives. The key to a happy SCSI chain is proper termination (see page 33).

impatient person, a 680x0 series Mac (from the original Macs–if they have an FPU–to the Quadra lineup) may be fine. Models made before the Quadra series (Mac II, IIci...) can handle the job, but may be agonizingly slow, especially when it comes to rendering the final product. The Quadra family would handle most needs adequately but true speed improvement comes with the PowerPCs. Macs with LC processors, such as a Performa 630–which has a 68LC040 processor lack an FPU chip and should be avoided.

One great advantage with building a 3D system using a Mac is the ease in which you can cannibalize an older system and make it fit into an upgraded new one. Keep this in mind when buying your system. Instead of opting for an internal CD-ROM, for instance, you might choose to buy an external unit. Some equipment does not move well and this needs to be considered. RAM, for instance, from the Mac II and early Quadra line uses 32-pin SIMMs, while later Macintoshes use 72-pin SIMMs.

The Macintosh PowerPC line is really the best way to go for work in modeling and animation. The PowerPC acts as if it was tailored to work with 3D calculations with rendering speeds up to four times faster than the best 680x0 Macs.

AV Macintoshes combine traditional computer monitor output with NTSC video input and output, allowing the user to both import and export video from the Mac. To animators, the output is the most important angle, as this allows them to "print to tape" their final product.

As with many of life's situations, you get what you pay for, and video quality is certainly no exception. Many video output cards and devices exist on the market; some fall within the industrial quality range and a few within the broadcast quality spectrum.

If your concerns are for broadcast quality animations for video, you might not want to buy the CPU with the AV option. Even if you are just creating models on the CPU you are planning to purchase, you would be wise to get the same type of video output as the Mac that will do the final output. This way you will have fewer surprises from inevitable color shifts. One well-deserved TV-world adage is that "NTSC stands for Never The Same Color."

On the other hand, using any NTSC encoder is better than none at all, since the difference between NTSC monitors (your TV set) and the computer screen representation is great.

Port connections on Macintoshes are standard and similar to those on other Macs, so you should not have any problems in this area when shopping for a CPU. PowerBooks have a variety of port options, but a PowerBook is not the recommended platform on which to create animations. Although processing speeds, RAM, and disk size are all within working range, the screens are too small to give you the elbow room you need to work. In addition, PowerBook screen refreshes can be frustratingly slow. Duo docks offer relief with FPU support, SCSI ports and larger video support.

All Macintoshes support AppleTalk or Ethernet. If you are working on your own, and have only one computer, you might not be too concerned with your computer's network capabilities. If you have more than one Macintosh and you spend any time rendering images, you will be interested in checking out network rendering software which takes advantage of all the Macs available on the network. If this is the case, look for a Mac that has either built-in Ethernet support or plan on using a slot for an Ethernet card. Network rendering moves at a snail pace over LocalTalk.

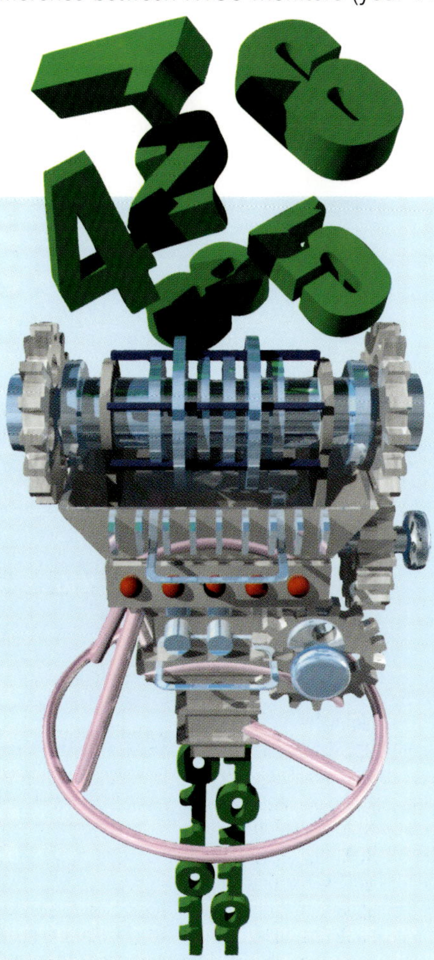

FLOATING-POINT PROCESSOR – THE NUMBER CRUNCHER

To desktop modelers and animators, the floating-point processor unit (FPU or FPPU) is the key technology which allows them to do their work quickly. The FPU does the high-end math so the computer can keep up with your creation speed.

Earlier, when discussing CPUs, we looked at the main box. For the FPU discussion, the CPU is now the little chip. The FPU is an assistant to the CPU (co-processor).

Explaining an FPU is complicated. When you dig back into computer history, you cannot help but be amazed at how everything works. Without boring details, here is a simple explanation of what an FPU is.

The computer has three ways to retrieve and process information for you. Each method is designed to handle one kind of information–characters, integers and floating-point numbers.

Letters, words and names are processed as one kind of information. Whole numbers (negative and positive) and zero are handled as a second type.

Those numbers from advanced algebra and calculus–the ones which continue without an endpoint (for example, the value of pi, 3.13159...) or those with scientific notation–are processed by the FPU.

In order to work efficiently, the computer handles each category of information differently–mainly because each category requires different amounts of processing brainpower. The most labor intensive category is the work of the FPU. If your computer does not have an FPU, high-end art or science processing (for example, rendering a 3D image) will be slow, so slow that your project may never get out the door.

Some programs will not run without an FPU. Other programs may run, but they will be painfully slow.

RAM, STORAGE AND VIDEO NEEDS

Three-dimensional animation is a RAM intensive activity. A complicated 3D model with a few texture maps will drain a Mac dry of RAM before you can say "expensive memory upgrade."

In the 2D print world, large high-resolution images are replaced in working mode by low-resolution proxies. When you run a 3D program, the texture maps are either linked to, and subsequently loaded into RAM, or are imbedded into the document. Either way, 3D files tend to get large very quickly.

Rendering the model is also RAM intensive. The document being rendered needs enough RAM to load the entire file, texture maps and all. Usually, rendering speed also is improved with additional RAM.

Some editing programs that do not use low-resolution proxies or thumbnail sketches for editing animations together can require large amounts of RAM.

The amount of RAM you will require depends largely on the software you use and the quality of the animations you want to create. When deciding on RAM needs, have enough RAM to load your system, the program (or programs, if you plan to run several at the same time) and the document (including linked files).

TWO PROJECTS, TWO DIFFERENT RAM NEEDS

Many variables contribute to animation file sizes. The file sizes are a result of the modeling/rendering programs and the editing program. But screen size, image resolution and length of animation are the primary concerns when determining your RAM needs.

A full-screen, 640x480 pixels, in 24-bit (millions of colors), uncompressed animation that lasts a minute might use several hundred megabytes. A 160x120 pixel window, in 8-bit (256 colors) that lasts 15 seconds with medium JPEG compression (a standard format) might only use 100k. The full screen animation might be for broadcast and will be put to videotape, so the file size is largely unimportant. The smaller animation might be for a small inset window explaining a medical procedure that will be imported into a HyperCard stack for interactive screen replay where file size cannot be too large.

The tools to create both projects may be the same. But the RAM requirements would be vastly different. For the first project, anything less than 128mb of RAM might present difficulties. For the second project, 24mb of RAM would be fine.

How you allocate your RAM also will play a role on how much you need. If you run a single program, planning your RAM needs can be based on your most RAM intensive tasks. Running several programs at the same time may increase your productivity, but it can put heavy demands on your RAM.

If you have the working RAM space, it is nice to run your key programs all at the same time. Modeling programs can often tap into the power of other programs, such as Illustrator and Photoshop. Being able to keep all of these running at the same time can help keep your creativity flowing. You become a beast of burden when you have to "Save." Wait. "Quit." "Open." Create. "Save." Wait. "Quit." "Open." Wait. "Import." With all your main programs open and function keys designed to streamline importing, running two or three programs can feel like they have all been integrated into one package.

Allocating your RAM largely depends on your programs' needs and how many programs you would like your Mac to juggle at one time. To change the memory allocation, select the program in the Finder (highlight it, do not open it) and choose Get Info from the File menu. Choosing About Your Macintosh from the Apple menu in the Finder will tell you how much RAM you have.

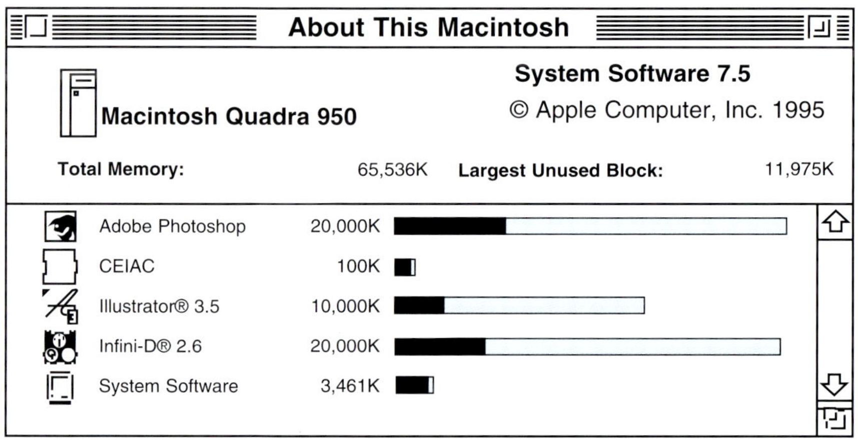

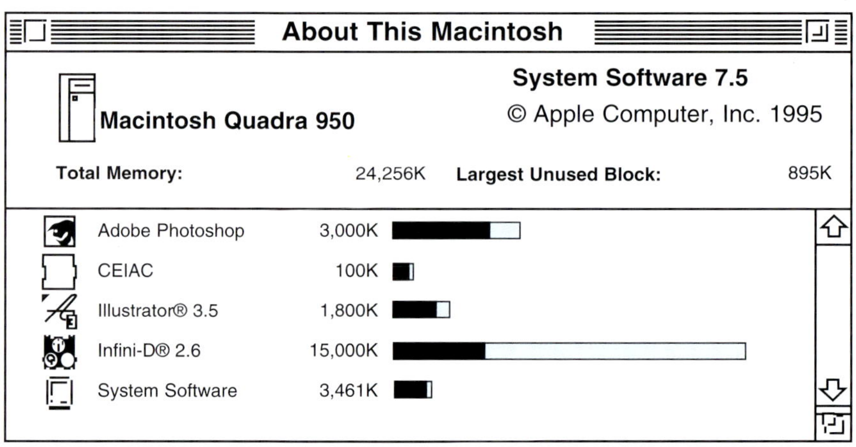

If you are running one program, allocate all the RAM you can to that program. If you want to juggle programs, weigh the importance of each program against the other. Leave some space for the system, miscellaneous control panels and utilities. Two possible spreads (above) are outlined for a modeling session setup. In an editing session, you might be juggling between movie-editing and photo-editing software.

YOU SAY SCSI AND I SAY "SCUZZY"

The SCSI (pronounced "scuzzy") chain quickly becomes an animator's best friend. It makes expanding the existing system a painless, often plug-and-play experience. There is room for six additional devices on the chain. Your CPU always reserves #7. Four key rules apply for a happy SCSI chain: 1) The overall length of cable should not extend over 7 feet. 2) Buy the best cables you can. 3) All devices *must* have a different address. 4) The last device on the chain *must* be terminated. Problems arise when the user does not know whether a device is terminated internally or not. Read the manual which came with your device, and disable internal termination on every device but the first and last one. Most likely, your internal drive is terminated already, so you just worry about the last device on the chain. It is that simple.

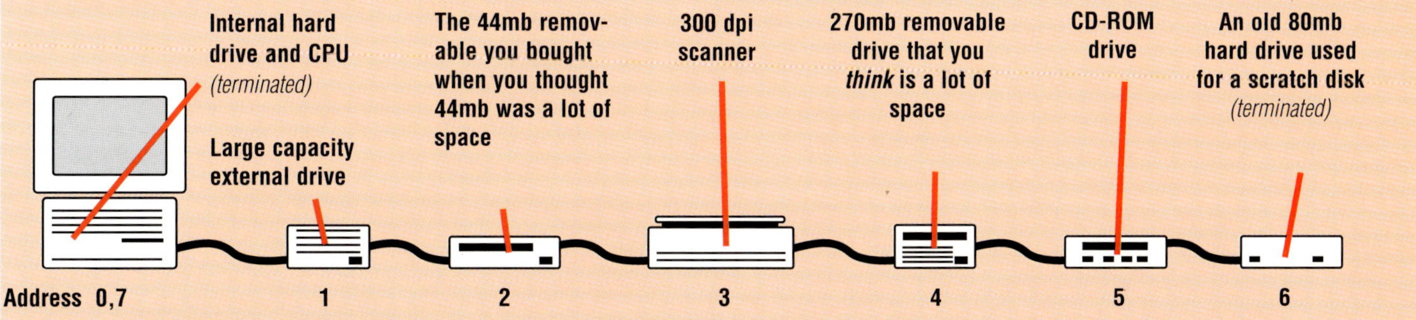

This is a typical animator's SCSI chain. Setting your address in the order that they are on the chain will help you troubleshoot later.

Do not max out your RAM allocation. If the largest available block reads 18,000K, set your program to 1,000K or 1mb less. Your system will require fluctuating RAM amounts depending on what you ask it to do while you are in the program, so leave a little room–1- or 2mb should be fine.

For instance, if you use DiskDoubler and try to import a compressed texture map, DiskDoubler will need enough room to do its work. If you want to change printers, networks or monitor resolutions while you work, you will need some space to be free for those functions.

Not giving your system breathing room can result in system errors. If you begin running into Type 1 errors (a memory error) and you have already increased your RAM allocation as far as you can safely go, it is time for a RAM upgrade.

The little bar in the About the Macintosh dialog box will help you figure out where you stand. The bar's hollow part represents unused RAM that has been allocated for your program. The solid part is the approximate amount of RAM being used. Go to your Finder every so often and look at this display to give you a basic idea of how much RAM is free on your computer. Fill up the bar–you have used up your allocation. If you cannot increase your allocation, you have run out of RAM.

Using virtual memory is an option, but not a good one. Virtual memory fools the computer into thinking part of your hard disk is actually RAM. Complex modeling runs even slower with virtual memory. If it is a last-ditch "need-to-get-the-project-done" effort, use it, but make sure the program you are using supports virtual memory.

Workspace: This is the hard drive where you have your System Folder, applications and your documents. The drive that came with your computer usually serves this purpose nicely, as long as it is big enough to handle the job. Even though your needs may not seem large, they will be. Your texture files will be much larger than your model files. Your rendered output, whether QuickTime or PICS, will be huge and your final movie file will be massive. Animation files have a way of snowballing in size. Along the way you may not want to trash your work files because you may want to use them later to re-create your final product. To create a 20mb animation, you will easily eat up 100mb.

Scratch Disk: If you are doing animations, you will be dealing with Photoshop to

RAM
What you can do with...

8mb: Run most modeling packages with few to no imported texture maps. Rely on the program's on board procedural map tools. Almost no editing capabilities– so plan on your rendered output as being a final product.

16mb: More sophisticated models possible but not too extravagant. Keep imported textures to a minimum. May have less definition in 8- or 16-bit maps than 24-bit maps but will be able to add more of them. Limited editing capabilities.

32mb: Now complex models can be created and loaded easily into RAM with detailed texture maps. Editing of 24-bit movies possible, but challenging. Two programs can be run simultaneously without difficulty.

64mb: Huge complex models with lots of texture maps are no problem. Editing of large, high-resolution animation clips limited only by length of animation (*always* a limitation). Run three programs easily when modeling.

A large primary monitor will give you enough room for the many palettes and windows used in the process of building animations.

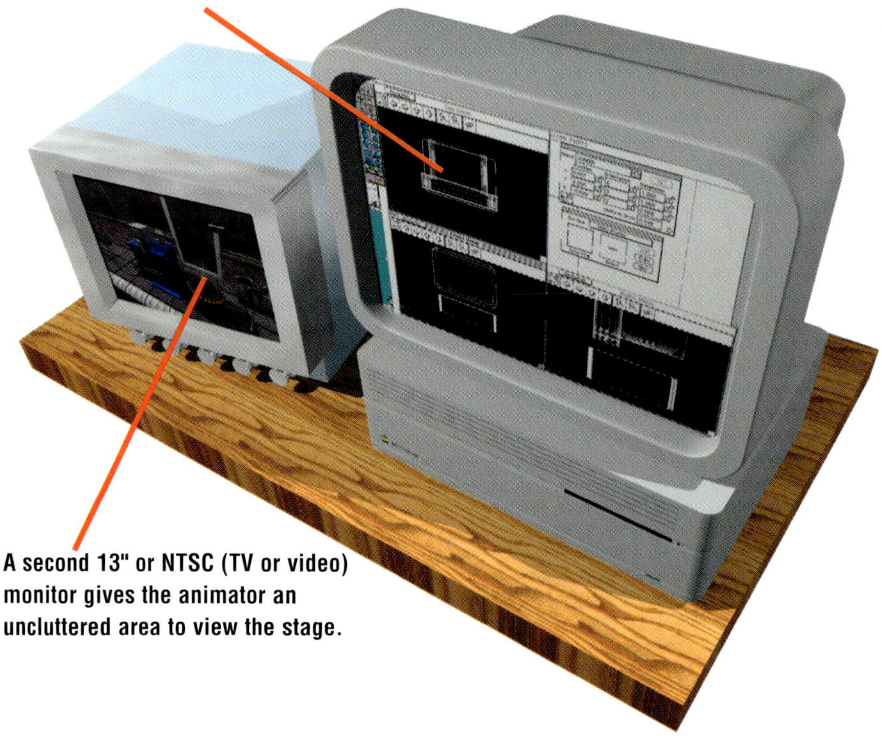

A second 13" or NTSC (TV or video) monitor gives the animator an uncluttered area to view the stage.

create texture images and edit still files. Photoshop uses a virtual memory scheme of its own and requires a scratch disk. Depending on your file sizes, your scratch disk may be a couple of extra megabytes on your work disk or an entire hard drive of its own. If you work mostly with low-resolution images, this should not be much of a problem. But if you render high-resolution models for print, you will need some scratch disk space. A 300 dpi image like the cover of this book needed an 80mb scratch disk.

Storage Space: Animation files are huge. Unless you have an unlimited budget, it is hard to find free disk space for a growing pile of animations. In some cases, you also will want to save the work files you have used to create the animations. Removable media is the best solution for this. Higher capacity removable drives in many cases are as fast as regular hard drives.

Also, removable media are wonderful for organization. As your source files grow, you will need a place to store textures, backgrounds and models where you can get to them easily. A removable drive dedicated to these specific tasks makes it easy to get the files you need without too much hair pulling. Optical media are slow and with huge files, speed counts.

Archiving and Back-up: Nothing is forever–except optical media. Over time, magnetic media loses its data. Tape back-ups, when possible, are recommended. Most important is to make sure you have a second copy of all your models and their texture maps. In some cases, whole movies can be recreated totally from models that have been saved with all their key frame information. Removable media makes good back-ups and if used with compression programs, they can make retrieval relatively painless.

Realistically, floppy disks are outmoded for use in 3D animation storage. Most of the software you buy will come to you on floppies. Models are small enough to fit snugly on a floppy, but if you have texture maps with any semblance of detail, that is a different story. Most likely, the resulting animation files will be several megabytes, ruling out floppies for all but the most basic animations. Most compression software allows you to split large files for placing on floppies, but the cost per megabyte will push you to removable media.

Service bureaus can take your animation files and place them on professional quality media. They usually have a wide range of both magnetic and optical removable devices that they support, including tape drives. Before purchasing a removable media drive, you might want to inquire about your local service bureau's system, even if you do not have any plans to use them at the moment. Investing in the right format now may save you money later.

If you have one hard drive, you might consider partitioning it to set aside room for a scratch disk.

An *ideal storage system* would include:

– a basic drive for programs, fonts and utilities,

– a 500mb internal hard drive (as a start),

– an external 1 gigabyte drive (practical workspace for your animations and portability with huge files),

– a large capacity removable media drive (such as a SyQuest) in the 270mb range (quick storage access and easy to ship across the country), and

– an optical drive or tape backup for archiving. (Optical media has a shelf-life far superior to magnetic media.)

VIDEO

As with RAM and disk space, your video requirements will depend on your animation needs. Animators whose final product is animation clips for importing into video games may not need more than the on-board output of their Macintosh combined with a 13-inch monitor. This setup forces animators to stay within the "least common denominator" restrictions of the lower-end user base.

On the other hand, an animator concerned with presentations and promotional work may desire a larger, 19-inch monitor combined with a video accelerator card to drive it. In between lies a wide field of possible video systems, each of which, thanks to an easy-to-expand NuBus system, can be custom tailored to the user's needs.

A system preferred by many animators is a two-screen system (above). Screen #1 (right, above) is your working screen, where your normal desktop is found. If possible and if your on-board video can handle it, make this screen at least a 16-17" monitor. This will give you plenty of room to organize your various palettes and windows.

A second screen (above) serves as your

display window. Video standards are the same size as a 13" monitor (640x480 pixels); therefore a standard Macintosh screen will do the job. Both screens should be able to display 24-bit color (millions). If you are working with a video encoder, either an external box or a NuBus card, this makes a great second screen. If you are working on animations for video, this will help keep your colors in check because there is a big difference between a computer's non-interlaced and an NTSC's interlaced appearance.

For video output, professional quality NTSC monitors will give you the best results. Short of that, you can buy a consumer TV set that has a video input jack. Although the quality may not be the best, it will still give you a better feel for your video image than a computer screen image.

IMAGE INPUT DEVICES

Image input devices allow you to bring in bits of the real world and apply them to elements in your 3D computer domain. You can survive without having some type of image input device, but it can make your work easier and more realistic.

Video input boards will allow you to dump images from your camcorder into programs like Photoshop for editing and then mapping to surfaces of models. Macintosh AV models have built-in video boards that can handle this job as well. Some digital still cameras also require input boards while others plug directly into a serial port. Scanners and CD-ROMS also provide an excellent route for grabbing textures and bringing them into your photo-editing software.

Animation images tend to be low-resolution. Video resolution tends to run at roughly the same line rate as your computer monitor, in the 72 dpi range. Because of this, the texture maps you import or create also can be low-resolution without reducing the quality of your final image.

Most scanners on the consumer market start at 300 dpi and work their way up to the 2400 dpi range. A 24-bit color scanner with 300 dpi more than satisfies an animator's scanning requirements. Flatbed scanners handle most jobs well, as long as the object you are scanning is flat. Three-dimensional scanners, with camera elements mounted on a stand above the image allow you to capture textures from real-world 3D objects.

If you do not have a CD-ROM drive, buy one. CDs are quickly replacing floppies as a software company's distribution method of choice. While you still may be able to load the latest upgrade of your favorite software with floppy disks, you are missing the fun stuff that is being crammed onto the CD-ROM version of the upgrade. This often includes filters, demos, tutorials and tips files.

CDs are also a valuable resource tool. A handful of CDs are dedicated specifically to textures and backgrounds. Hundreds of reasonably priced CDs packed with royalty-free photos also are available. These CDs are a boon to anyone working in animation or multimedia. A CD-ROM drive that supports the Kodak PhotoCD format also makes a powerful image input device. You can photograph your own textures and have a local photo lab digitize them for you.

INPUT	THE CPU	OUTPUT
While it is possible to create animations with no input devices other than your mouse and keyboard, other devices will be of assistance.	This is the box where it all happens. While almost all Macintoshes with an FPU can handle modeling, rendering and animation, some do it better. For instance, AV Macs supply input and output capabilities and PowerPC Macs supply a great deal of power.	Animations can be output to the computer screen or converted to a video signal using internal or external conversion boards.

AV (Audio, Video) Macintosh, available in both 680X0 and PowerPC
These Macs provide both video input for capturing still and moving images as well as NTSC conversion for TV output to videotape.

INPUT	THE CPU	OUTPUT
Scanners 24-bit color scanners can capture flat textures or import photographs into the Mac.	**68020 Macintosh CPU** If it has an FPU chip, a 68020 Macintosh (Mac II, IIcx) can be used for modeling and animation. The slow handling of medium and large models will have you banging your head against the wall and even simple renders may take days.	**Built-in Video** Most Macs come with built-in computer monitor displays–although these may lack in both resolution and speed.
Video Capture Boards Images from still or motion video cameras or full motion images can be imported into the Mac using video input cards and used as textures or backgrounds for animations.	**68030 or 68040 Macintosh CPU** This range covers a wide range of Macintoshes, from the IIci to the Quadra 840. The 68030 Macs handle modeling relatively well, but rendering time is still excessive. 68040 Macs can handle both tasks well, although rendering still can be painful.	**Add-on Video** NuBus boards can give you accelerated video and better resolution for more impressive computer screen results.
CD-ROM Drives Commercially available still and animated textures and photos from your own camera can be imported into your programs from CD-ROM discs.	**The PowerPC Macintosh** The rendering time in this class jumps up not in mere percentages, but by three- or four-fold over the 68040 machines. Modeling huge, complex models on even the slowest PowerPC is a snap.	**NTSC (TV) Video** Conversion boards let you export your product to video tape. Some offer hardware compression for full screen real-time playback.

SOFTWARE: SOUL OF THE CPU

The most notable element that differentiates various 3D software packages is user interface.

Historically, Macintosh software has followed a carefully designed user interface. One of the strong points of the Macintosh system is the similar use of devices such as menus and icons to help familiarize the new user to unknown software frontiers. These common denominators help reduce training time and increase cross-software adaptability. In general, 3D software throws a cog into this carefully designed interface gear.

Rules that formed a standard platform for 2D illustration packages have taken a back seat to the devices that 3D software developers have employed in attempts to deal with the added third dimension. No firm interface standard has been developed in dealing with 3D. The result is a series of different devices that allow the user to manipulate the viewer's position as well as elements within the world they are creating.

Illustrators who work with 2D software can painlessly hop from Illustrator to FreeHand to MacDraw without much problem. The interface is common in dealing with the X,Y axes. The tools often perform the same function and many of the command keys are identical.

The same cannot be said for 3D software. The tools and controls are different in various 3D packages. Some modeling programs, such as Infini-D, allow the user to work in "three space." Three space permits a modeler to view, simultaneously, a scene from three distinct viewing planes. This provides useful and immediate feedback on perceiving exactly what is going on from each vantage point.

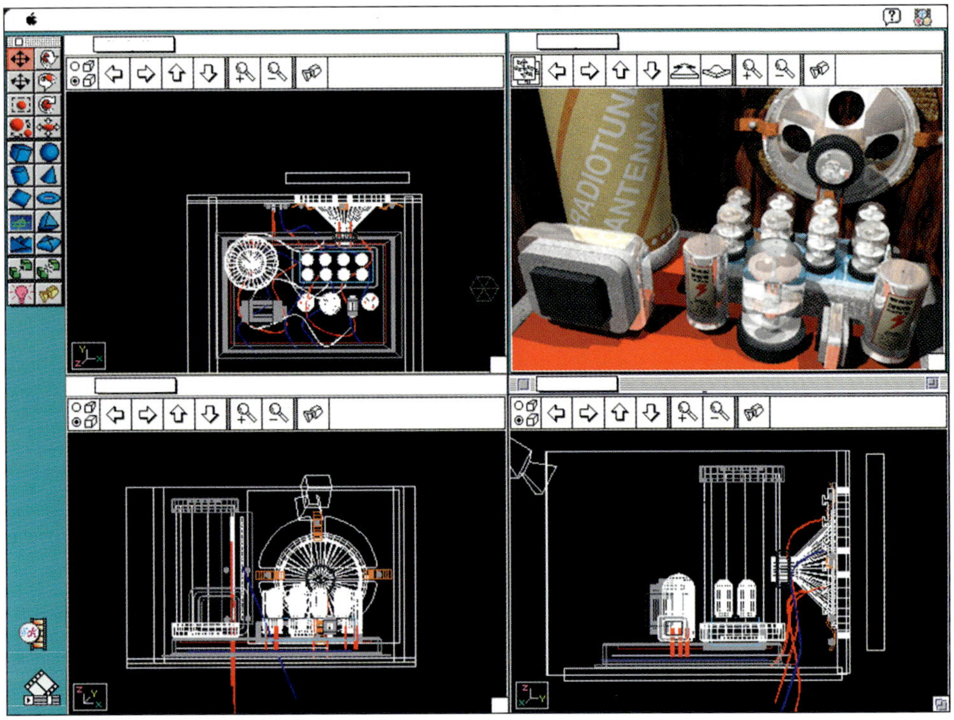

Programs like Infini-D offer multiple windows that give the viewer immediate feedback to show what is happening from each view. The drawback is the amount of screen real estate they take up.

We work on computer (flat, single-view) screens, thus we lack the binocular vision into the 3D world that would allow us to see that the vase we are putting on a table goes on the center, not on the edge. By working in orthographic mode with three windows showing us the top, front and side, we can get immediate satisfaction that our vase will not fall off the table. However, working with three viewing windows and a camera view does eat up valuable screen space. One solution to this is working from a singular viewing plane.

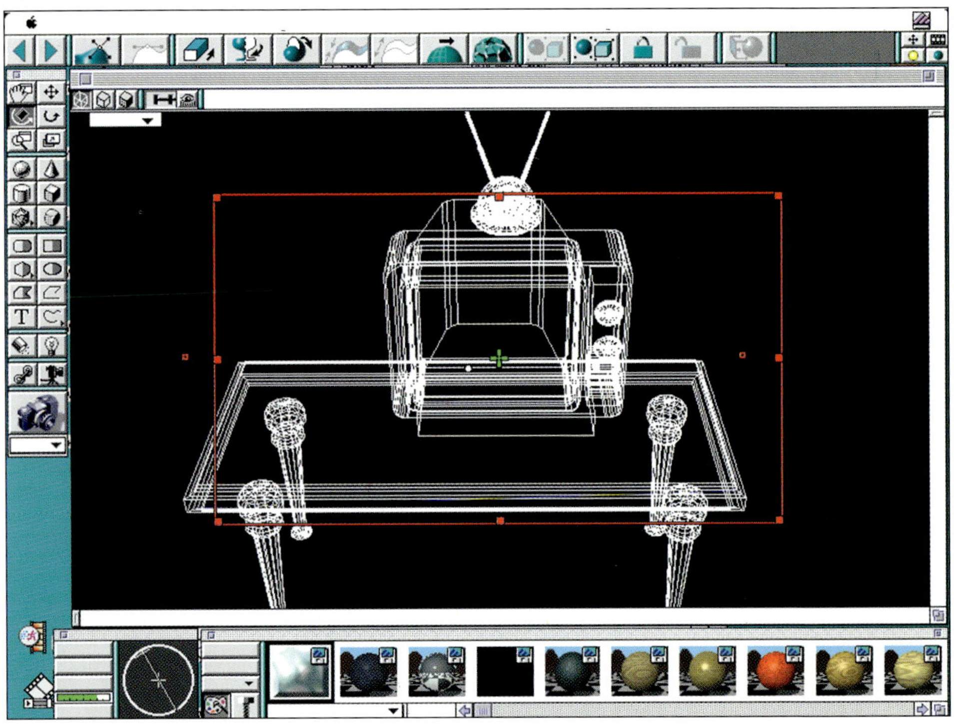

Single window working planes allow the user to fill the screen with the scene, using menu selections or navigation windows, like the one shown here in red from Strata StudioPro to change the viewing plane.

The single world view is a device employed by many programs (form•Z, StrataVision 3D, StudioPro, MacroModel, Swivel 3D Pro and Ray Dream Designer). This view is a single plane which allows the user to change quickly from top, bottom, front, side or a variable angle. The user moves around the model (changing views) via menu selection, navigational arrows, mouse manipulation or a virtual trackball. This system's advantage is that it allows the viewer to work with a single, large window.

Even these modes are not carved in stone. In Infini-D, you can close all the small windows and work from the camera view, using virtual bookmarks to zip from one view to another. Strata's software allows the user to create multiple windows, each can be customized to mimic the multiple, 3-space viewing scheme.

Shortcomings abound since no best way to deal with creating 3D images from your computer screen's 2D plane exists. Until we can strap on our sensor suits and walk into a virtual sculpture studio, we will have to deal with the frustrations of user interfaces that limit us to using our screens as windows.

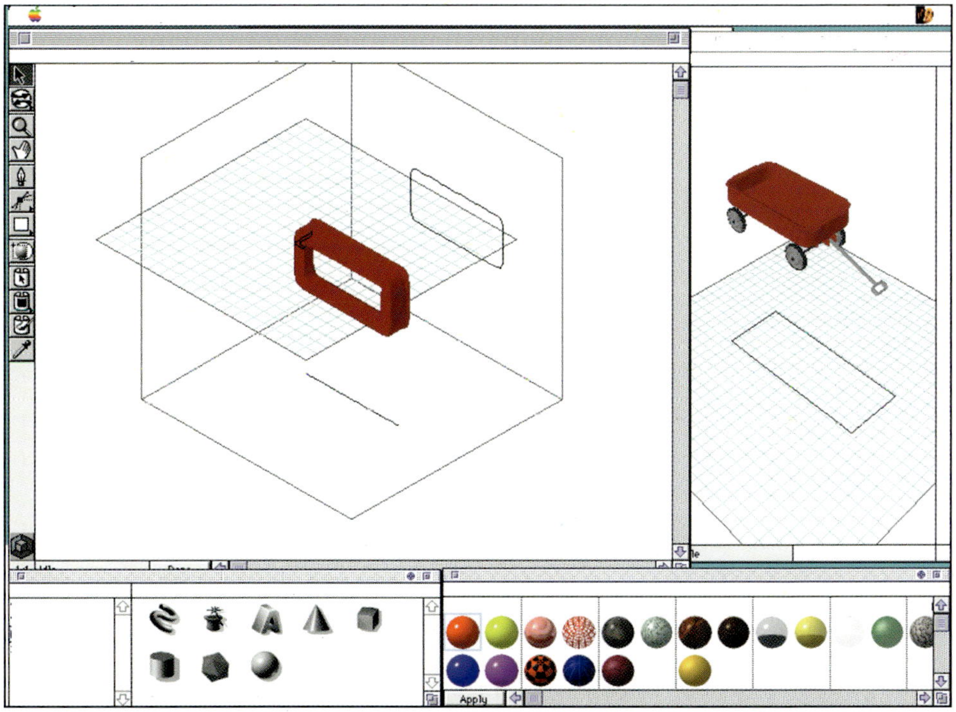

Model courtesy of Ray Dream

To create individual shapes, Ray Dream Designer (above) incorporates a "hands off" template modeler. Shapes are formed by manipulating templates on surrounding working planes.

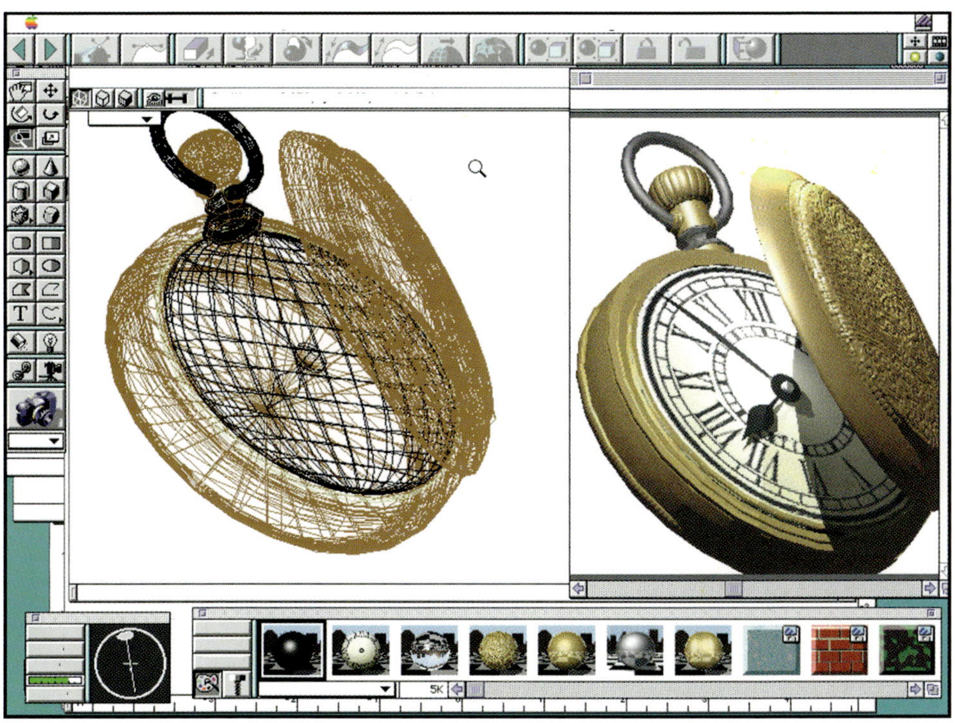

Model courtesy of Strata

Most modeling programs, like StudioPro (above), offer a direct "hands on" approach. The user interacts directly with the objects.

Getting various software packages to work together is a relatively simple matter, considering all the variables involved. Although a dozen formats are available, almost all of the *image imports and exports* can be handled in five formats: QuickTime, PICT (PICT2), PICS, EPS, and DXF.

QuickTime: Apple's system extension combines video, sound and still image compression into a single package. You can create a QuickTime movie as a final product, full of animation, complete with transitions and robust with sound or use it merely to create an animation file to be imported into another project, such as Premiere. Still images also can be saved with QuickTime JPEG compression.

PICT: More accurately known as PICT2, it is universal among animation and imaging packages. Texture maps imported into animation software generally use PICT files and editing software such as Premiere or Director will gladly import them.

PICS: This is a tidy file format that contains all the PICT frames of an animation. PICS does not allow compression methods like QuickTime, but does keep the quality of the image intact. Most animation programs and utilities support the PICS format.

EPS: Drawing programs, which are useful for creating detailed texture images and shapes, save in EPS format.

DXF: 3D objects can be moved between programs as well in DXF. Some programs offer direct support for other native formats but DXF is considered the common denominator among 3D programs.

Whatever format your software supports, the conventions are still the same. Image files (PICT) are mapped to model surfaces; models can be exported (DXF or native) to set up animation sequences or choreographed inside an integrated modeling animation package. The resulting animation is imported into an editing program (PICS or QuickTime).

ASSEMBLING YOUR TOOLBOX

In the early Mac days, the choice between software packages for creating images was easy: MacPaint for bitmap images and MacDraw for object-oriented drawing. The images may have been a bit crude in those early days, but the choice of which package to use was a snap.

Times change. By exploring today's options for 3D animation software, you will find quite a bit of crossover between program functions. For instance, Illustrator, while not a 3D program, can play an important role in 3D animation. Illustrator can create image files to be exported into Photoshop and then placed on a 3D surface. Shapes drawn in the program can be imported directly into modeling programs and be used to quickly build complex shapes.

A variety of 3D modeling programs allow you to build, animate and render models and animations. Some editing programs will take you from importing the animation clips to controlling a high-end video recording deck to transfer the animation to tape.

The chart (below) illustrates the functions of some popular software. By no means does it represent all the off-the-shelf packages

<table>
<tr><th>CREATION[1]
Tools for creating color, texture maps and shapes to import as definable objects.</th><th>MODELING[2]
Software used for creating 3D Models.</th><th>ANIMATING
Applications used for choreographed models for 3D animation and mapping surface textures.</th><th>RENDERING
Software for creating final shaded versions of animation and outputting the desired file type.</th></tr>
<tr><td rowspan="15">Photoshop
• PICT files for mapping surfaces and creating backgrounds

Illustrator
• EPS files for creating shapes
• Image creation for surface mapping

MacDraw
• PICT files for shapes[3]
• Image creation for surface mapping

PixelPaint Pro
Color Studio
Painter
• PICT files for mapping surfaces and creating backgrounds

FreeHand
• EPS files for creating shapes
• Image creation for surface mapping</td><td colspan="3">Infini-D</td></tr>
<tr><td colspan="3">Vision 3D and StudioPro</td></tr>
<tr><td colspan="3">PixelPutty</td></tr>
<tr><td colspan="3">Animation Master</td></tr>
<tr><td colspan="3">Shade</td></tr>
<tr><td colspan="3">Extreme 3D</td></tr>
<tr><td colspan="3">Presenter Professional[4]</td></tr>
<tr><td>Sketch![5]</td><td colspan="2">Showplace/MacRenderMan</td></tr>
<tr><td>Designer[5]</td><td colspan="2">Macromedia Three-D</td></tr>
<tr><td>form•Z</td><td colspan="2">Morph[6]</td></tr>
<tr><td>Sculptor/Sculpt 3D</td><td colspan="2">Metaflo'[6]</td></tr>
<tr><td>MacroModel</td><td></td><td>BackBurner[7]</td></tr>
<tr><td></td><td colspan="2">Electric Image</td></tr>
<tr><td></td><td></td><td>Render Pro[7]</td></tr>
<tr><td></td><td></td><td>MacRenderMan[8]</td></tr>
</table>

NOTES

1. In most cases, you can survive by starting with a good modeling program. Most modeling programs have tools available to create colors and often textures, as well as a host of tools to create shapes. Reaching outside of the programs to other software packages can increase dramatically the strength of your toolbox. 2. 3D modeling packages usually have built-in rendering schemes. 3. Swivel 3D ships with Swivelizer, which allows you to take PICT objects and import them as shapes. MacroModel also supports PICT import. 4. Presenter has built-in support for Macrenderman as a rendering engine. 5. Some 3D illustration programs have strong modeling tools, but their rendering capabilities are focused on still images. Most support DXF exports which you can bring into your animation program. 6. Some special effects programs create animations by importing either still or moving images, manipulating them, rendering a final sequence and outputting them, usually as PICS or QuickTime. 7. BackBurner is a network renderer that works only with Infini-D. RenderPro processes only StrataVision 3D and StudioPro files.

available. This chart only gives you a selection of products often used by animation professionals. Dozens of more defined and task-specific programs are available to help create animations for niche markets such as virtual architectural walk-through or character-based animation packages.

Macintosh-based software provides a great deal of mobility between programs. Because of this, most of the packages below can be used in conjunction with one another. For example, to produce an animation, you might: 1) Create labels in Illustrator. 2) Import them into Photoshop. 3) Map the labels to a surface in Infini-D where you set up the animation to render in BackBurner. 4) Import the work into After Effects (where you might employ a Photoshop filter) to create a QuickTime movie. 5) Access the QuickTime movie with a HyperCard stack. Then, a viewer at a kiosk could interactively push a button and see your animation.

You could also build and render an animation entirely in Swivel 3D, import the resulting PICS file into JAG II to remove jaggies, run that resulting file through DeBabel-izer to resize the file and apply a distortion filter and export the results as a QuickTime movie.

EDITING Takes the resulting file, usually PICS, PICT or QuickTime, and creates a final movie.	PRODUCTION The movie is then ready to be displayed on screen, or laid to tape resulting in...	OUTPUT ... a file format that is transportable between many applications, resulting in...
Photoshop[9]		
Premiere		QuickTime movie
After Effects		QuickTime movie
Avid[10]		QuickTime movie with real-time playback
Media 100[11]		QuickTime movie with real-time playback
Avid VideoShop		QuickTime movie
VideoFusion		QuickTime movie
Jag II[12]		QuickTime movie & PICT/PICS
DeBabelizer[13]		All imaginable formats
Macromedia Director		QuickTime movies, PICS, tape deck control for recording
	HyperCard	Multimedia, computer screen display
	SuperCard	Multimedia, computer screen display
	Apple Media Kit	Multimedia, computer screen display

PRODUCT

...a file that is either kept digital for applications such as CD games or broadcast production.

QuickTime Movies (digital)

Apple's video and animation format is a boon to creating animations. It creates a standard for moving and storing images synchronized with sound. The final product can be, with the right hardware and software, played back in real-time, full screen at 30 frames/second. The movie also can be kept digital for playback in an action sequence on a CD-ROM game or in a short film on the flight of a bumblebee for an electronic encyclopedia. The movie could even be re-imported right back into most editing programs for even more tweaking.

Video/Film Production (analog)

With proper hardware and software configurations the final output can be edited down to professional-level linear editing stations, recording frame by frame, or played back via a non-linear editing system to virtually any video source. Most editing packages and video boards produce broadcast-legal NTSC (television standard) signals.

Multimedia (interactive)

QuickTime, PICS, PICT and sound files can be imported easily into most of the multimedia packages available. The results are an interactive kiosk in a shopping mall, an employee training lesson or a multi-screen presentation. The portability of most of the digital files makes it a simple matter for your computer to juggle movie clips, sound bites, scanned photographs and music scores.

8. MacRenderMan can process animations from programs that support the RIB format. The RIB format is a Macrenderman format that can be used to transport files. 9. Exported still images from editing files can be edited in Photoshop to take advantage of its powerful image manipulation. 10. High-end Avid systems require Avid hardware, as well as software. 11. Media 100 requires proprietary hardware to use its software. 12. Jag II is a utility that anti-aliases single images or whole animation files. 13. DeBabelizer is a powerful, cross-platform tool that can open most file formats, manipulate them with similar capabilities and the same filters as Photoshop and save the results in any number of file formats.

PULLING IT ALL TOGETHER

All 3D animations start from 3D models. All 3D models begin their journey as shapes. Usually, the shapes are 2D elements that are lathed, swept or extruded. They also can be 3D primitives, like a sphere that is reconfigured similar to a soft ball of clay which is pushed and pulled into the desired shape. Whatever the genesis, the model is the building block from which all animation is born.

BUILDING THE MODEL

While some programs offer strong drawing tools to create the basic elements of the shapes, many animators prefer using the strength of dedicated Postscript drawing programs such as Illustrator or FreeHand to create more complicated shapes.

Modeling programs that offer PICT support can use applications such as MacDraw or Canvas. The information from these imported shapes, or shapes and primitives derived from the modeling program, form the objects that are either stand-alone models or parts of a complex form.

The model can have its attitude adjusted–rotated clockwise or counterclockwise, leaned backward or forward and swung from left to right. Usually this pivoting takes place from the object's center axis point.

After an object is created and adjusted in attitude, it can then be attached to other objects in a process that is known universally as *linking*. The links between objects can be a firm lock that allows no repositioning of an object, or it can be dynamic, allowing free pivoting on one or more axes.

The relationship between objects is commonly referred to as *child* and *parent*. The child can move independent of the parent. When a parent moves, they all move. An example of this is the model of a doorway. The child-parent structure would be: doorknob, door, hinge, wall. The doorknob could rotate freely without affecting other elements because it is the child of the door. When the door swings open, the doorknob moves along with it. The door is linked to the hinge, which stays in place because it is linked to the wall. The link between the door and the hinge can be constrained so that the attitude of the door can be adjusted in only one direction, swinging on the Y-axis to simulate how a door really opens.

The ability to create a shape, change its direction, link it to an object and subse-

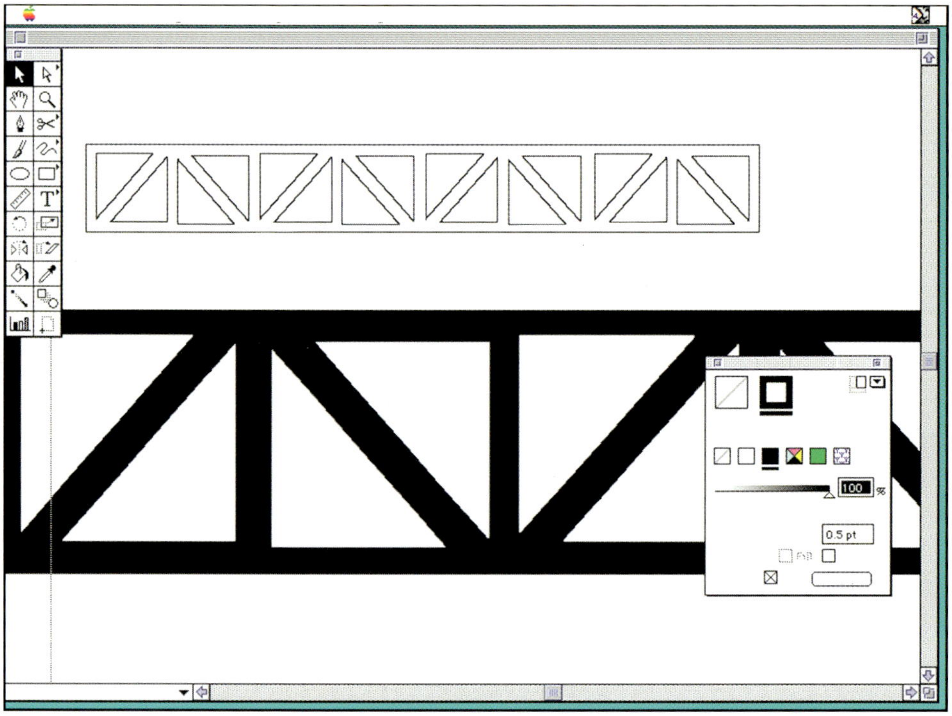

2D drawing programs, such as Illustrator, allow the animator to use a range of powerful shape creation tools that usually are not available inside modeling programs. Using black-and-white files will not make a difference in the shape, but it can be used as a good organization tool to see how the form is structured (above).

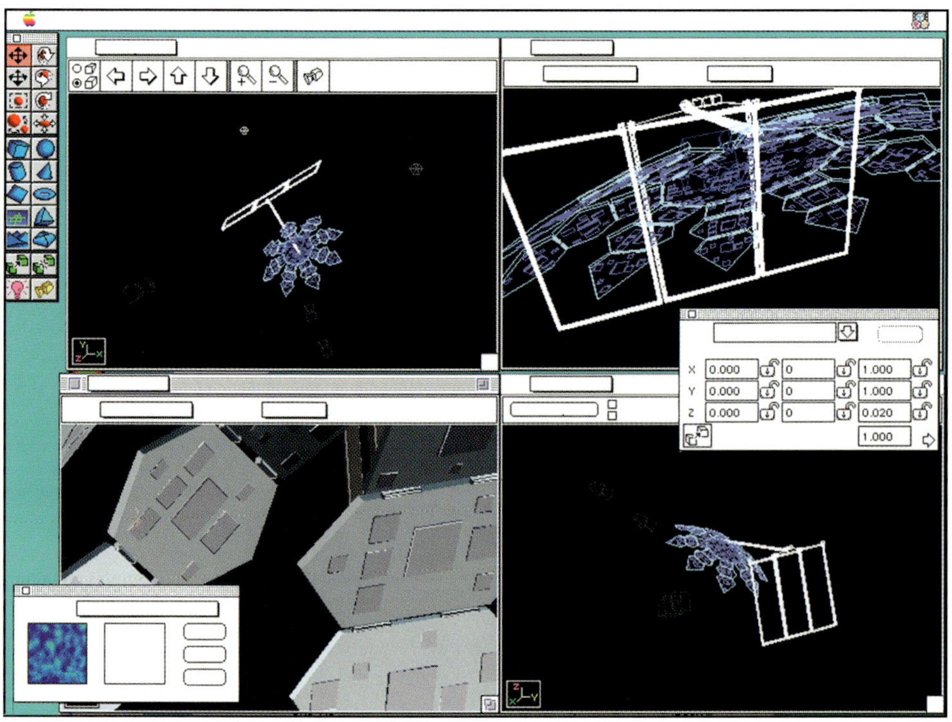

The shapes are imported or created inside the modeling program then links are established. This process of putting together shapes is where the structure of the model begins. In Infini-D (above), three windows help orient the user to working in three dimensions. The fourth window (upper right) is the final camera view. Fast shading (lower right window) helps give a feel for overall form and lighting.

quently other objects gives the animator the capabilities to create almost any conceivable, and inconceivable object.

CREATING THE TEXTURES

To bring an object to life, the animator applies a texture to the surface of the model. Two types of surface textures exist: computer-generated procedural and imported images, usually PICT files.

Procedural textures are generated by the computer. By using a set of variables, the program alters the object's color, highlights, bump maps, reflections and transparency.

Image files that are created outside of the modeling and animation software are called imported texture maps. These files have the bonus of being applied to the surface of an object to give it a high degree of realism.

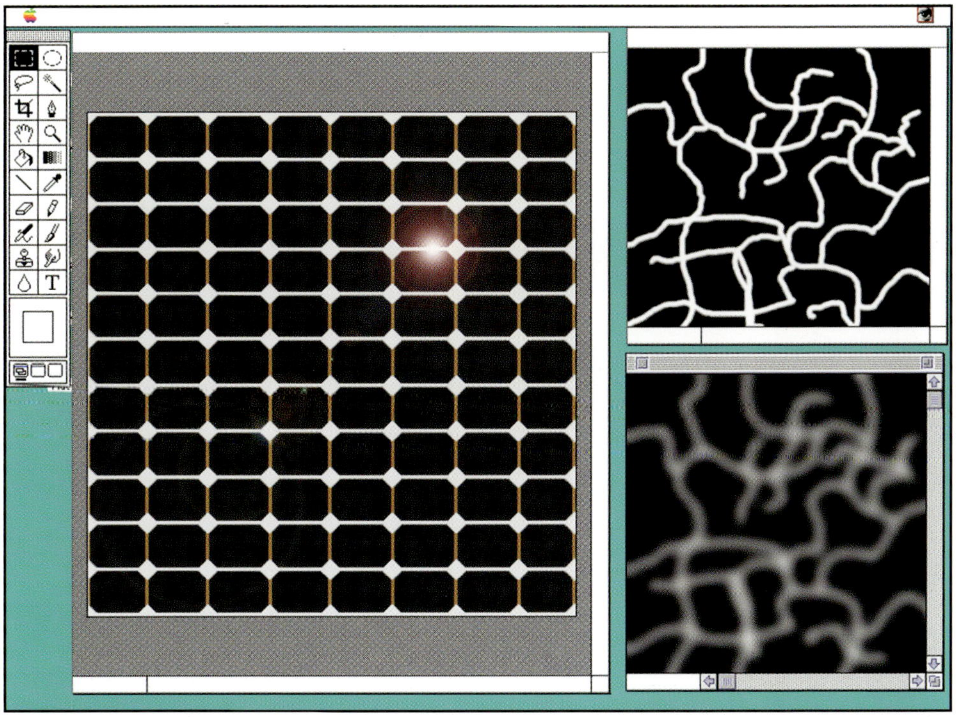

In an image-editing program, such as Photoshop (above), textures for the model can be created or edited. The satellite model uses two texture maps: the solar cells for the solar panels and a chrome environment map to help give some of the flat surfaces a little sheen. The environment map is in its first stage (top right). The map is blurred for its final image (lower right).

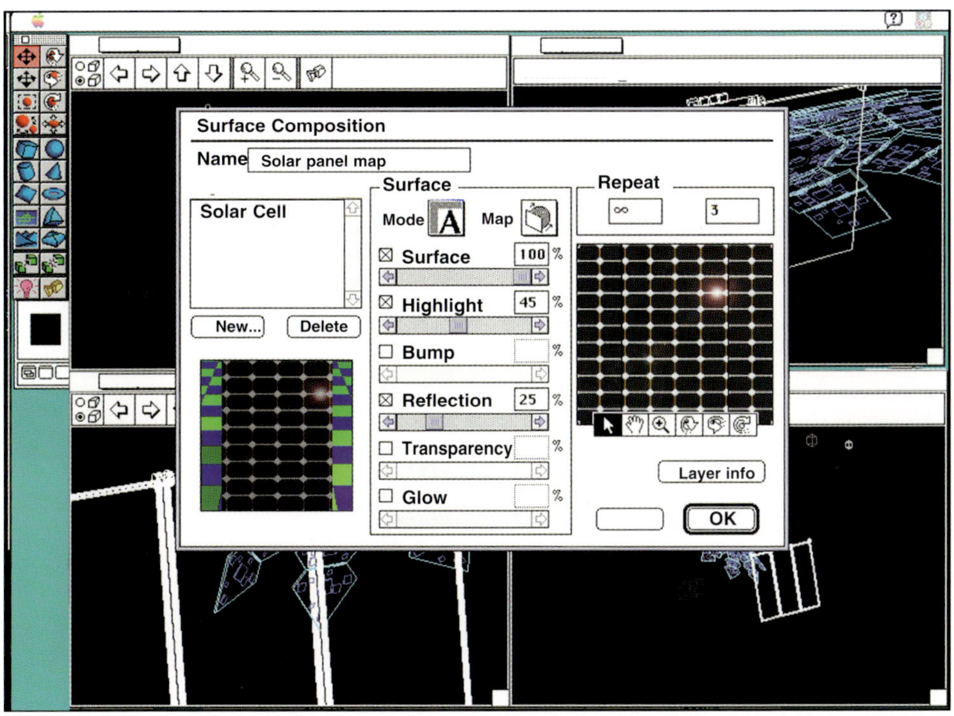

Texture maps are then imported. Textures can be applied in stand-alone animation programs like Three-D or Electric Image, or inside integrated modeling-animation packages like Infini-D (above) or Stratavision 3D and StudioPro. The texture map is applied to individual shapes–for example, the solar cell texture that is being applied to only the solar panels.

Imported texture maps come from many sources. A soup can label may be created inside a 2D drawing program and converted to an acceptable import format, like PICT. An image editing program like Photoshop might be employed to create a grainy surface using its Noise and Emboss filters to make a beach surface. A photograph can be taken of a lumber sample and applied to a whole house to make a log cabin.

Models usually have a combination of different texture treatments. A block wall might use an image texture of a concrete wall from a CD-ROM. The window would use the modeling program's on-board surface creation tools to make the glass.

Once a texture has been created, whether from inside the program or from an external source, it must then be applied to the model. Procedural maps are volumetric in nature–they are applied to the entire model. (If you cut a model in half with a procedural map applied, the texture would be the same on the inside.) Image maps are applied to look the best only on the surface of the model. Applying image maps is like applying virtual wallpaper.

Different mapping technique settings are available to apply to different surfaces. Spherical mapping, for instance, is designed for wrapping an image around a round image, like stitches on a baseball. Flat mapping is designed to place an image straight on a flat surface. The modeler must choose which surface mapping technique to use with each object. Since the world of potential models is so diverse, this can be a hit-or-miss effort as the user experiments with different possibilities.

The image map is not the only concern when applying texture maps. The modeler is also responsible for deciding a host of other surface variables. Does he or she want the surface to be shiny? If so, the user must boost the specular highlights. If the object is transparent or translucent, the user must adjust the surface tools accordingly. In the real world we do not spend a lot of time thinking about surface treatments, but when creating a photo-realistic image, each object's surface variables should be adjusted.

SETTING UP THE ANIMATION

The next step is adding motion to your

model. Animations really do not move. It is an optical illusion relying on the eye's visual retention to see motion in what is really 30 still images flickering each second on the screen.

To animate a computer model, move the object around the screen and let the computer do all the hard work figuring out how to get it from point A to point B. All animation programs, whether stand-alone or integrated, use a timeline-based method to choreograph the objects as they move over time. An important element of this timeline is the keyframe.

A keyframe is a reference point in the timeline where an event occurs. Example: If you had an animation of a hammer hitting a nail, you might have two keyframes for the hammer movement. The first would be with the hammer pulled back, poised to strike. The second would be the hammer hitting the nail.

What happens next is a process called *in-betweening* or *tweening*. You tell the computer to create the motion. Example: Poised to strike (first keyframe), the head of the hammer is linked to the handle and will move wherever the handle goes. The handle will pivot in an arc and hit the nail. So at the 30th frame, or one-second mark, the hammer's handle will be positioned at the point where the head of the hammer is at the nail (second keyframe). The 28 frames between the raised hammer position to the strike point will be figured out by the computer. This is another area where the power of the computer really benefits the user.

To help give natural and smooth motions to these objects, the animator is given ease-in and ease-out as well as spline curve controls. Ease-in and ease-out adjustments can put more frames of an animation at the beginning or end of a sequence. The effect is an object slowly accelerating into its move, or slowly decelerating when it is finished. Spline curves allow the motion at peak points to be smooth instead of sharply defined.

RENDERING THE ANIMATION

After the model has been sequenced, it has to be rendered. Until now, most of the work has been done in a lower rendering mode such as wireframe. Wireframe mode allows the animator to work quickly without having to wait for screen redraws. The final product will be rendered using a more sophisticated and timely rendering mode such as Phong or ray tracing.

Integrated modeling-animation programs have built-in rendering capabilities, as well as optional network rendering software. Stand-alone animation packages such as Three-D, MacRenderMan or Electric Image import models, apply textures, choreograph, then render. In any case, the variables are similar. The user must decide what level of image quality is needed by choosing the level of sophistication of the rendering algorithm used.

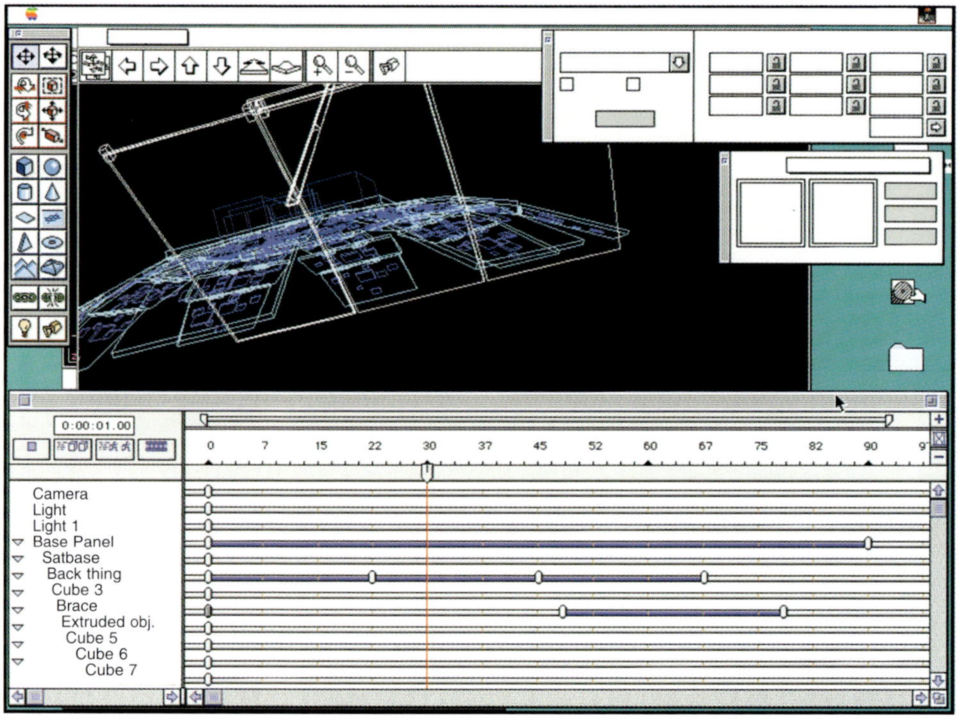

Animations are placed in motion by moving models in the scene at different points along a timeline. In the Infini-D sequencer (above, screen bottom), different objects are in the vertical column on the left while the timeline is played out from 0 to 90 frames (30 frames per second). The event marks locate where an adjustment has been made to an element, whether it has moved, changed in scale, rotated, changed textures or morphed in shape.

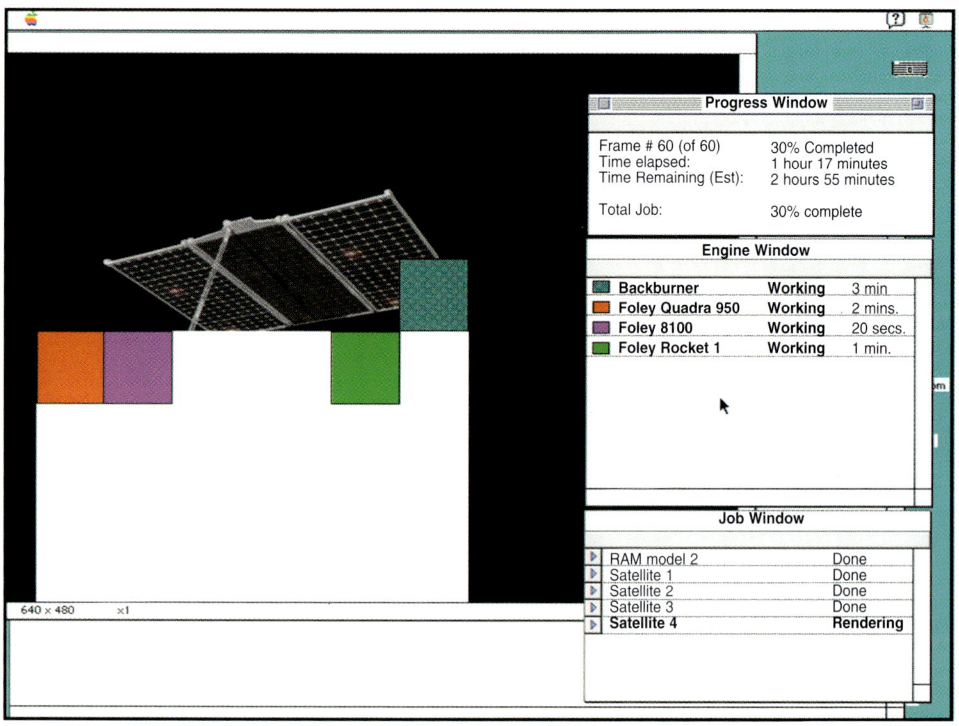

After the choreographing of an animation is complete, the file must be rendered. The model (above) was rendered using Infini-D's optional network rendering software, BackBurner. This program allows for distributed rendering, also known as network rendering. This shared rendering places the burden between available Macintoshes on a network or dedicated co-processing boards. The image of the satellite is being ray traced with medium anti-aliasing.

Ray Tracing is the best, but takes a heavy toll in rendering time. *Phong Shading* does not support some of the features of ray tracing, such as transparency or reflections, but might support texture mapping and shadows, depending on the software used. *Gouraud Shading*, another option usually available, is a fast shading mode that allows smooth rendering and accurate lighting, but usually does not support texture maps or shadows.

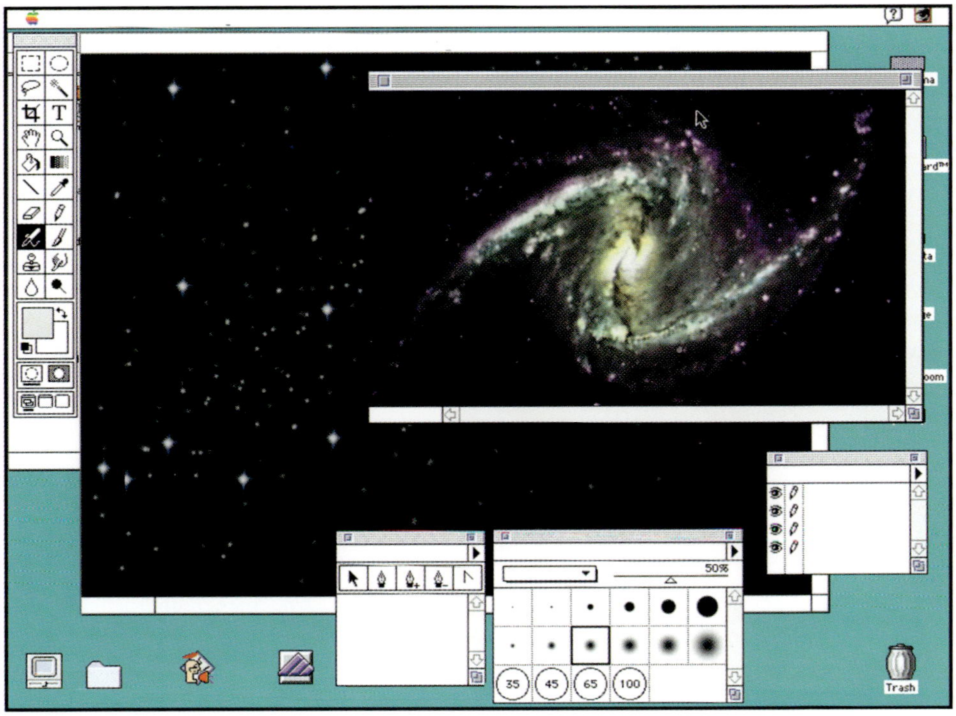

Backgrounds (2D elements) can be created or edited in programs like Photoshop (above). Rendering the animation with an alpha channel will allow compositing of several elements in the editing process, such as the satellite on top of a space background. These are considerations that must be planned out before the editing process. Rendering the image without a space background will give the animator more flexibility when compiling the animation later. It also will make for a faster render and a smaller animation file.

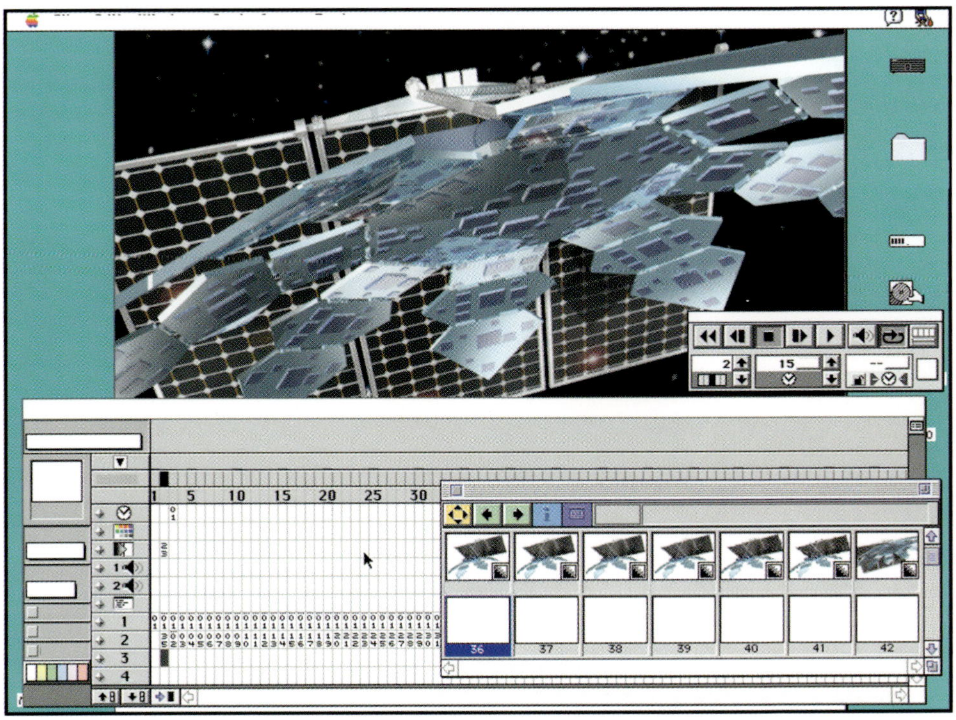

A single animation can contain several animation files, background images and even 2D elements that also move (only on the X,Y-axis). The editing program is where all these files come together. Most editing programs, like Director (above), use channels on the vertical left hand column to introduce new cast members. The timeline across the top shows how the cast members are placed in time with the movie being created. The structure is very similar in concept to how a sequencer in an animation program works.

Another alternative is *anti-aliasing*. When the computer renders an image, it does its best to give objects clean, defined edges. However, a problem arises when it draws the edge, the point where one object ends and another begins. Close inspection of any unrefined computer rendered image will reveal a jagged edge. The stair stepped ridges are called *aliases*. Rendering programs incorporate a technique called *anti-aliasing* to remove these edges.

This much-needed process takes time, however. To get the sharper edges, many programs employ a technique called *supersampling*, where a much larger image than that being rendered is created and used to define a tighter edge. The larger image takes longer to render, but using it will assure higher quality.

Another solution is post-render anti-aliasing by using a product like Jag II to remove the edges. This software looks for contrasting edges you would find in the stair step and averages them out. The quality may not be as good, but it is quicker.

A final render can be done on a single Mac or networked over a group of Macs. The render also can utilize a single Mac with parallel processing boards, like Radius Rockets or YARC boards, in available NuBus slots. Rendering is the most time-consuming process. It is best done during the computer's down time, such as nights or weekends.

EDITING THE ANIMATION

The output of the render usually is a QuickTime movie, a PICS file or numbered PICT files. The output can be imported easily into most editing programs.

Output from the render might be just what the animator wanted. But the animation often is part of a larger project, or needs to be edited by compositing the animation onto a background, adding text labels or combining several animations into one movie.

Animations are often a combination of several animated files that must be layered together as well. All these tasks can be handled inside editing programs like Premiere, After Effects or Director. These programs can import other files such as photographs, live video and CD-ROM images that can be incorporated into a final product.

THE FINAL PRODUCT

The resulting file from the edited animation can go in any number of directions.

Animations recorded in QuickTime and designed for full-screen (640x480 pixels) playback can use special hardware compression coder/decoders (CODECS) to help speed up the animation playback. The resulting animation can be viewed straight from the computer in real time. The files also might be played back onto professional video equipment one frame at a time for the best possible quality. Since only one animation frame is recorded at a time, it is not necessary to compress and decompress the file. This gives the image the highest possible quality. Recording frame by frame requires special hardware or software to control a frame-accurate recording device, such as a laser disk recorder or Beta video deck.

The animations may also be designed for multimedia playback. The files can be optimized to playback quickly from a hard drive or CD-ROM without any special hardware. Animation files can easily be incorporated into training materials or entertainment products. QuickTime offers a great deal of portability into all presentation and multimedia packages.

The following pages will go into greater detail as to how all these elements work together to create a final animation. A wide variety of tools and utilities exists to facilitate animation creation and implementation. This list seems to grow every day. The software packages you choose to purchase will dictate the tools and resources you can utilize. The adage "You get what you pay for" generally applies to software as well.

As you read though the following pages and use some of the tips and hints provided, keep in mind that creating 3D animations is not a simple A+B=C situation. It often involves a great deal of problem-solving that can best be accomplished by the person putting together the animation files. Because the software mimics the real world in all its complexity, the solutions can be equally complex. One of the most frustrating aspects to creating 3D environments is that most of the time the computer is doing exactly what you are asking it to do! If something is not looking right, before blaming the computer, examine what you told it to do.

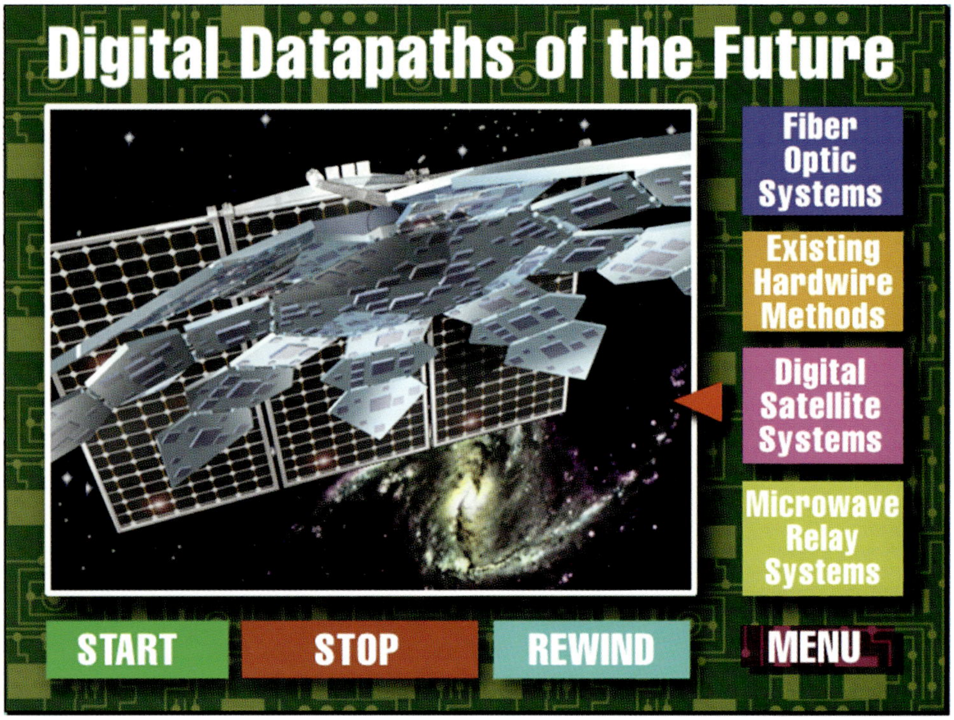

Animations can be kept in their digital format, often as QuickTime movies, that can be played back in a wide variety of applications. Programs such as Hypercard, Director, Supercard and the Apple Media Kit allow users with limited programming experience to create their own interactive multimedia presentations. The final product can be used for entertainment, education, inspiration, presentation, training, archiving or just about any imaginable purpose.

With special hardware, Macintosh animations can be output to videotape or played back live in real time. Many video companies have products that output a broadcast standard, NTSC, signal. Two tricks apply to getting the Macintosh to successfully output full-screen video at a sustained 30 frames a second. The first is using separate co-processor boards that can compress and decompress the video signal fast enough. The computer processor is not fast enough to handle this. The second is playing the animation to a frame-accurate tape deck that is controlled by a software or hardware device, writing a single frame to tape at a time, assuring smooth playback.

3. 3D MODELING

ANATOMY OF A MODEL

3D models are the foundation of computer animation. Artistic craftsmanship and precision engineering, combined with smoke and mirrors, join to create photo-realistic models.

Every curve, angle and shadow should be conceived by the modeler. Working in the computer's 3D environment does present some interesting surprises as the scene begins to take on its own life. Truly successful scenes are almost always the result of careful, overall planning combined with meticulous attention to detail. The path to success is through trial and error, along with understanding the capabilities of your hardware and software.

The following chapter serves as both a visual primer on what tools and features are available to the animator, as well as a guide to tips and techniques that will add polish to your models and animations.

A few general rules apply to 3D modeling that, if followed through in every model you work on, will become habits to aid you throughout your animations.

Work in orthographic views. This removes the perspective from your viewpoint so you can get a clean, accurate alignment between elements. Perspective, although desirable in your final render, can make it difficult to line up objects. Things may look right in perspective, but in reality, the objects may be in the wrong place. (See figure at the top of p. 47).

Work in multiple windows, whenever possible. If your software allows you to create multiple windows: create one for your top view, one for your front view and one for your left or right view. This may use a good deal of your screen's space, especially if you are using a 13" monitor, but you will be able to work much faster and your models will be easier to assemble.

Name everything. Name each piece of your

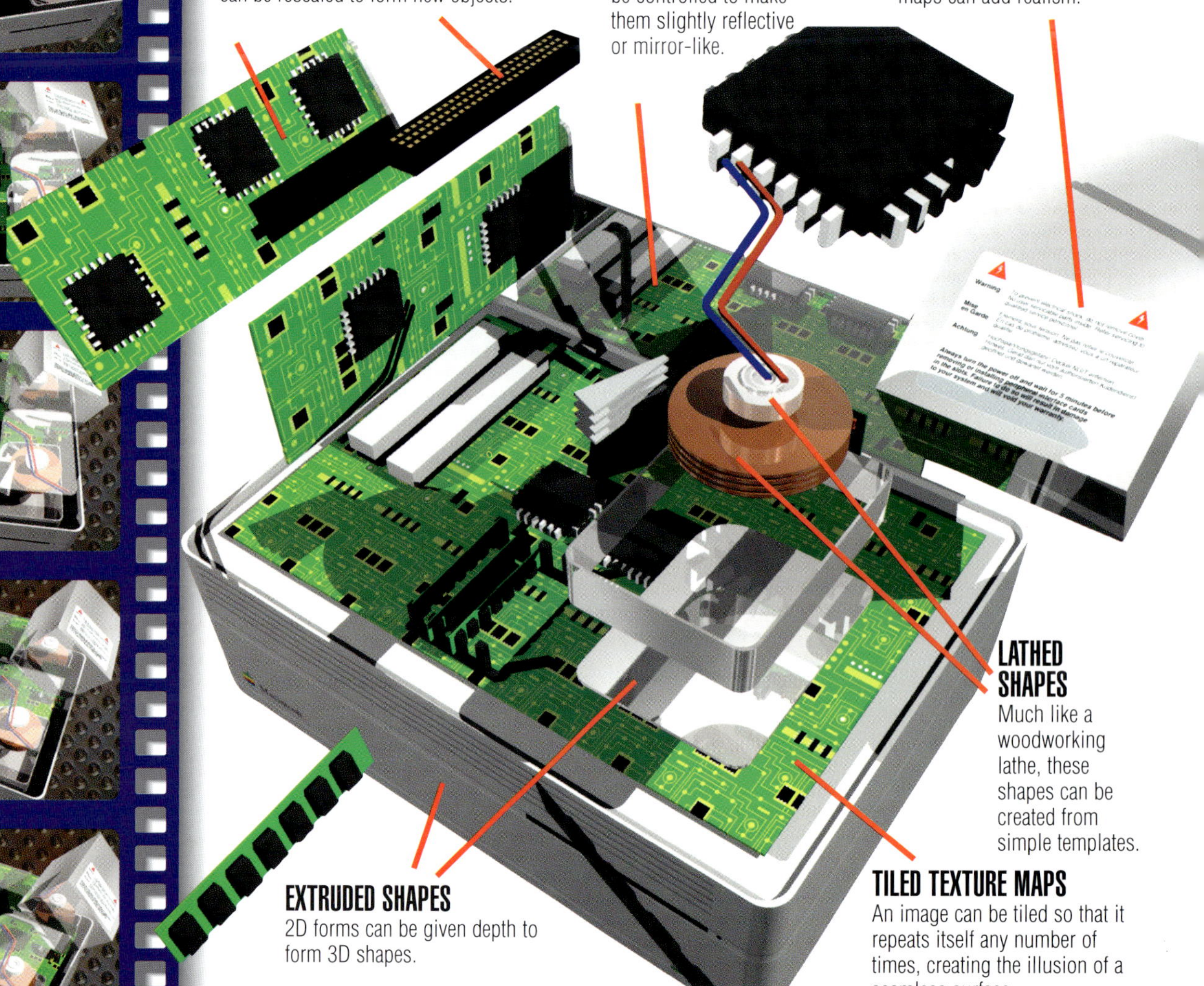

model. Name each color. Name each texture. With simple models this may seem like overkill, but it is one of the most important habits you can establish, so start early. When you have built a model with 200 parts, things can get a bit confusing. With all of the parts named, it makes it much easier to edit and animate your model.

Establish a naming technique for your associated files that makes sense to you. If you render an animation file, you might call it "File name.PICS." An image file you created to map to the side of a surface might be called "File name.PICT." Your resulting animation may be a QuickTime movie that you call "File name.QT." Some files may be created just to edit or experiment with, these might be called "File name.edit."

In the process of creating animations you will generate dozens of files. Some may be linked to your model as an imported surface; others just may be stray edit files. When you clean up your folders, you will know which files can be trashed and which ones *must* be kept. Animation files are huge. The last thing you want is unneeded files choking your hard drive. Actually, the *very* last thing you want is to throw away a file that your model needs to render or the final edit itself. A careful naming technique, diligently followed, will go a long way in keeping you out of trouble.

Keep associated files in same folder. It is tempting to make a single folder for all your textures, but it will kill your mobility. A few large files may be an exception. If you use a surface map of the planet Earth, you may not want more than one copy of this 1- or 2mb document.

For most associated files, like tile maps that compress to 10K, try to keep things nice and tidy by creating a folder for each project. If you work with a removable cartridge drive, which is almost mandatory if you create many animations, you will quickly find that your files get spread all over the place.

Create a stationery pad. To set preferences for your modeling software, open a new document and import files you use regularly, such as specific environment maps. Create a palette of colors you either like, or that work well with your final output. Set up a couple of lights and adjust your camera angle at a 45°-angle offset from the center, creating a nice, natural opening stage from which to work. Set your windows, if possible, to view from three sides orthographically and your camera at a normal lens setting (30-50mm). Once you have established this file, quit the program and select the document. Choose Get Info from the File menu. Check the Stationery Pad check box and close the dialog box.

To take this even further, save this document someplace safe and make an alias of it. Place the alias in your Apple Menu Items folder inside your System Folder. Now you can choose your stationery file at any time. From this point, it is easy to create a function key in a macro program that will choose this item from your Apple menu with a single keystroke. (Note, when you open it, you will choose Save As and name your new project!)

WORKING IN ORTHOGRAPHIC VIEW, TO KEEP PERSPECTIVE

The perspective image (below left) shows a TV with rabbit ears on top. Working with a side view reveals the rabbit ears actually are floating far back from the TV set (below right).

Perspective, rendered

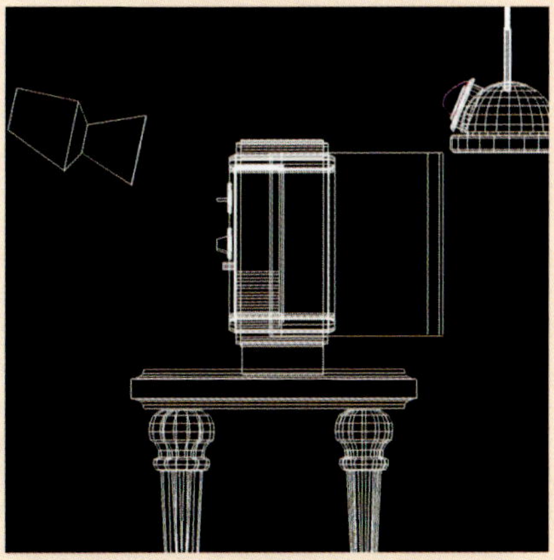

Orthographic, wireframe

BRINGING THE SHAPES TO LIFE: SURFACE TEXTURES AND MAPS

The computer model (page 46) used four different image files to create most of the surfaces. The circuit board color, on both the NuBus cards and the mother board, is made of a simple Photoshop-generated image and tiled to cover the entire surface. The NuBus slots had the pinholes mapped on them instead of creating a model with dozens of real holes poked in it. Real holes would have increased the file size as well as the rendering time.

The power supply label was created in Photoshop and mapped directly to a squashed cube. Or, just as easily, it could have been scanned into Photoshop at 100 to 200 dpi resolution and used as a decal in the same manner.

The front cover is a flat surface map that has fake vents drawn on it. Once again, this not only makes construction of the whole box simple, but it also keeps down the file and rendering size. Keep in mind when creating fake-3D surfaces where the light sources in the final model will be placed. Doing this will ensure your color import will match, or at least have the same feel as the rest of the scene.

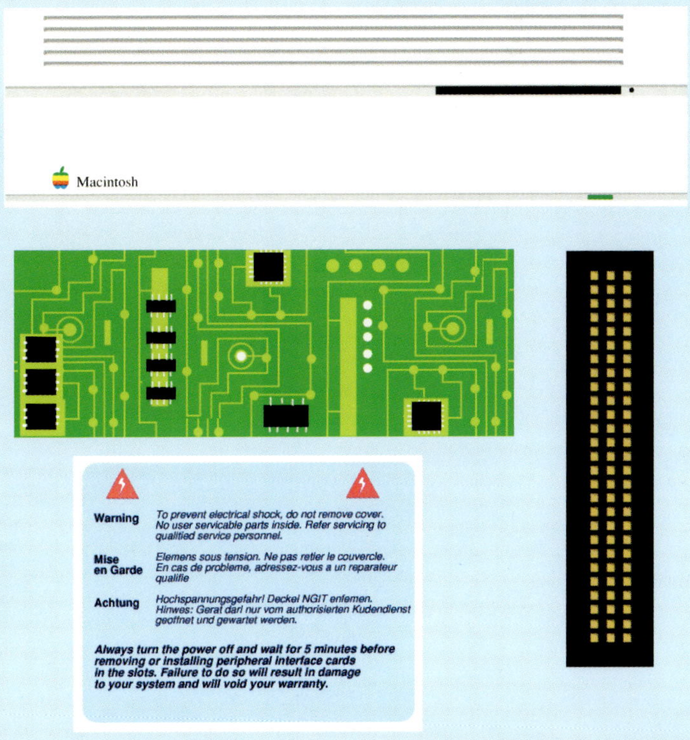

PRIMITIVES

Most modeling programs include a bundle of elementary shapes that can be used when creating models. These shapes, or *primitives*, provide a useful variety of easy-to-use forms that can be rendered quickly.

While primitives provide an easy stepping stone towards creating a 3D world, they also have advantages for advanced users. More sophisticated tools can replicate these simple shapes, but often at the cost of rendering time and file size.

If you need to make a telephone pole, using a cylinder instead of a lathed object will work well. (Lathe objects take longer to render.) If your scene requires 50 telephone poles you will soon see the importance of primitives.

Even though primitive forms may be simple, the detail may lie in the color map. Simple form does not mean simple image. Nine-tenths of creating a successful, realistic model is in the color map which is applied to the form.

BASIC BUILDING BLOCKS Simple objects can form realistic images. Like its more sophisticated family members–lathe, extrusion and free-form tools–the success of using primitives lies in the skillful use of color maps. For example, the same cube that creates a wall also becomes a magazine. The forms used to make the above images are shown below. The color-coded inset (below left) shows the primitives used to create the scene.

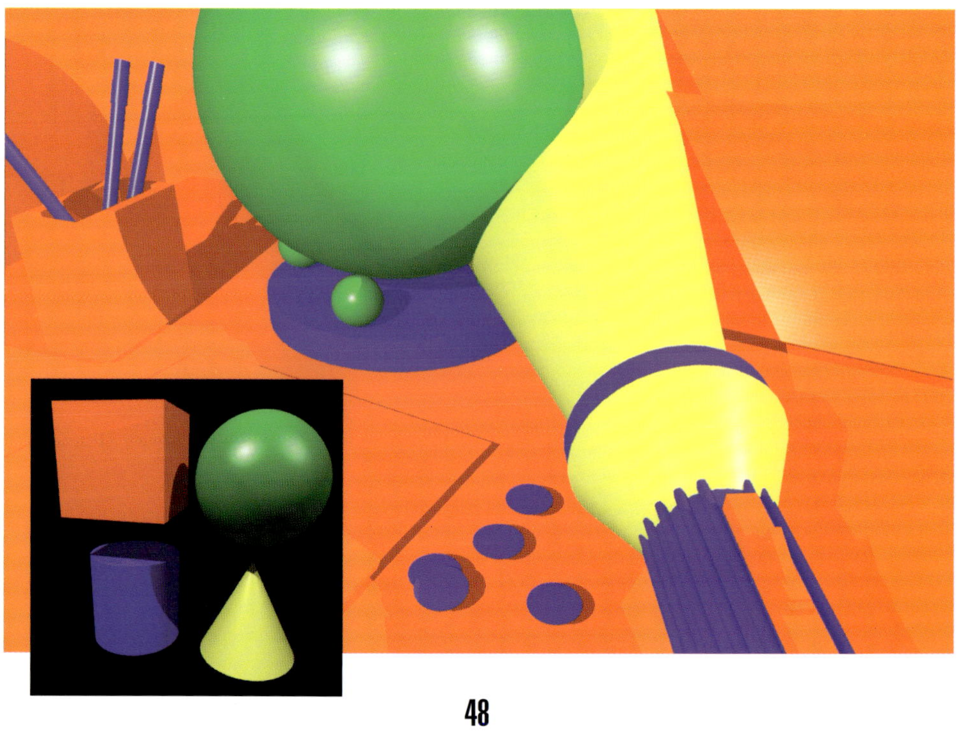

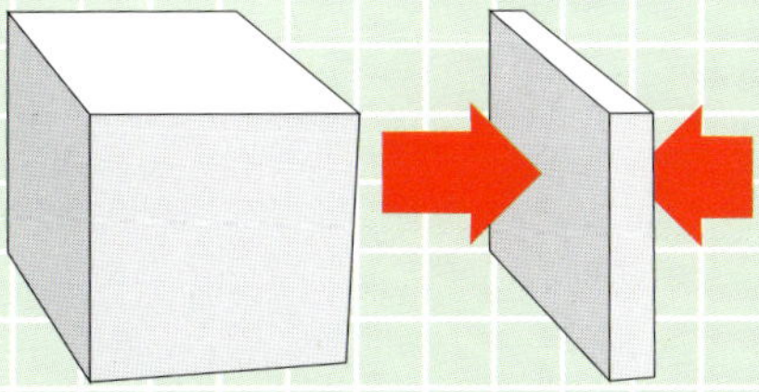

Squeezing down a cube on one side makes a flat surface.

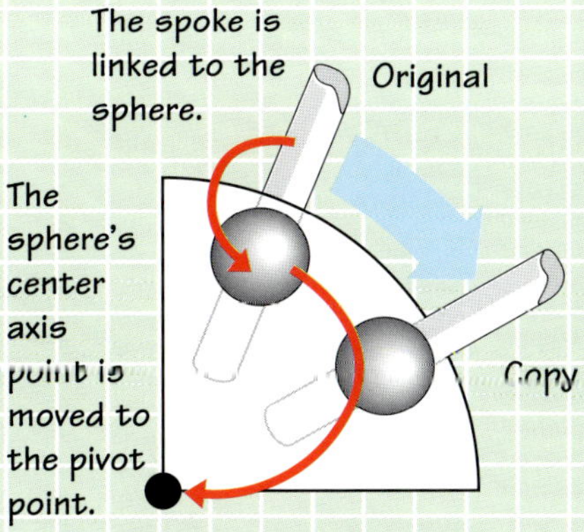

The sphere is then copied, pivoted (17° in this case) and linked to the original.

A single image file can wrap itself entirely around the sphere.

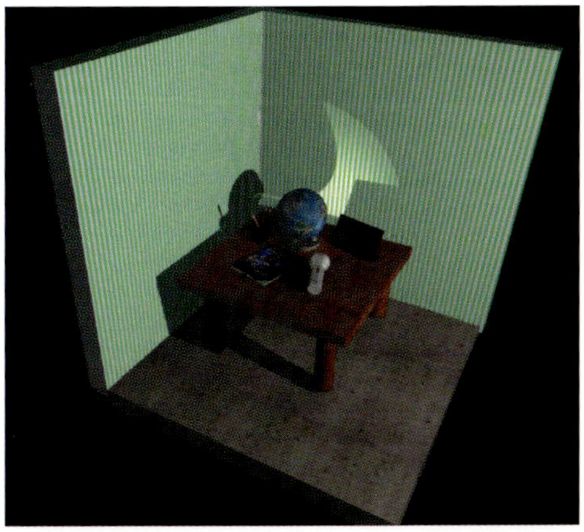

DOWN AND DIRTY STAGES

Very seldom do you want your background color showing through in your scenes. To create realistic images you have to create a believable stage. The simple cube is a quick, painless way to achieve that goal. Reducing the proportions of one side, you get a flat, mappable surface. By copying and rotating that object a few times, the walls, ceiling and floors quickly take shape.

DETAILS, DETAILS

The thrifty nature of the primitive makes it perfect for detail, especially repetitive detail. Spheres used as is or slightly squeezed make perfect rivets. Because of the economy of the shape, you can use many spheres. Cylinders make great ropes, wires, posts and spokes (left). In this example, both the rivets and the spokes were established. Then, using a "make-child-like-parent," or "replicate link" function, the image to the left came together with a dozen keystrokes. Remember, the computer can do a lot of your work–if you let it. Know your software.

ROUND THINGS

If you create balls and globes using the lathe tool, they can get bulky in short order. With no corners, bevels or defined shapes, this is one case where primitives rule supreme. The key, of course, is what you put on the sphere. Cylindrical wraps work well for globes where the top and bottom of the texture map pinches in, such as a Mercator projection map. Other textures, such as a tennis ball map, use a standard wrap that affixes an image onto the sphere much like a bumper sticker.

BEAUTY IS ONLY SKIN DEEP

Forget what your mother told you. It is not what is on the inside that counts–not at least in a computer's 3D world.

Primitives, by their nature, are very simple. But that does not mean primitives cannot be used to produce remarkable models. The surface texture mapping brings primitive models to life.

Although the image mapped to the surface is important, the technique used will reflect on the final product as well. Fortunately, most programs make it obvious which mapping technique to use.

With the expanded surfaces (right), the cube uses a 4-sided cubical map. The cone works with a cylindrical map, but beware of pinching at the top. Cylindrical wraps are well-designed for cylinders, and spherical maps for balls.

You do not always have to follow the rules. Sometimes it is fun to draw outside the lines. For instance, an image of a building facade may wrap nicely around a cube using a cylinder wrap.

EXTRUDED OBJECTS

One of the most dynamic, flexible and easy-to-create shapes is the extruded object. Think of it as giving depth to a 2D object, like plywood. To cut the virtual plywood, you need a virtual jigsaw.

At this point, you can cut out a shape of any size and dimension. When you have completed the extrusion, you can make the extruded plywood cutout any depth you want. It is virtual plywood so you can cut doughnut holes and the middle will stay in place.

For a flat and seemingly lifeless object, extrusions can take on a life of their own and add a wonderful amount of detail and form to a model.

As shown below, a single plank with the proper texture can become a keyboard. Another simple shape becomes an entire fireplace. Just as it is possible to build an elaborate house with two-by-fours and plywood, it is also possible to create some of the most complex models with one of the simplest tools.

USING FLAT SHAPES TO MAKE A 3D WORLD All the shapes used to create the image (above) are flat, extruded objects (below) created in Illustrator as exported 2D shapes.

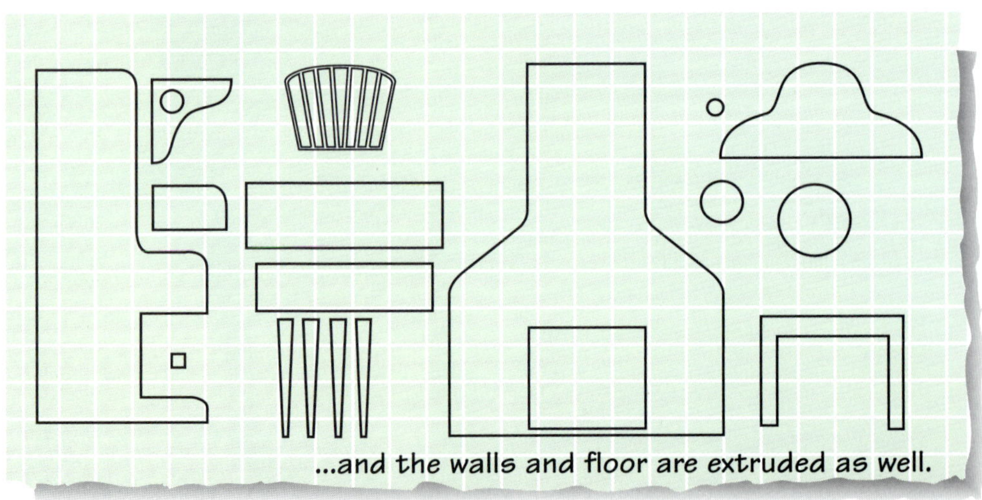

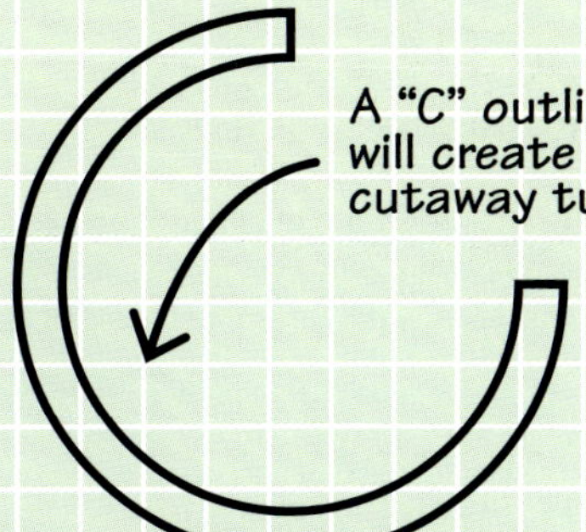

MAKING PIPE/TUBE CUTAWAYS

A simple outline that resembles a "C" takes on a dramatic shape when given a good amount of depth and viewed with a wide-angle lens. This technique is useful for creating see-through veins and arteries, tunnels, wires, cables and pipes.

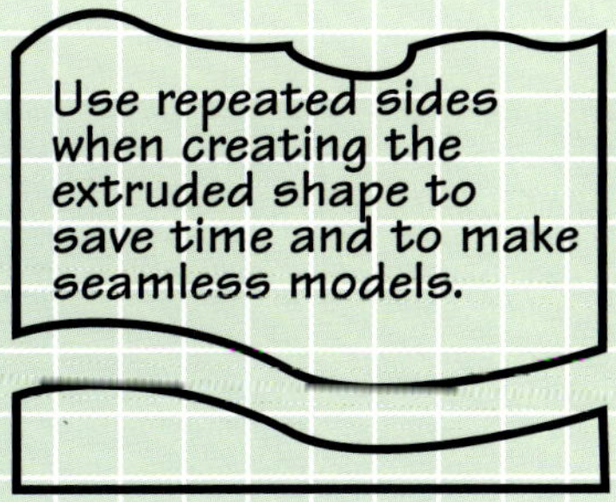

EARTHY CHUNKS AND OTHER FORMS

Smooth, undulating surfaces are created easily by using extruded objects. Make a duplicate of an original shape and re-edit it to recycle adjoining sides. This technique helps create a seamless junction between the shapes. All the layers (left) were created from edges of the adjoining layer. This makes modeling a snap and the images fit together perfectly.

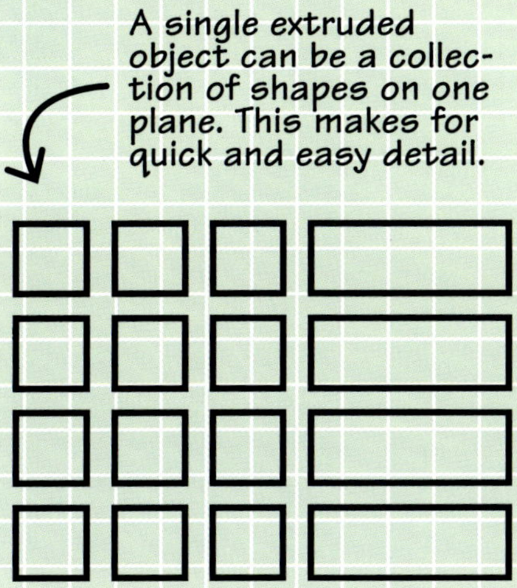

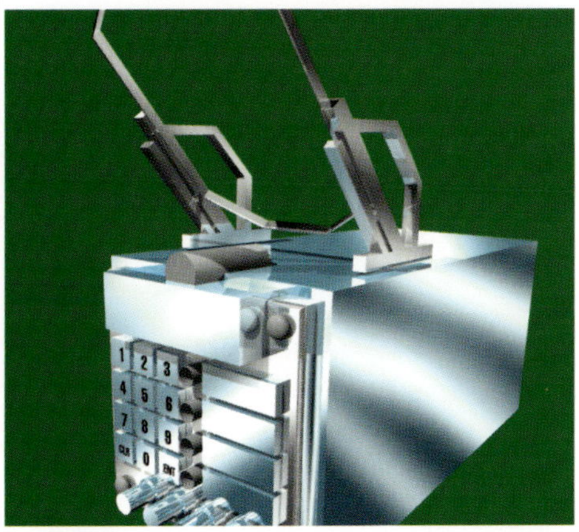

EXTRUSION DETAILING MADE EASY

The key to creating interesting and believable images is detail. A single extruded shape can be a cluster of bumps, knobs and hatches that give a model the detail it needs without too much effort.

APPLYING TEXTURES TO EXTRUDED SHAPES

When mapping a surface to an extruded shape, the map can go straight through the shape–you see it on both sides. Sometimes this effect is desirable, such as the texture map on the radiator (right). The radiator grill uses the same texture on both sides.

Other times, and almost always when text is being mapped onto a surface, it is undesirable for the mapping to go straight through the shape. The railroad crossing example (left, rear signs) shows the sign map through the back. One solution for preventing type from showing through is to sandwich a blank object between the two sides.

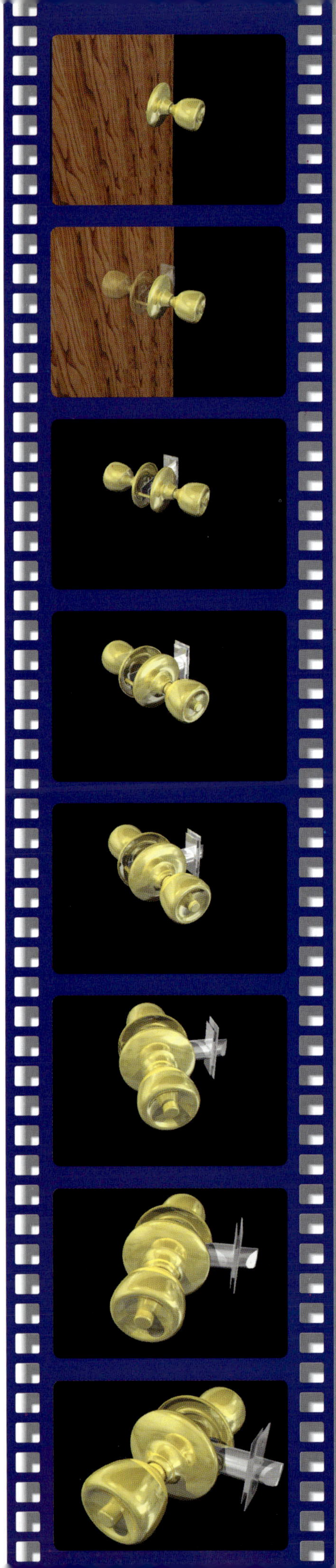

LATHED OBJECTS

In a 3D modeling program, the lathe tool gives you more options and less sawdust than its real-life counterpart.

A real lathe takes a piece of wood, spins it on its axis and shapes it into an intricate chair leg. In a modeling program, you also work from a template to describe the final shape you want the object to become. Once the template is established and imported into a 3D program, the shape is swept around an axis. The result can be a simple soda can or a complicated satellite dish.

Lathed objects can be the final product or building blocks to more complex shapes. In their most basic, unedited form, lathed objects can make a great many of our real-world objects. Light bulbs, dishes, glasses, tires, compact discs, lamps, steering wheels and doughnuts all can be formed by simple unedited lathed objects. With a little tweaking as free-form objects, a lathe can transform itself into an asteroid, a pie tin or an artery.

A COMBINATION OF LATHED TECHNIQUES The doorknob (above) borrows from several lathing techniques: traditional, doughnut and free-form. The overall polished gold effect comes from a highly reflective surface and a soft chromium environment map.

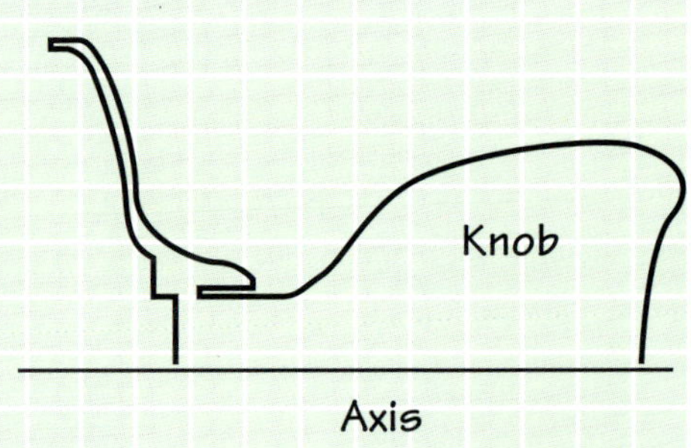

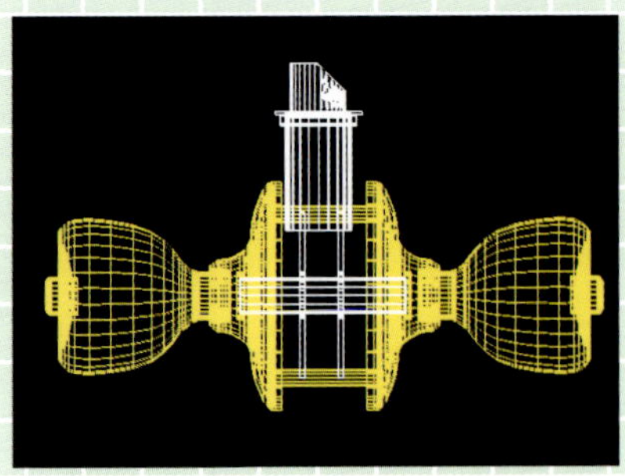

DRAWING THE TEMPLATE

All modeling programs have built-in drawing tools to create the lathed template, but using a dedicated drawing program also has advantages. Programs such as Illustrator or FreeHand have top-notch drawing tools that allow precise template editing. The template (above) is drawn in 2D and imported into a 3D program. The shape is then rotated about its axis to create the doorknob and base plate.

WORKING SMARTER NOT HARDER

The bulk of the doorknob image (above) is actually two lathed objects repeated one or two times. After duplicating and linking the original knob shape, it is a matter of rotating the image on the same axis at 180° to get the second knob.

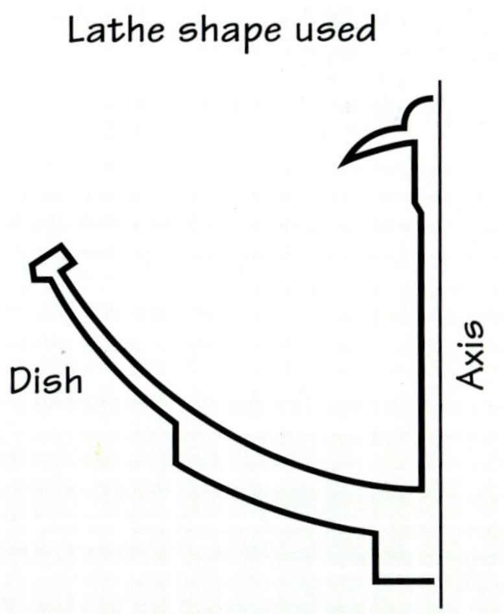

STANDARD LATHES

Pivoting around an axis, a standard lathe is one of the workhorse tools that transforms a simple line or curve into a completely modeled surface. It is tempting to create complex and intricate shapes when you are dealing with a simple line to adjust, but if CPU or rendering speed is a concern, try to be conservative. A single line will be replicated dozens of times as it lathes its way around the axis.

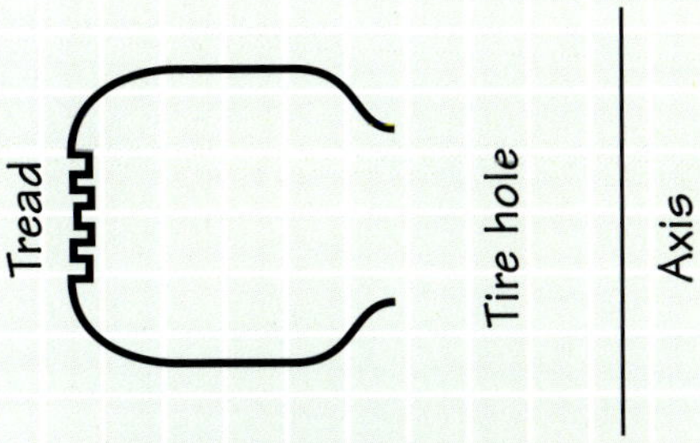

DOUGHNUT LATHES

If you want to make a hula-hoop, then the lathed object is the tool of choice. This shape, as well as rings, tires, tubes and doughnuts, can be formed easily. Placing a closed or open object away from the axis will rotate the shape in a complete circle.

An edited portion of a "doughnut" makes a clean artery.

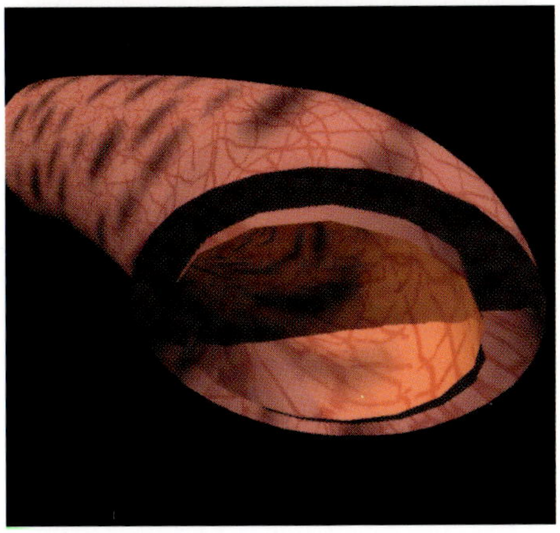

EDITED LATHES

Creating a lathe and editing it as a free-form object results in a completely new shape. This technique is valuable when doing cutaway images such as motor housings, artery diagrams or subway tunnels. A doughnut shape (in white, far left) was edited by deleting three-fourths of the circle, leaving only the segment that then had an organic blood vessel texture applied to it.

WRAPPING SURFACES ON LATHES

One of the advantages to creating a lathed object is the ability to wrap a texture around the surface, giving a dramatic, photo-realistic quality to the image. Flat images created in any program that can output a PICT file can be used.

CREATING THE MAP

Flat surface maps can be created in drawing programs to give the technical precision (above). Then the image is output to a paint program to be sized and saved as PICT.

THE FINISHED PRODUCT

Finished maps for lathed objects can use a number of different wrapping styles. The most common style is a cylindrical wrap (right).

FREE-FORM OBJECTS

Some shapes defy the constraints of form that extruded and lathed objects offer. These shapes are called *free-form* objects.

Some programs allow the creation of an object that permits editing of points on all its faces. Others let you begin with a lathe or extrusion which can be edited as a free-form. The free-form tool can be the most liberating and dynamic tool in the object-creation toolbox. It can also be the most challenging tool with which to work.

Free-form objects are usually edited using three views–top, front and side, allowing for a kind of digital sculpture.

FORMS THAT WORK Some shapes, like a boat's hull, can present a hurdle for a modeler. The hull illustrated here began as an Illustrator file drawn from a scan of the boat's deck plans. An Illustrator export of the top view started the model out as an extruded shape. It was then converted into a free-form object. Using the scans as templates for the side and front views, the hull came together quickly.

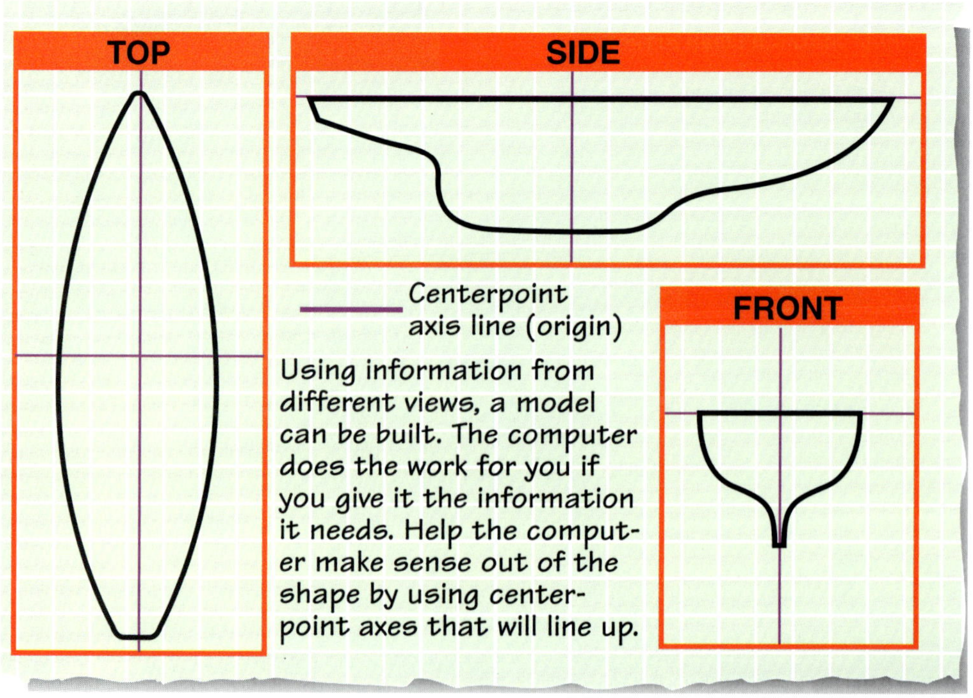

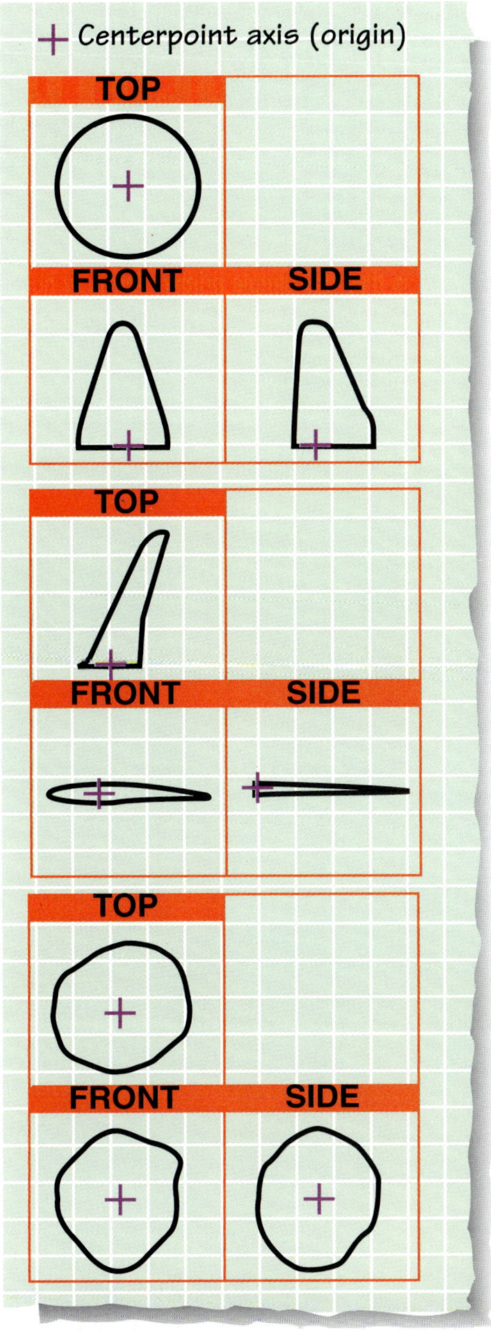

FREE-FORM FROM SCRATCH

One shape which demands absolute precision is the nose of a plane or shuttle (near left). If you get it right, the nose looks well constructed. If you get it slightly off, you can end up with an object that screams of imperfection. In this example, the top view matches the outline of the rest of the plane's body. The front view replicates the overall shape of the structure sides. The side view is the profile of the craft. Note: The nose point on the top and side views both meet on the axis. This is an important juncture that is critical in making the shape work properly.

FREE-FORM FROM EDITED EXTRUSIONS

Working from the basic building tools, such as extrusion or lathed objects, allows you to lay down the fundamental shape of the object. Further editing as a free-form object gives you control over the shape and form of the object from all perspectives. The airplane wing (left), for example, starts out as an extruded object that reflects the overall shape of the wing. A bevel might give it smoother edges, but not a true airfoil shape. Editing the front view of the wing into the desired shape gives it a true airfoil design. The top view outlines the wing; the front view shows the width and the side view shows the span.

FREE-FORM FROM EDITED LATHES

Editing a lathed object works in much the same fashion as editing an extrusion. The original form used for this asteroid was a bumpy half circle. In free-form edit, additional bumps were added to the front and side views to give it an irregular shape.

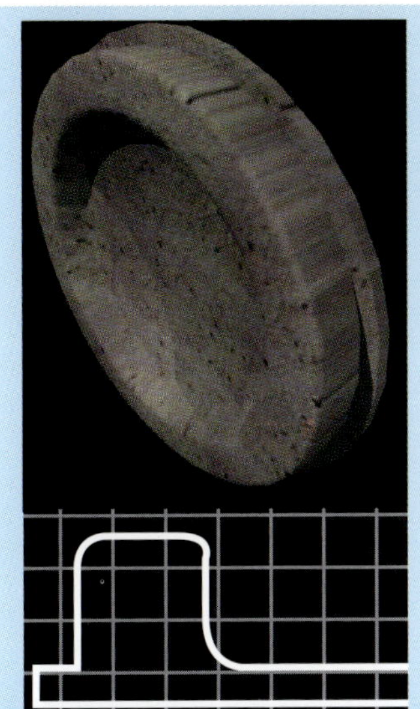

Original Lathed Shape

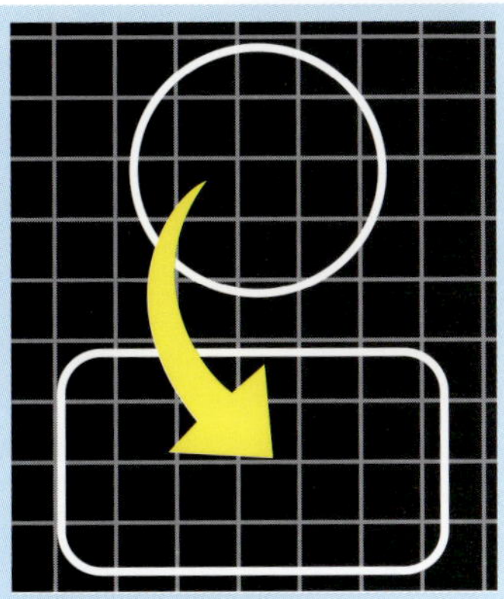

Change top view...

...to create a new shape

The final image

PRESTO, CHANGE-O

In some cases, editing free-form shapes can be done by using the drawing tools in the object's workspace. Four-sided boxes, with a bottom, for example, can be made from one object using the lathed tool initially to create a hollowed out area. Its top view is then changed to form the circle into a square. This same technique was used to create the smooth-shaped concrete blocks in the subway scene (above). When using this technique you can substitute any variety of shapes– squares, ovals, stars or any polygon–for the circle.

SKINNED/SWEPT OBJECTS

The world is filled with irregular, twisted and otherwise odd shapes. In 3D modeling, one of the most difficult tasks is attempting to replicate those forms. Two powerful tools for the creation of irregular shapes are *skinned* and *swept* objects.

Skinned objects perform much as you would imagine from their name. They wrap a skin over "ribs" to form a solid object. The ribs are usually a series of 2D shapes that have been edited to form an underlying structure.

On the other hand, swept objects can take the geometry of one shape, say a circle, and make it follow the geometry of another form–such as a curved line. The result is a linear, but irregular shape that could form an object like a coiled garden hose.

The common denominator between the two tools is they use simple primary forms to build upon, resulting in difficult-to-construct models.

In animation, most programs that support skinned and swept objects allow you to alter the position or shape of the underlying forms over time, creating a flexing effect. This can be a powerful aid in mimicking real-world motions.

TWIST AND SHOUT Several of the forms in the above scene illustrate the importance of skinned and swept objects. To get the "I" beam support post, a letter "H" shaped form was swept up the post. To get the fake dented support post, the "H" shape was told to "Extrude Along a Path" or follow the form as it swept up.

2D ribs used to construct the underlying form of the pump.

With skin applied, the ribs create a solid model.

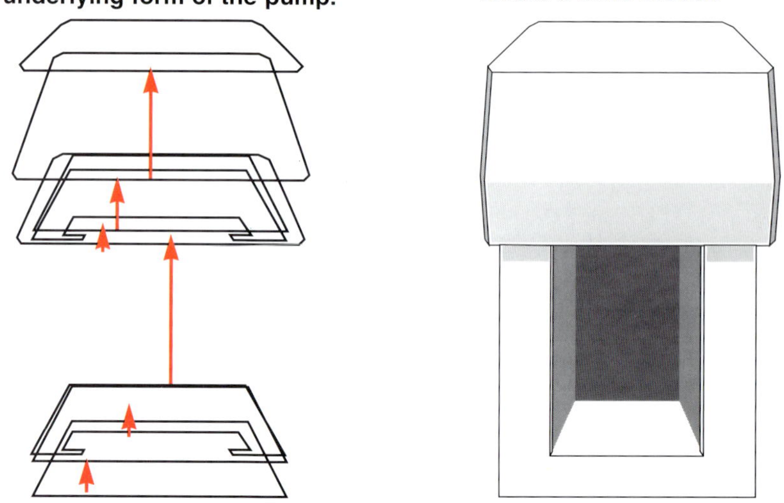

The order in which the ribs are linked is very important. The red arrows (above left) indicate the order of the links. The order creates a path the skin will follow as it envelopes the ribs to create the shape (above right).

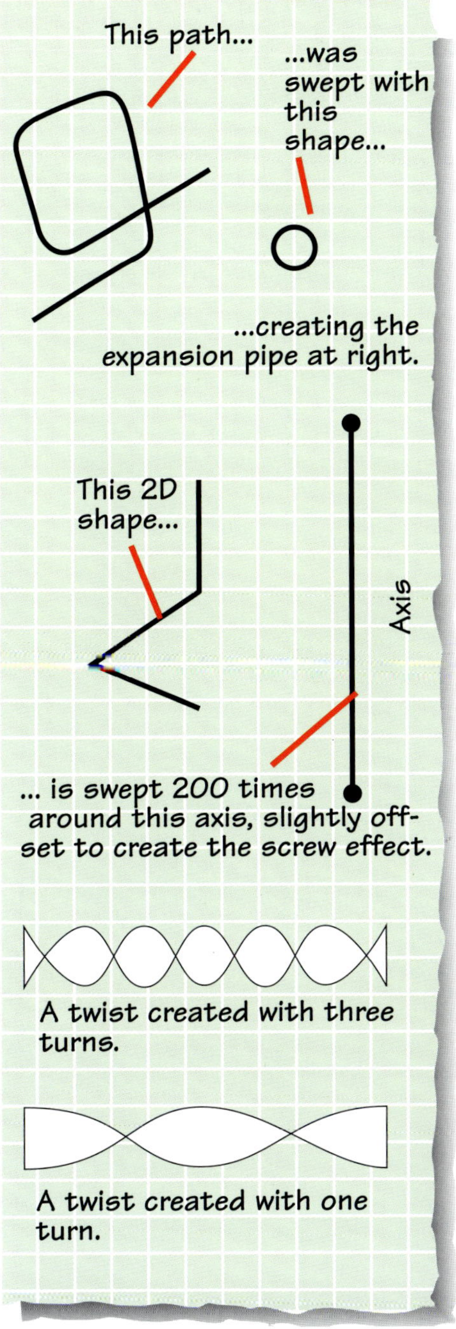

SWEPT OBJECTS

The expansion pipe (left) was created by building a series of 2D paths that, joined together, created the guide path to form the overall shape. The sweep shape, in this case, a simple circle, was created and then instructed to sweep along the guide path. Some programs allow the user to define the proportion of the beginning and the end of the sweep. This allows the modeler to create a tapered or expanding sweep for even more complex models. This tool is also called "Extrude Along a Path" since it takes a 2D object and uses the guide path as a template to create an extrusion.

LOOSE SCREWS

Some programs control the sweep function by allowing the user to define an axis, much like a lathed object, and the number of steps that a 2D shape is swept. By adjusting the vertical and horizontal distance and dimension of the sweep, a variety of shapes can be constructed. This screw (left) has 200 steps. Each step moved .05" vertically. The result is a continuous screw thread that wraps itself around the defined axis until the preset number of steps (200) runs out.

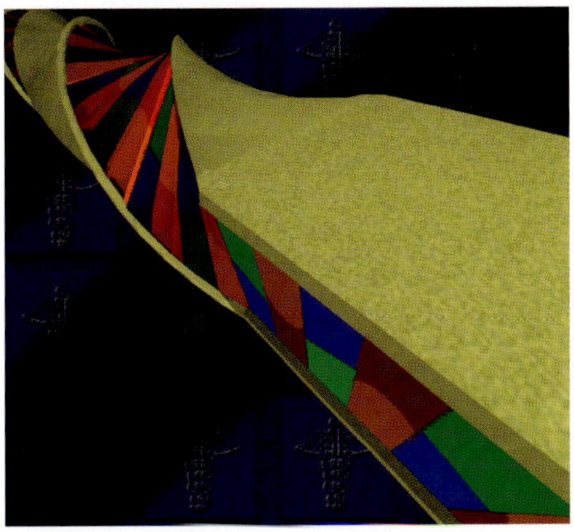

ROLLER COASTERS

When "Extrude Along a Path" is used in conjunction with a twist or warp deformation, the result can be a complex sweeping twist like this DNA chain (left). In twist deformations, the number of rotations that are made in the length of the object can be controlled to create either a sweeping arc, like the DNA chain, or twisting spiral. Examples of twist deformations can be found in objects like flypaper, spiral staircases and roller coaster rides.

CREATING A SKINNED INFRASTRUCTURE

1) Use the computer's strengths to help create complicated frameworks for skinning. Start off with a 2D cross section (above).

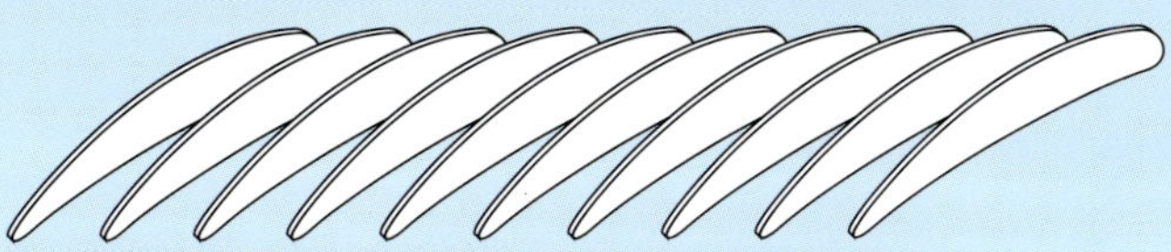

2) Replicate the form using your "Step-and-Repeat," "Transform" or "Duplicate Link" function.

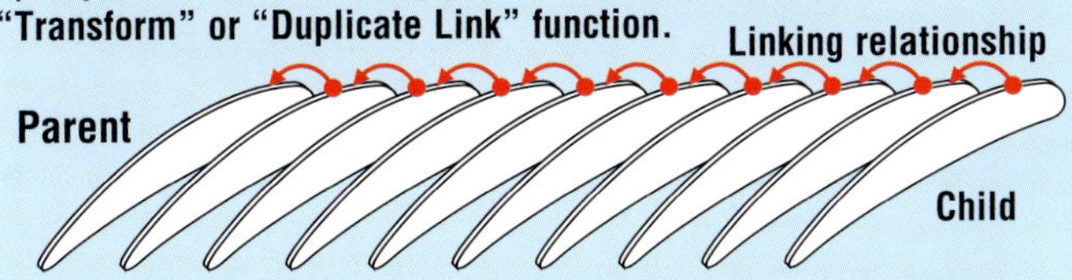

3) Maintain the parent-child link. In this example, the far right cross section is at the bottom of the parent-child hierarchy. Any dimensional change in objects up the line will affect the last rung.

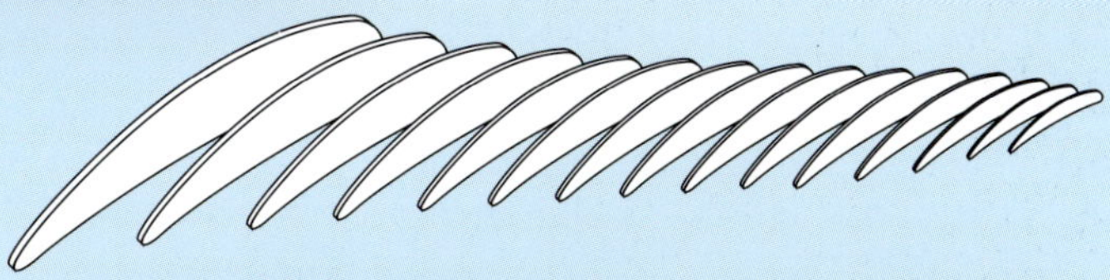

4) By reducing the size of the second cross section from the left, all the following cross sections will be reduced. Each cross section can be slightly adjusted–with the succeeding parts in the link following suit. Positions can be altered slightly in the same manner.

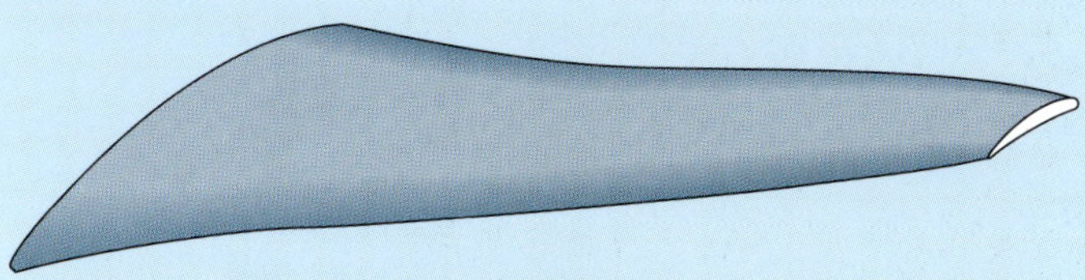

5) Placing a skin on the final grouping will result in a smooth, carefully constructed form. This technique can be effective in creating a variety of shapes–from airplanes to fish.

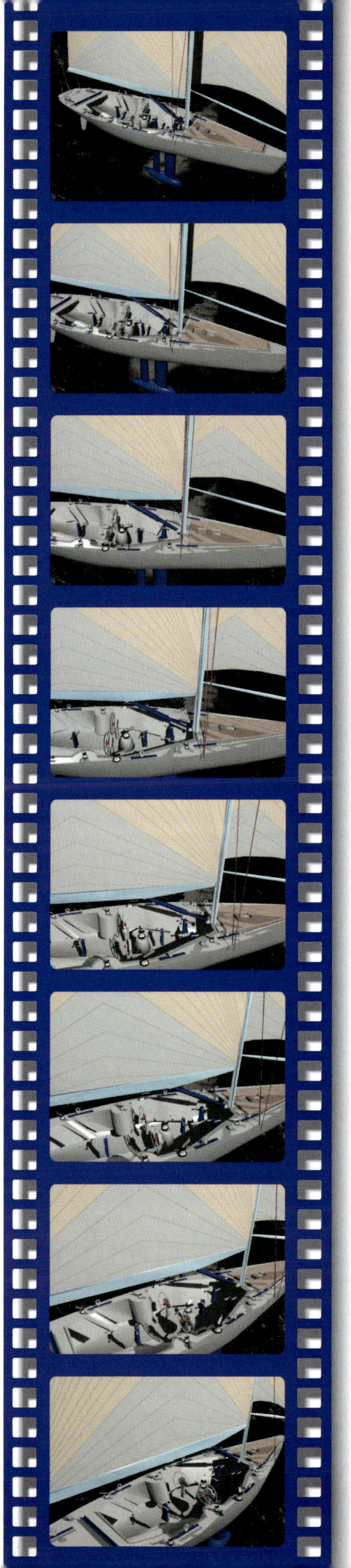

BOOLEAN SHAPES

Software that supports boolean modeling gives the user one of the most powerful tools available. Boolean operations determine how existing shapes interact with each other. One impressive function of this tool takes the shape of one model and uses it to remove a portion of another model. The subtractive process is not so much a carving out as it is a molding–where one shape defines or redefines another.

Boolean functions can be used to join two objects together. The effect may seem similar to just jamming two shapes together yet the result of a joined boolean shape allows the two shapes to share a seamless texture map. The resulting shape's intersecting mesh can be adjusted to help form a more natural union.

Because of their ability to allow shapes to interact together, booleans can be used to create shapes that would otherwise be impossible to create.

A perfect example of boolean use is creating a bolt and a nut. While the bolt can be simply created using a sweep tool, making the matching thread inside the nut is a challenge. With a boolean function, you simply remove the bolt from the nut.

CREATING COMPLEX, OTHERWISE IMPOSSIBLE SHAPES Shapes like this boat hull (above) would be incredibly difficult to construct without the aid of booleans. Using StudioPro, the hull was created from two forms, the hull shape itself, and a shape which was formed after the cockpit area in the boat. To create the finished shape, the boolean function was used to remove the cockpit shape from the hull shape.

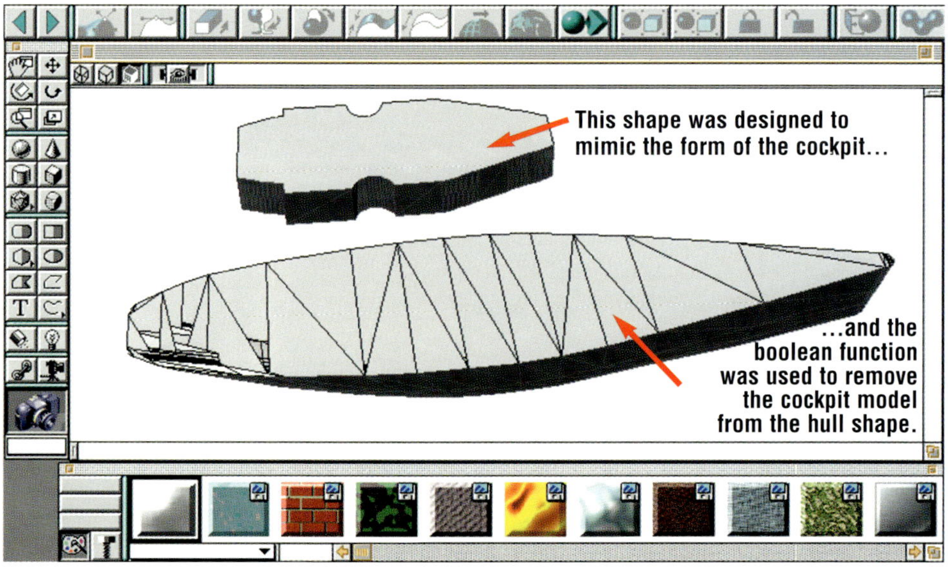

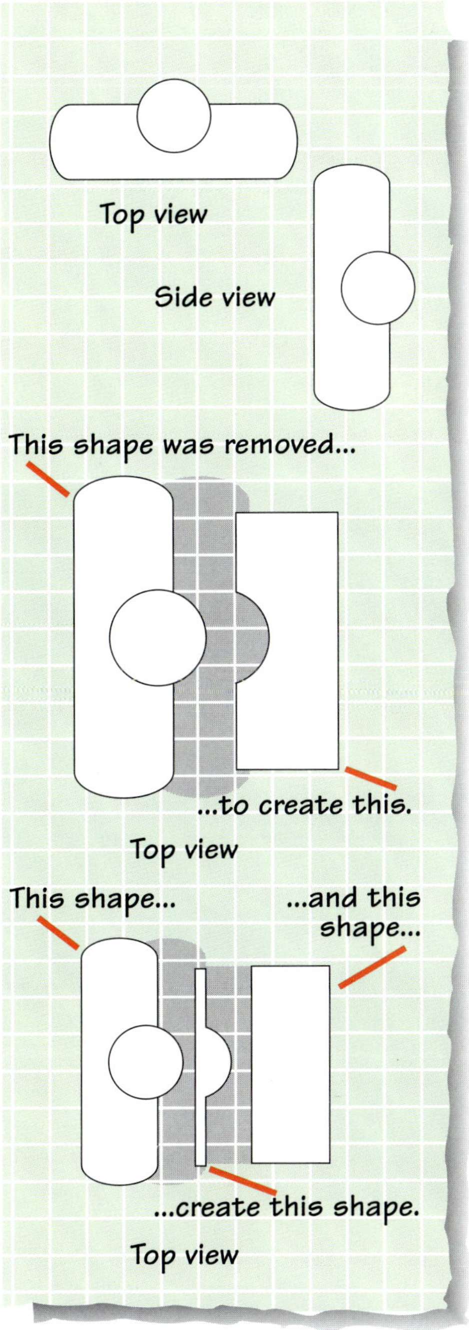

ADDITION

In additive mode, boolean functions can take separate objects and merge them into a single form. The advantages of this include the ability to map a single texture to a single object instead of attempting to map the same texture map to two objects and try to line them up so they are seamless. Also, creating complex forms in one chunk allows you to further take advantage of boolean functions by removing the new shape from another form. For instance, the shape (left) was created from two single cylinders. Joining them together as one allowed the new shape to be removed from a single cube, creating the form below.

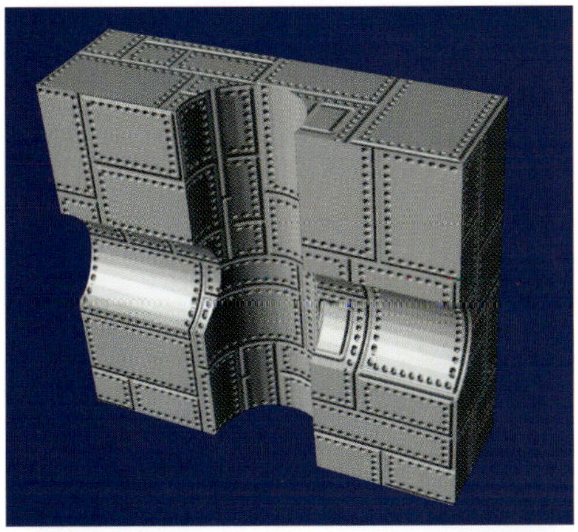

SUBTRACTION

The subtractive mode lets you carve one form out of another. The example (left) shows a single cube as the base, and the cylinder form from above used as the subtracting form. Using subtraction, you can poke holes in buildings to create custom windows, dissect portions of machinery for examination and create textures and grooves in otherwise flat objects.

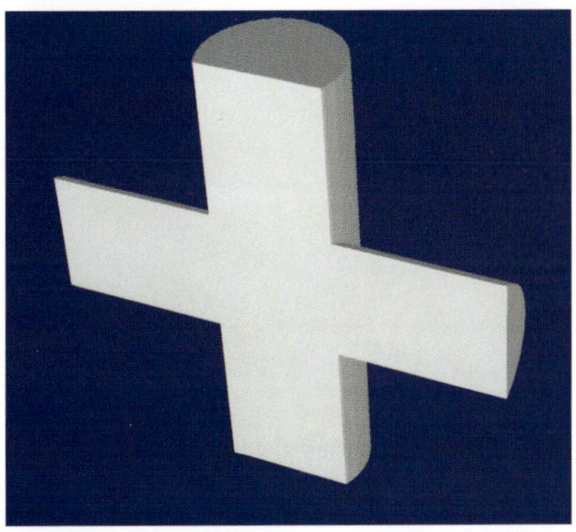

INTERSECTION

This function leaves the remainder of two shapes. The example (left) took the cylinder shape and the cube and left the user with all the parts of the form which intersected each other. If a model was created that needed to seamlessly fit into another form, like a ship's hatch cover, using the copies of the forms combined to create the subtracted form could create another form which would fit snugly into it.

USING BOOLEANS TO CREATE OBJECTS THAT FIT TOGETHER

Objects that need to fit together perfectly, like a piston in an engine or a bolt in a nut, can take advantage of boolean functions.

First, create the object that will serve as both a model and a form used to create the hole. In this example (right, 1), it is a bolt. Then create the object that will have a portion of itself removed–in this case, the nut (2). Duplicate the bolt (3) so the original remains untouched. Then use a boolean function to remove the bolt from the nut. The original bolt can be reintroduced to the scene, allowing for a perfect fit. Two other booleans were used to create this image. The head of the bolt was made by removing the shape of a squashed cube from a lathed half sphere. The pre-booleaned nut was cut in half using the form of a simple cube, and then the bolt was removed.

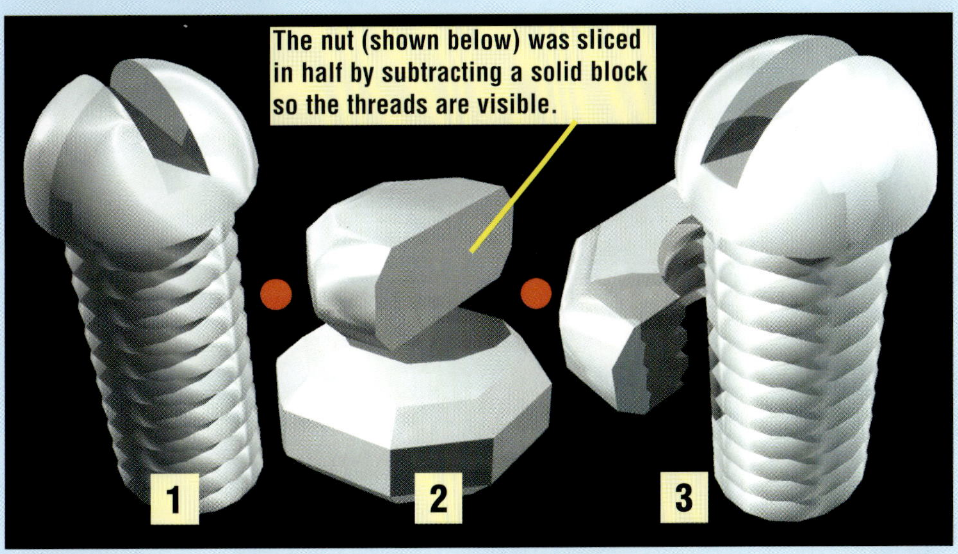

TERRAINS

Accurate terrain mapping can serve two purposes in 3D modeling and animation. First, in cases where it is important to reflect the undulations in terrain, such as architectural modeling or land-area fly-through, it is possible to imitate accurately both the topographical contours, as well as the geographical coloring.

Terrains can be created by painstakingly following contour maps to create accurate elevations of real world geology. They also can be wholly fictional, with the modeler or computer generating the landscape. Some software programs even allow the computer to generate fractal landscapes, forming whole mountain ranges and canyons purely from mathematical fractal formulas.

Secondly, terrains can be used to create hard-to-model forms, such as human faces or loose, rolling surfaces like a quilt on a bed.

NATURAL TERRAIN A flowing, smooth terrain is important in the overall believability of a terrain surface. One of the key ingredients to this is accurate topographical information and attention to detail.

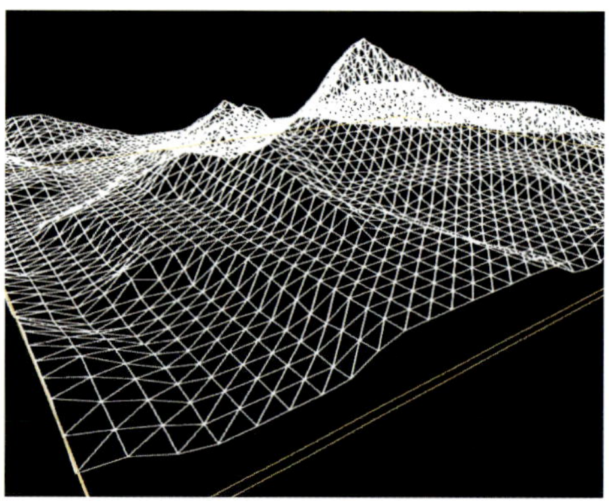

THE TERRAIN GRID
Terrains are handled by the computer as a polygon mesh. The wireframe view (above) gives a good feel of how the mapped image tightly follows the topographical features. Overall height or depth can be controlled by adjusting the Y-axis parameters.

THE SURFACE MAP
Creating a believable surface map is just as important as creating an accurate topographical scale. This can be achieved by layering rock, grass, forest and other types of stock surface resources on top of each other. Projected from the top downward, the surface wraps itself around a shape.

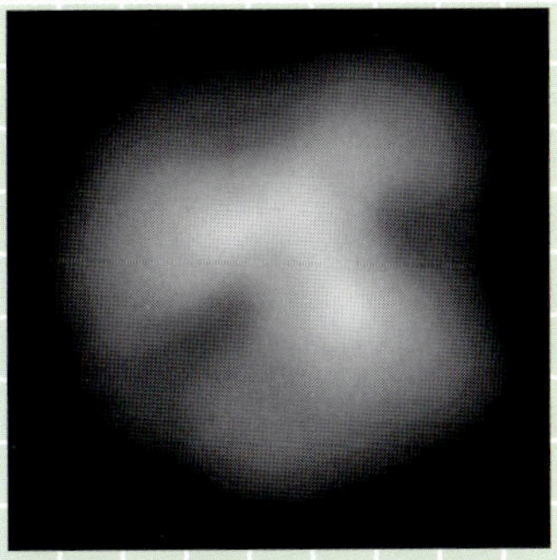

White pushes up a mountain...

...while an image like this creates a sinkhole.

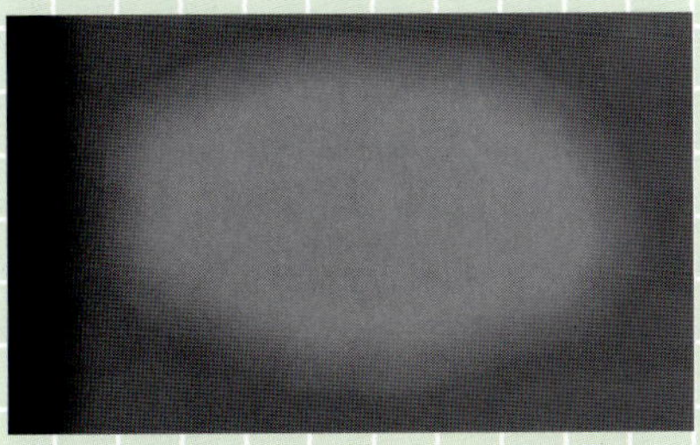

Gray undulations form shape

MOUNTAINS AND VALLEYS

To push a hill or mountain out of the flat form (left), create a grayscale image in a bitmap editing program such as Photoshop. The black images will remain flat while lighter shades of gray to white will push up from the surface. One easy way to do this is to use the Feather tool set at 10-30 pixels and to change the selected area by altering the levels. This will keep the transitions smooth without causing the abrupt change in values that you might find if you used differing fills of gray. Using a darker area surrounded by a light field would create the effect of a hole.

THE BRYCE OPTION

KPT Software makes a great tool for creating terrains. The program, Bryce, only exports a rendered PICT image or QuickTime movie, but this could be imported as a background into an editing program. The landscapes that can be created are truly fantastic. The program gives the user control over elements such as fog, water, clouds, sky and, of course, the terrain.

CREATING ORGANIC SHAPES

To create shapes that otherwise might be impossible with the modeling tools, terrain mapping can simulate anything with a smooth bump or shape. The man under the blanket (left, on bench) shows one use of this technique. In this style it is possible to take a photograph of a human face, and create a texture map out of it. As long as the nose is light and the recesses of the face are darker, you can create very accurate organic models.

TERRAIN SURFACING MADE SIMPLE

Flat contour maps that clearly define the shape of the terrain can be translated accurately into a 3D model. Use a scan of a map, for example a US Geological Survey map, as a template in a 2D drawing program. The resulting image is then imported into a 3D program.

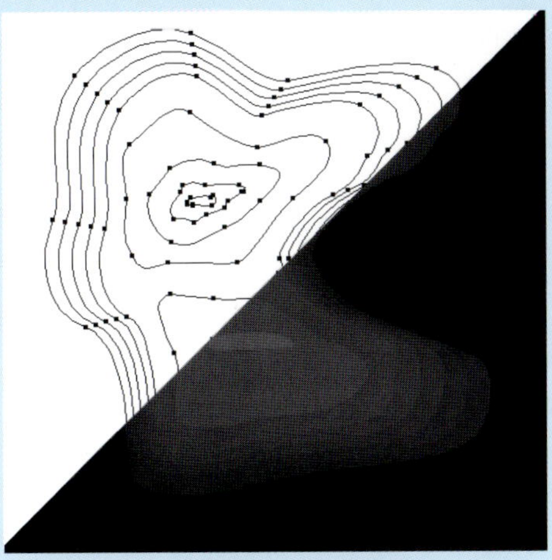

START WITH A DRAWING PROGRAM

Use a 2D drawing program such as Illustrator or FreeHand to create the initial bands. Lighten them softly, beginning with 100% black and working your way up. The lightest band (above) is 60% black.

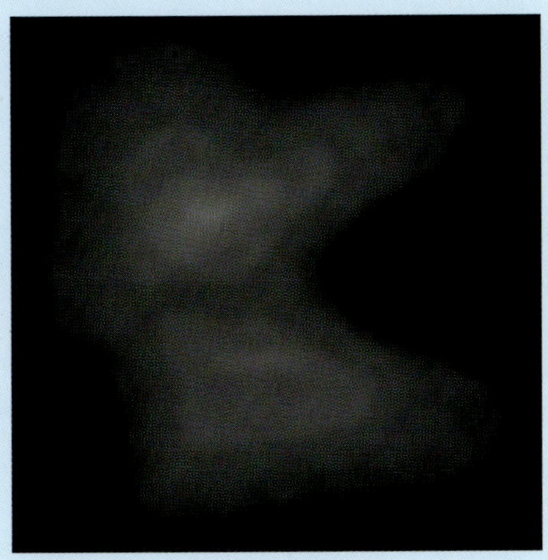

IMPORT INTO A PAINT PROGRAM

Import the file into a paint program that can blur an image, such as Photoshop or Color Studio. Blur the image from 5 to 30 pixels (above), depending on the crispness and detail needed.

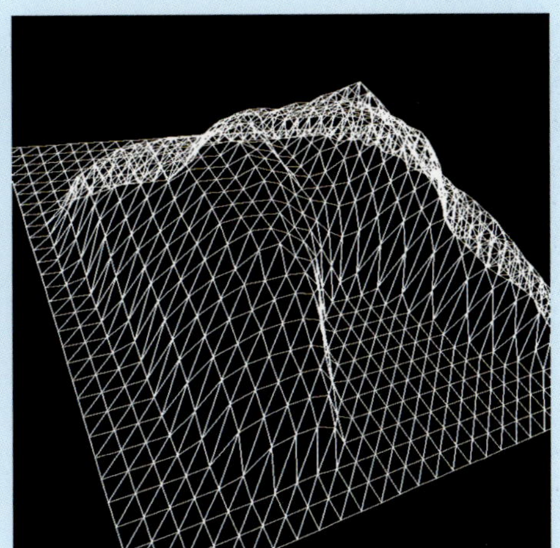

CREATE THE TERRAIN

Import the file into your modeling program and use the Y-axis editor to increase or decrease the height. If a mountain runs into an edge, but you still want it flat all the way around, put a 1-point black rule around the image before you import.

IMPORT/EXPORT

One advantage of 3D modeling on the Macintosh is the easy access to dozens of programs that can aid an animator in completing a project. Fortunately many of the software developers have included filters that allow easy transport of documents between programs. The closest thing modelers have to a universal format is DXF (Drawing Exchange Format or File). Although DXF, created by AutoDesk, will move information on the shape of an object, the data on textures and procedural maps will be lost.

For example, a program like form•Z may offer wonderful modeling tools but not include any serious texture creation or mapping tools. In this case you might export the form•Z model as a DXF object. Import it into a program such as Infini-D and take advantage of its surface editing tools. In this way your Macintosh multiplies its usefulness. Your two separate programs act almost as modules to a single package. With enough RAM, you can even keep both programs open at the same time.

Model by Viewpoint

EASY IMPORTING OPENS THE DOOR FOR 3RD PARTY IMAGES In many cases you might need a model that is either beyond your scope to create or one needed for a fast turnaround. Companies such as Viewpoint or Acuris might be your answer. Both companies have libraries with thousands of models which can be purchased in CD form or on individual floppies. This Triceratops was imported into StudioPro and wrapped with a single PICT file. The background came from Corel's Trees and Leaves CD, saved as a PICT file and imported into the file's alpha channel.

Example A—Using imports to introduce a foreign file

Viewpoint —DXF→ StudioPro —Native→ Render Pro —QuickTime→ Premiere

A Viewpoint model was imported as a DXF file into StudioPro. After applying a texture map and setting up an animation sequence, the file was exported in its own native mode to Strata's network rendering software, Render Pro. The resulting QuickTime movie then was imported and edited in Premiere.

Example B—Using import/export to enhance productivity

form•Z —DXF→ Infini-D —Native→ BackBurner —PICS→ Director

A model was created using the powerful tools in form•Z, then imported into Infini-D because form•Z lacks serious texture tools. Then BackBurner rendered the finished file which can be exported as PICS to be edited in Director.

DXF file polymesh close-up.

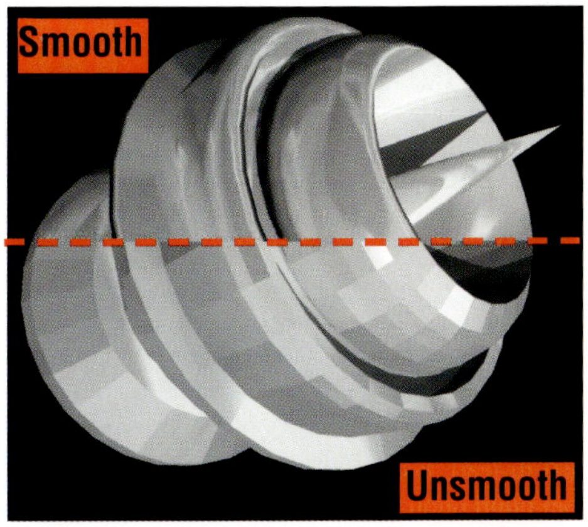

SMOOTH, UNSMOOTH DXF IMPORTS

When importing a DXF file, you probably will be given a choice to smooth the import or not. Smoothing the file may be what you want, especially if your object is organic in nature (top half of image on left). On the other hand, if your object is mechanical, you may want the advantages of an unsmoothed DXF import and its more abrupt edges (bottom half of image on left). With unsmooth, you also may have to live with visible faceting that shows the definition of the polygon mesh (polymesh) shown in detail on the far left.

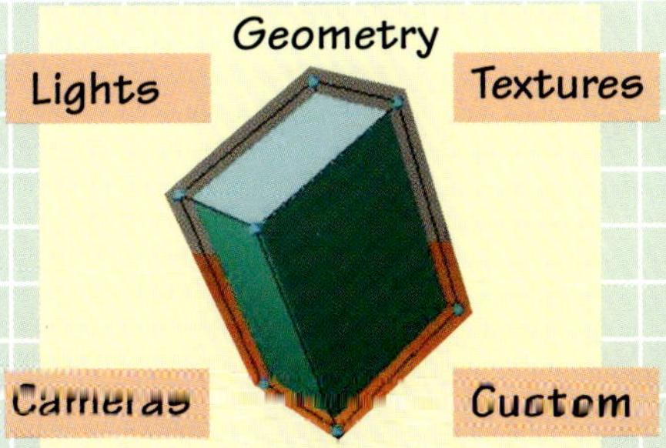

QuickDraw 3D file format supports both geometric and appearance information.

APPLE'S MULTI-DIMENSIONAL FORMAT, QD3D

QuickTime helped define the multimedia boundaries between programs by offering a solid foundation for motion/sound presentation as well as a consistent import/export format. QuickDraw 3D promises a similar revolution in solving the dynamic problems presented in crossing 3D boundaries. Once the major 3D modeling companies incorporate the new technology, a cross-platform 3D interface will finally exist. Moving 3D images will be as simple as cutting and pasting objects between programs. QuickDraw 3D will also speed up rendering times and open up the Mac's architecture for add-on rendering acceleration devices.

Image courtesy of Apple

EPS IMPORT: THE EASIEST WAY TO CREATE AND IMPORT COMPLEX SHAPES

Not all importing and exporting of shapes has to be done between 3D programs. Programs which are 2D, such as Illustrator, FreeHand, MacDraw and Canvas can also be used to create shapes. These 2D programs are limited to making 2D shapes, but most of the work in the 3D world starts out as a 2D shape anyway. Drawing programs that are dedicated to creating 2D shapes do a much better job than the 2D workspaces in modeling programs, allowing the user to quickly and painlessly create complex shapes. Importing is usually straightforward. Most modeling programs offer direct support for import of Illustrator or FreeHand files saved as EPS. Some programs offer PICT object support from programs like MacDraw or Canvas, either directly or using packaged utilities. Below is an example of how Illustrator can be used to create a 2D extruded shape.

1) You can draw from scratch or use a template, such as a scanned rough draft or perhaps a schematic drawing or blueprint. Save the template as PICT.

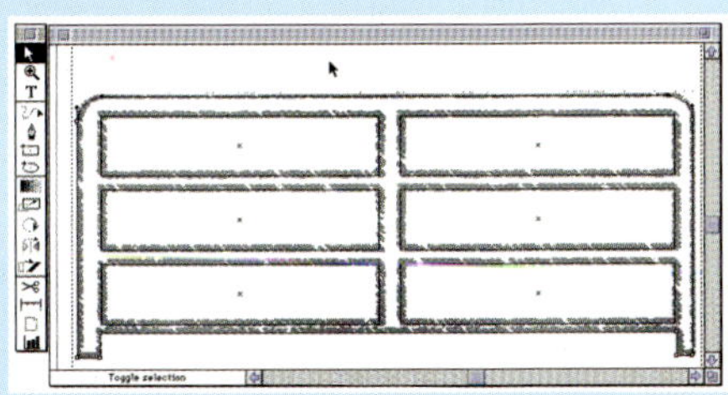

2) In Illustrator, it is a simple matter to open a template.

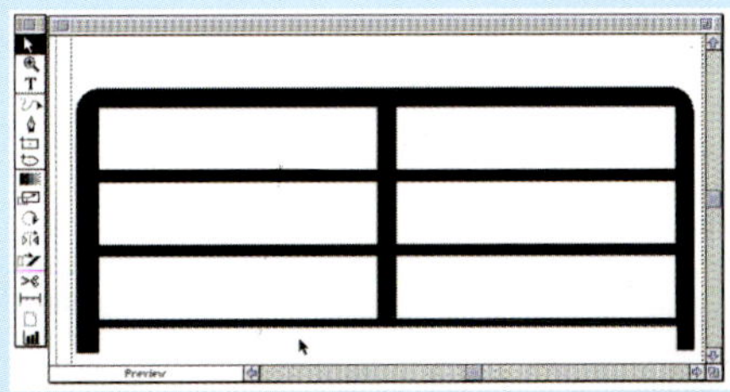

3) When drawing your 2D outline–whether from a scan or from scratch–use color fills to help you see what you are creating. In the final export, the fills you choose will be disregarded–but while you are creating, they can help you keep your place. In an EPS export, any objects that you draw inside the first, external object will poke a hole through the extrusion. If you are making a complex, full-of-holes shape, make your first shape black. Make the next shape you draw white. In preview mode this will show you what will be solid and what will be hollow. If you wanted to put a solid object inside the draw hole, for instance, color it black. In the final render it will be solid.

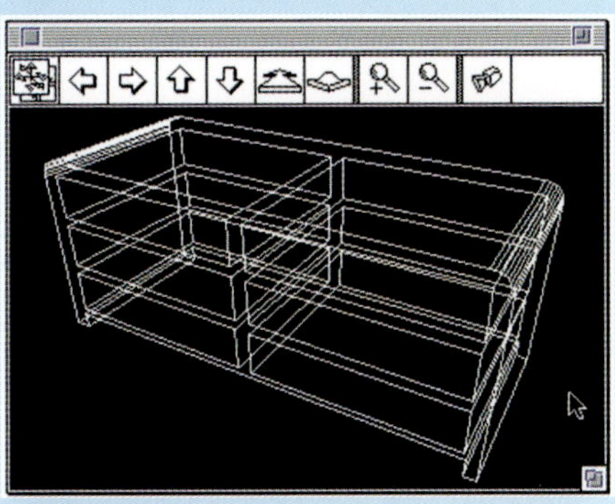

4) Bringing the shape in as an extruded shape will create the whole, complex shape in 3D, allowing depth adjustment.

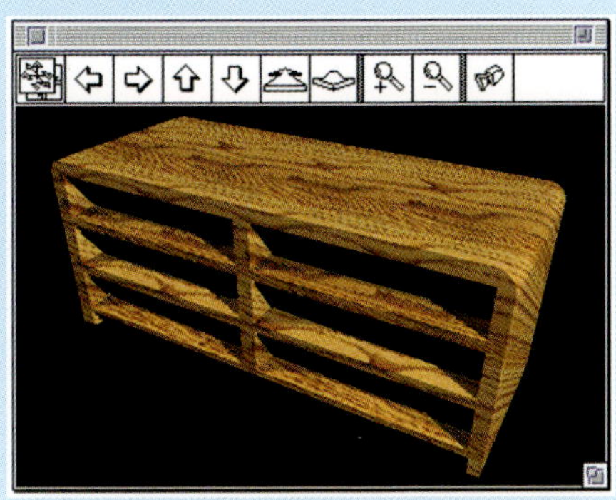

5) The final form (above) would have taken four times as long to draw using a modeling program's 2D workspace.

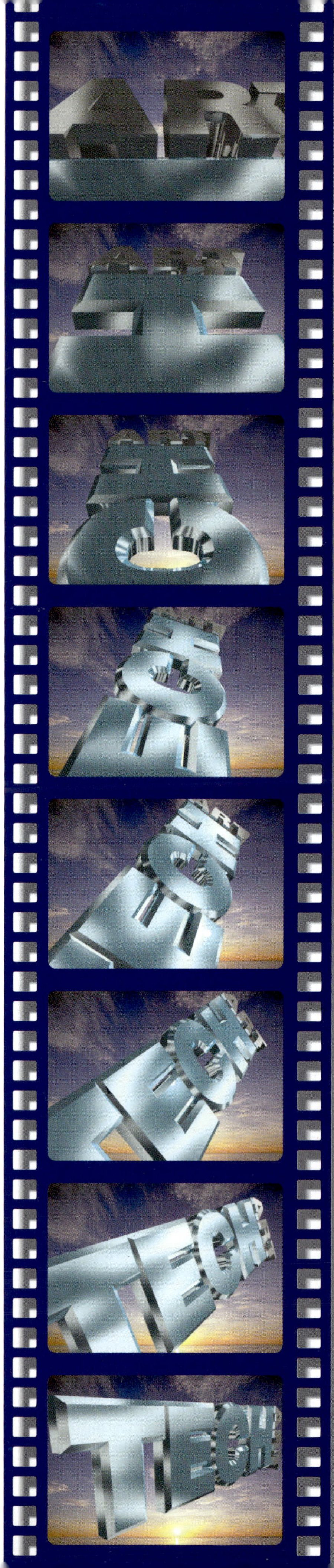

TYPE & LOGOS

When in doubt, put a shiny chrome surface on your type, bevel it and then spin it around a few times. This, of course, is the clichéd technique for logo animation. Yet it does provide some insight into some effective methods for handling type and logos on the screen.

In the 3D world, type becomes more than just text to read. It becomes a shape which an artist can build upon, take apart, shatter into pieces or simply fly by.

Programs that support bevels can quickly take a bland typeface and spice it up a little. The bevel is effective in catching angles of light and helping define the dimension of the form.

With chromium surfaces, the environment map is all important, since that will be the bulk of what the chrome type will be reflecting. With chrome logos, use ray tracing whenever possible so that the objects in the logo or type will reflect off of each other.

FLYING LOGOS Zipping over the ocean, this logo was created in an Illustrator file, imported as an EPS outline and rendered on black with an alpha channel that was later used to composite the logo over the photo.

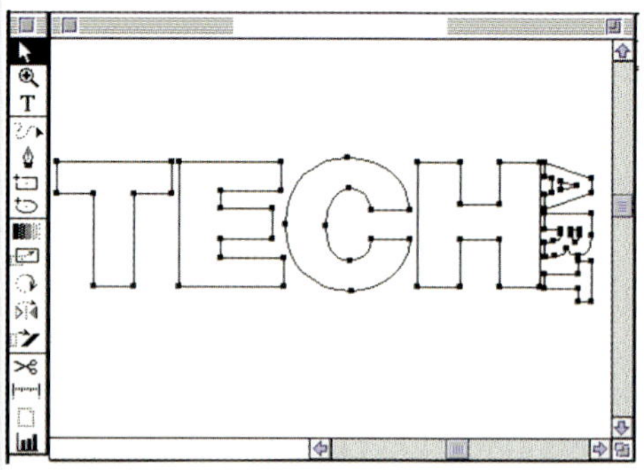

CREATE THE OUTLINE The outline for the logo was created using a standard font and then converted it to outlines. The result was saved as EPS.

IMPORT THE SHAPE Bring the file into the modeling program as an extruded object, and bevel the edges to help define and improve the shape.

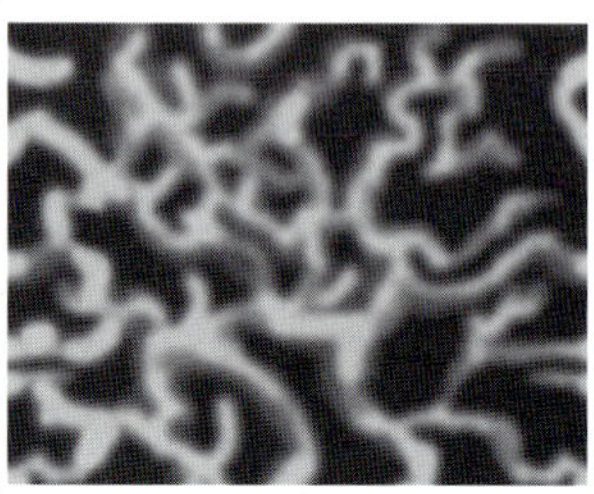

CREATING THE ENVIRONMENT The environment map (left) will reflect off shiny surfaces. The background image (middle) can be rendered at the same time with the model or composited later to make the image (right).

CREATING FACADES

Chrome is fun. It is a cheap and easy way to take simple shapes and fonts and bring them to life. Although using highly reflective surfaces has been done to death, it still looks good. Because of chrome's modern styling, it has a way to go before joining the overdone grid style of the '80s. One problem with chrome type and logos is caused by its reflective nature. The front and sides tend to blend together. Placing lights at harsh angles help define the edges, but sometimes a little contrast is needed between the front and side edges. To achieve this, simply copy the model, create a VERY shallow extrusion of the copy and place it on the front of the base. Tweak the color on the base by darkening it or reducing the reflection.

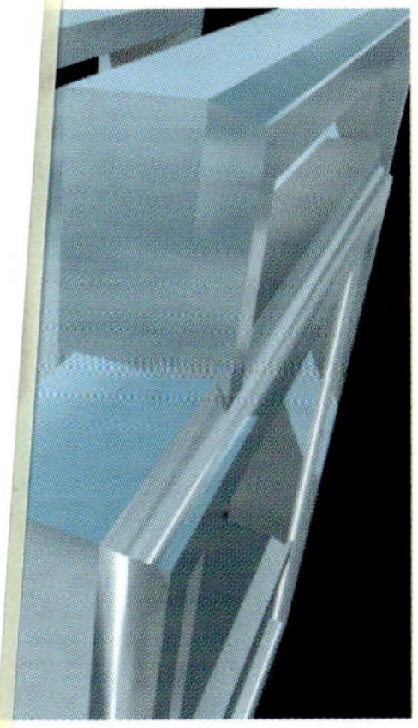

THE BEVEL—LOGO'S BEST FRIEND

Bevels have a host of uses in model creation, but one area where they excel is in logo creation. In general, to produce a company logo:

– recreate the stock logo which was done originally for the print world;
– import the logo into the computer's 3D realm; and
– enhance the logo by using bevels.

Most 3D modeling programs support bevels and give the user a great deal of control on how to transform the shape of an otherwise flat extruded shape.

cases, this may be the [illegible] results with objects that should have left the camera's view suddenly swinging back into view again when the parent does a slight roll.

One way to work around this problem, whether the model is a company logo flying apart or an F-16 firing a heat-seeking missile, is to create an invisible object to link with all the moving elements in the scene.

A cube is a good shape to work with because it is easy to see the general orientation. Spheres will do the job. But since a sphere looks the same no matter which way you roll it, it is harder to control.

Place the cube in the center of your elements and move it around to create the basic sequential movement the overall project will take. After choreographing the cube, you can start working on the individual pieces. When you are done, make the cube invisible. If your program lets you view invisible wireframes, this is a good mode to work in with this technique. The results will be a nice, smooth movement with all the elements acting independently and with no surprises.

The UN logo (right) was ray traced so that its many shapes and edges would interplay with each other to add interest to the model. The scene was rendered with an alpha channel, which was used to drop in the background. The invisible control cube was placed in the center of the rings.

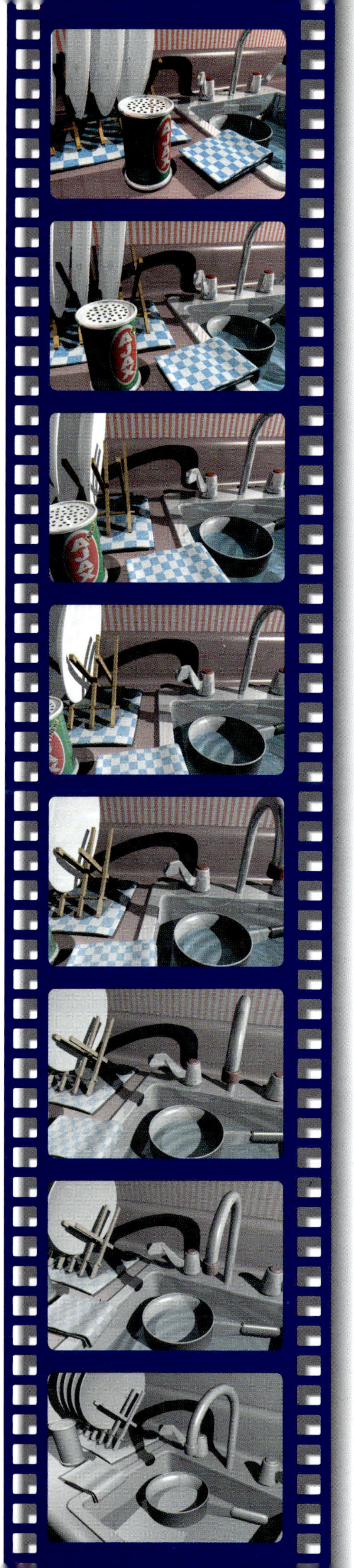

SHADING

Until the image is rendered, a three-dimensional scene is, technically, just an ugly pile of math. The step that makes the difference between a photo-realistic "so-real-you-can-touch-it" image and a disk full of algorithms is the rendering of the image.

One of the most important pre-rendering choices is deciding what shading selection to use. The high-end pick is ray tracing, where every pixel is calculated out, depending on how it is affected by the objects in the scene. Like everything else in life though, trade-offs exist.

Ray tracing, while the choice for professional quality output, also can take an eternity to render. The other end of the scale is bounding box mode. While this mode can run an animation in real-time, you will not have any idea of what you are looking at.

In between is a tidy range of rendering levels, each costlier in time as the quality increases.

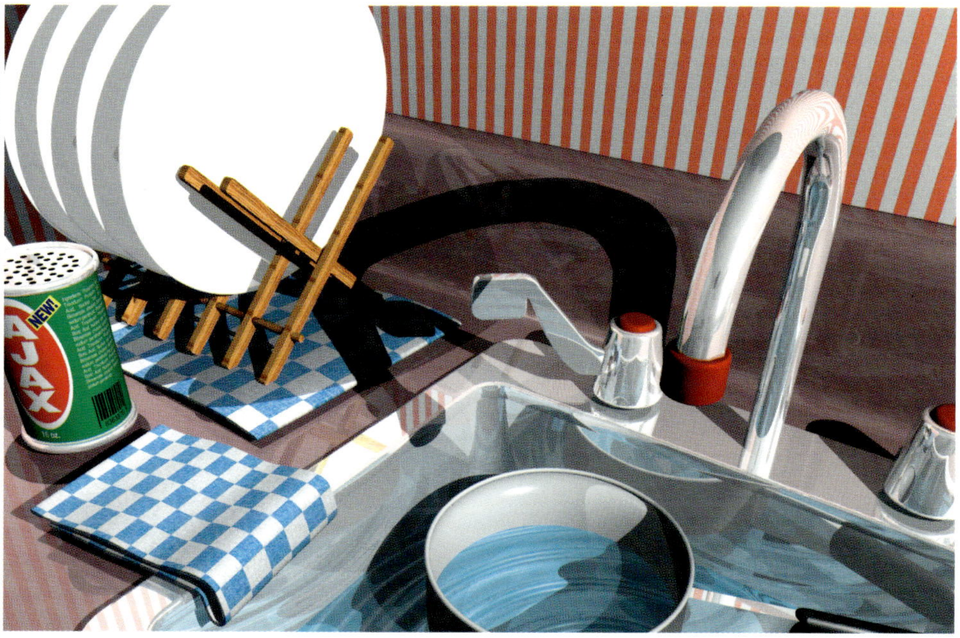

RAY TRACING This is the mode of shading that gives the most realistic appearance (above). Water is transparent and shiny things reflect all the other objects in the scene. Texture mapping and fog effects are also in full glory. Although this is the choice for most final renders, a price is paid in time for each additional light placed in the scene. The results are worth the wait.

PHONG SHADING You lose transparency in glass and water, as well as reflections, with Phong shading. Some programs allow Phong shading to retain environment-mapped reflections (above). Texture-mapped surfaces, such as the towel, Ajax can and wallpaper remain, as well as shadows and wave surfaces.

GOURAUD SHADING

At times you will need to render your animation or image quickly or without much detail. Gouraud shading (left) is the tool of choice for these jobs. When setting up an animation, it is important that objects do not mesh into each other, something that is not too obvious in wireframe or bounding box modes. With Gouraud shading, you can check element positions in far less time than in more detailed rendering modes. It is possible to work in this mode when creating less detailed scenes. The price paid for the speed is loss of shadows and texture maps, although general shading and highlights remain.

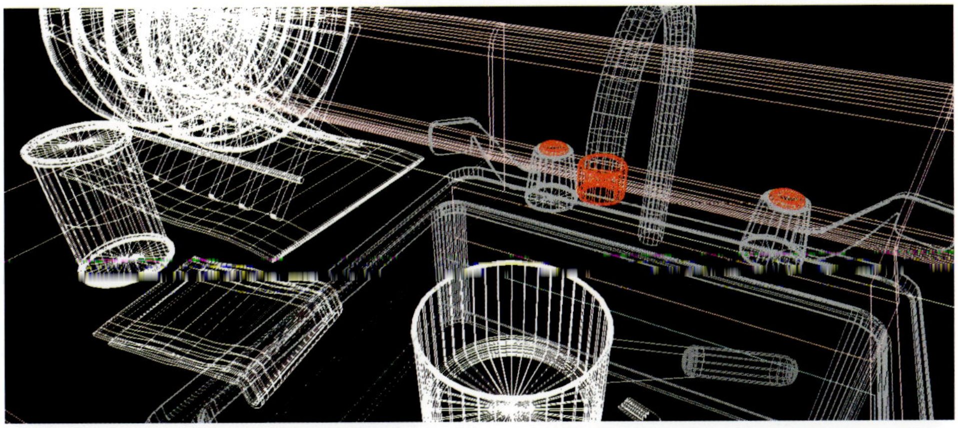

WIREFRAME

As your model gets more complicated you will find that wireframe (left) is a great working mode. Object shapes are still clearly defined, but the time to redraw the windows is much less than the higher rendering modes. Hidden objects used for pivot links can be seen easily and general color assignments are often represented in the color of the wireframe. Since wireframe mode renders so quickly, it is perfect for rendering a test animation to disk in order to check out object movements and timing.

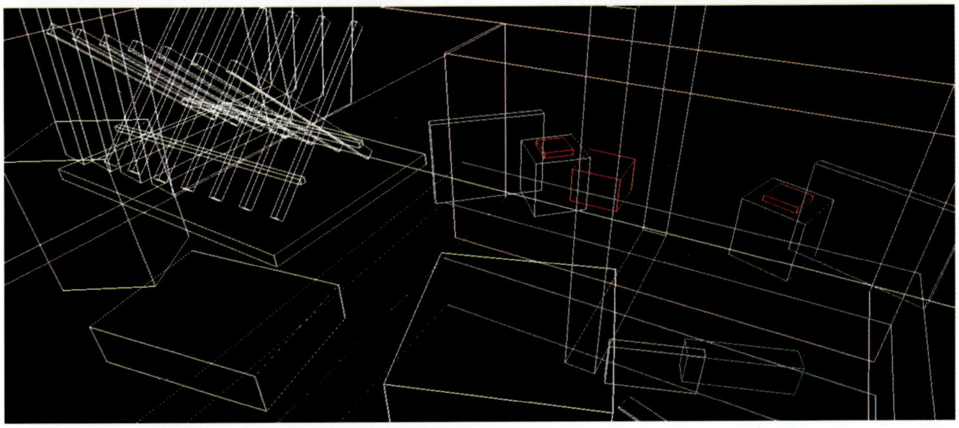

BOUNDING BOX

In this mode, each object is defined simply by a cube (left) that represents its exterior boundary. The most redeeming facet of this mode is speed. With very complicated models even wireframe can get sluggish. In bounding box mode even the most complicated scene can be easily moved around–a nice feature even if it is hard to tell what you are looking at. Animation previews play back in almost real-time allowing quick feedback on camera positions and object movements.

BLENDING SHADES FOR BEST RESULTS

To say ray tracing is the best shading mode under all circumstances would be akin to saying that champagne is the only drink choice for those who can afford it. It may be good stuff, but it is not going to be the best choice for all occasions.

Time is a deciding factor when choosing whether or not to ray trace a scene, but other considerations exist. Different modes of shading have different effects on models, depending on how the models were built.

With the Infini-D arrow model (right), no difference can be seen between the ray-traced or the shaded "best" models. Since there are no transparencies or reflections, the scenes look identical. The difference is the ray-traced scene took twice as long to render.

In the shaded "fast" scene, the terrain surface takes a beating; yet, this arrow could be argued to be the best.

If you are animating that arrow and it takes but a few minutes to render a few dozen frames, you might consider rendering the land in ray trace or shade "best." Then render the arrow in shade "fast" mode on black or with alpha channels in order to edit the land and arrow together.

Ray trace

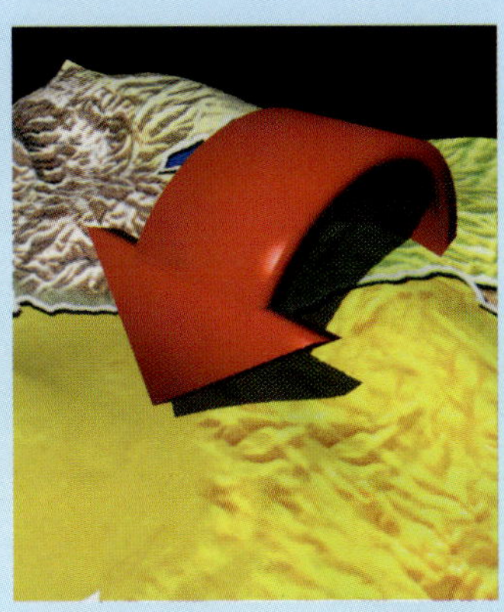

Shade "best"

Shade "fast"

CREATING TILED TEXTURES

Creating a believable texture to apply to the surface of a model is one of the largest hurdles to clear on the track to making photo-realistic images.

Tiled textures are small swatches of images, usually in PICT format that, when replicated side by side to cover an object, make a single seamless texture. For instance, if you were creating a wall, you could go to the effort of recreating the pattern of the entire wallpaper in one huge PICT file, or you could create a small tiled PICT file that repeated itself over and over again, with the same results.

In many instances, creating a clever pattern will save you a great deal of effort and rendering time. The tile pattern (below) allows you to use one simple shape, such as a cube, with a nice map instead of hundreds of little tile models that would give much the same effect.

TILING TILES The bathroom scene (above) relies on two small tile swatches to recreate an entire room. Both of the swatches were first designed in a 3D program, rendered and then edited in Photoshop to create a seamless tile. The same concept could be used to create wallpaper or a brick wall.

MAKING THE MODEL Tiles, vents, machinery, whatever–they all involve creating a model that will become a tiled texture. Avoid hot spots and shadows that will not work by using the tile concept.

RENDERING THE IMAGE Make sure your design is symmetrical enough so that right and left edges, as well as top and bottom edges, line up seamless with each other. Keep final resolution in mind, so render larger than you think you will need.

In Photoshop, use a couple of filters on top of a colored field and you can create a grass or grain surface.

Make sure lines and images on the boundaries line up with the opposite side.

This tube lines up...

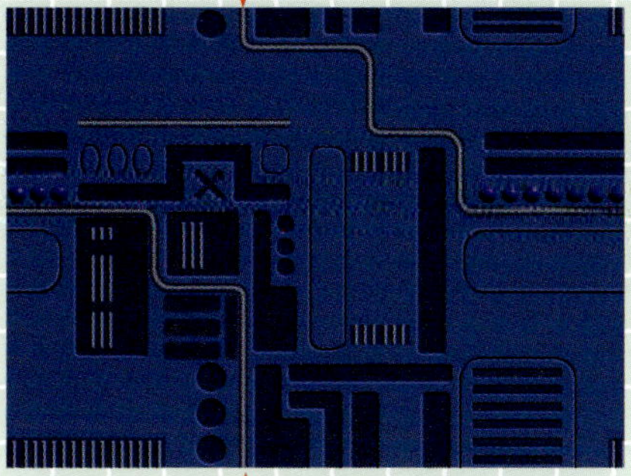

...with this tube.

Hard-edged computer models can take on an organic feel with the proper tile texture.

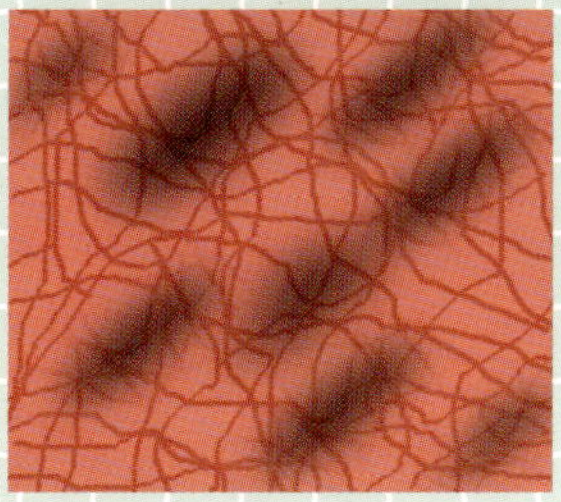

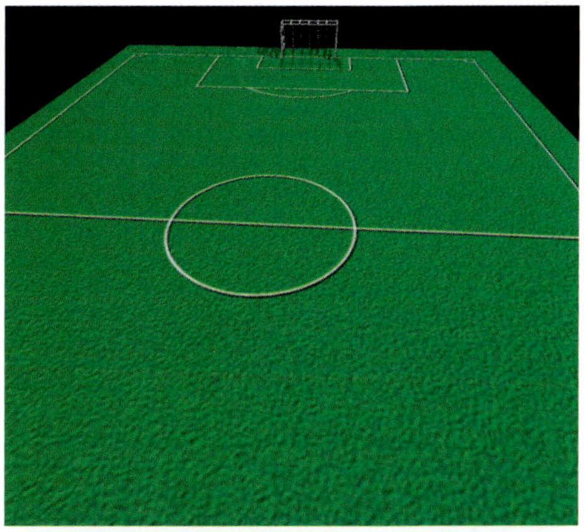

SCRATCHY STUFF

Photoshop and the wide array of filters available for the program make it a powerhouse for creating textures. Invaluable are the filter packages available from third-party developers. A simple grass texture, shown here, was created by first creating a small swatch of green, adding noise via the Noise filter, and then embossing the results. The end product is a grainy noise that has many applications, depending on the color you started with. Bump maps can be created easily from the file to add to the depth of the texture.

COSMIC TILES

A quick and dirty way to take a boring shape and bring it to life is with a tile map that has a fair amount of detail in it. The spaceship (left) is mainly a couple of lathed and extruded objects repeated several times. What gives it a little pazazz is a straightforward PICT tile. The image was drawn in Illustrator, imported into Photoshop where an overall noise was applied to give it a little tooth. An embossing filter was applied on most of the panels to give them a more dimensional feel. Careful effort was made to make sure that a tube going out of the bottom of the screen made its entrance at the top (far left). This ensures a seamless tile.

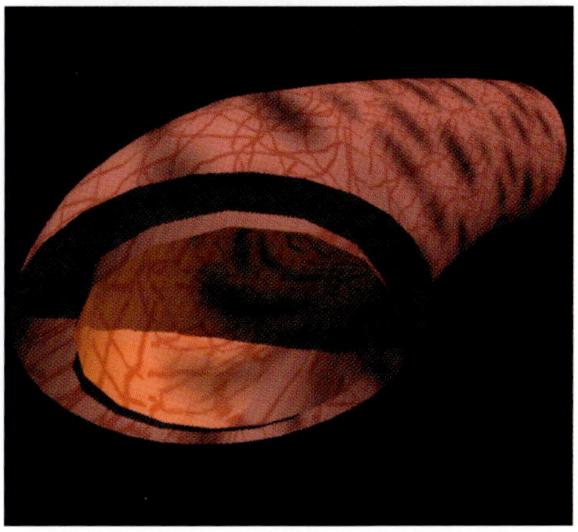

THE SOFT TOUCH

Simple forms (left) can rise above their primitive status with a clean texture tile that emulates soft organic images. A good tool to use when creating the tile in Photoshop is the feathered Lasso tool (see directions below). Selecting blotchy areas and lightening or darkening the areas with the "Levels" dialog box can help take off the hard edge that 3D models easily can get. It is easy when creating models to put a chromium polish or a slick marble texture on everything. The challenge comes when you try to overcome the computer characteristics of 3D models. Tiled textures with soft internal blends and blurs go a far way in achieving that goal.

MAKING ENDS MEET

Creating a pretty texture is just the first part of the battle. Your texture will lose all impact if the edges do not meet up perfectly and you end up with a little fault line all over your object. Fortunately, tools are at hand to help with this simple, but all-important chore.

After experimenting with your texture to get it just the way you want it, open it up in Photoshop. Check your tile by selecting Edit/Select All then Edit/Define Pattern.

Create a new document larger than the original texture. Select Edit/Select All, then choose Edit/Fill and select the Pattern button. The document should fill with your tiled pattern. If it looks good, as it will with some simple patterns such as the grass example (top of page), leave it alone.

If it is full of little defractions and edges, it is time to make it tileable. Double click on the Lasso tool and change the feather to 3. (Other settings may be better, depending on the image detail, so experiment.) Starting in the vertical center, just off the left border, draw a squiggly line to the top left corner, then straight down letting the border define the edge for you, and then back to where you started. When you lift up, the area will be highlighted. Option-drag this selection to the middle–this will copy it. Select Image/Flip/Horizontal. Drag the flipped image to the right side, to the edge, of the image area. You now have a horizontally tileable image. Repeat the process on the top and bottom to get a completely tileable image. Check the results by following the first step outlined.

Create the pattern.

Select one side with feathered lasso.

Flip it horizontally.

DECAL TEXTURES

When you were in college, it is likely that certain industrious young adults used to smuggle beer into football games. To disguise their ruse, they would wrap their beer with a thin rubber decal that had soda can markings. The results were quite believable and successful. Decal texture maps work much the same way.

These texture maps help create 3D models which mimic the real world. Think of non-tiled textures as bumper stickers. You can stick the texture down on a flat surface, roll it around a cylinder or wrap it onto a car bumper.

You also can go a step further by creating a decal that mimics a jet's control panel. You can create knobs and dials without the heavy time investment of having to build–subsequently render–all those little parts, with the final product image having the same impact.

A TALE OF TWO DECALS Decals turn a simple sphere and a lathed object into a baseball and a pile of cans. Notice where the label ends and the underlying surface begins. A highly reflective light grey mimics chrome. The background is a Photoshop document imported into an alpha channel.

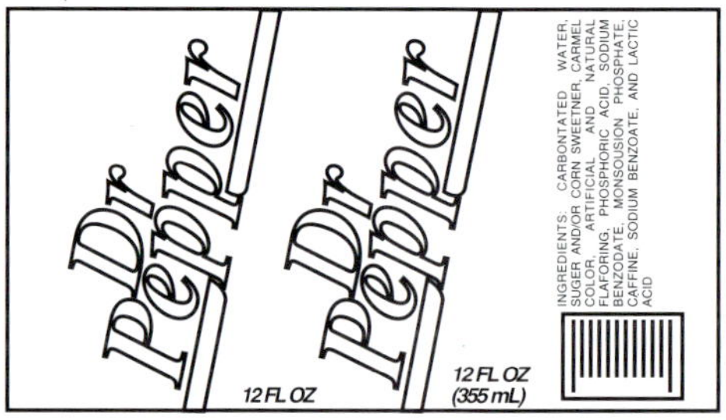

CREATING THE DECAL

The can decal was created in Illustrator using fonts that were sure to raster, or image, properly when imported into Photoshop. When the design is complete, enlarge the image so your final output resolution will be tight enough to match the final output.

EDITING THE DECAL

Open the file in Photoshop as an RGB document. The conversion from CMYK to RGB often leaves something to be desired. Bumping up the saturation in Photoshop usually helps brighten the colors. Save the resulting file in PICT. In the modeling program, import the file as a PICT map and use a cylindrical map to wrap it around the can model.

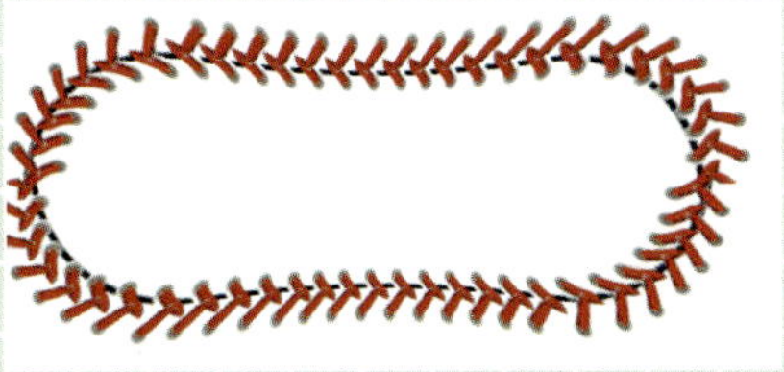

The stitch decal was wrapped around the sphere.

PLAY BALL

Decals do not always have to lie flat or roll over a surface. Texture maps, like the ball (left) can wrap around a surface as well. Objects such as golf or soccer balls are prime candidates for tiled maps, but decals for tennis and baseballs easily wrap themselves around a sphere. The baseball decal began as a long oval line in Photoshop. A single red string stitch was drawn and then repeated all the way around the line and then the stock Photoshop Pinch filter was used to squeeze the middle together.

The decal (below) was straight mapped to the surface.

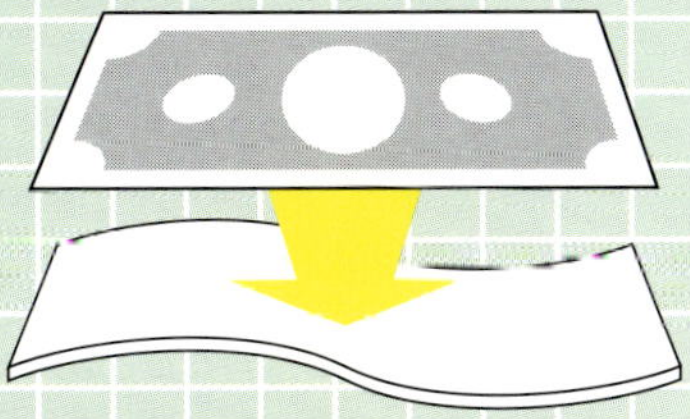

The model is an extruded wavy line, giving a folding paper feel.

IF YOU HAVE IT, USE IT

Scanning real world objects and mapping them onto another object's surface can add a dramatic edge. Anything you can lay down on a scanner bed makes an easy target. If you want to map the front of a house though, it might be better to take a photograph of it to scan. Covers of magazines, posters, baseball cards and the like are also good examples. But be sensitive of copyrighted material. The bill (left) was scanned at 400 dpi for print quality resolution. For an animation 100 to 150 dpi would be fine. The resulting PICT file was straight mapped onto a thin wavy shape that was deeply extruded to create the face of the bill.

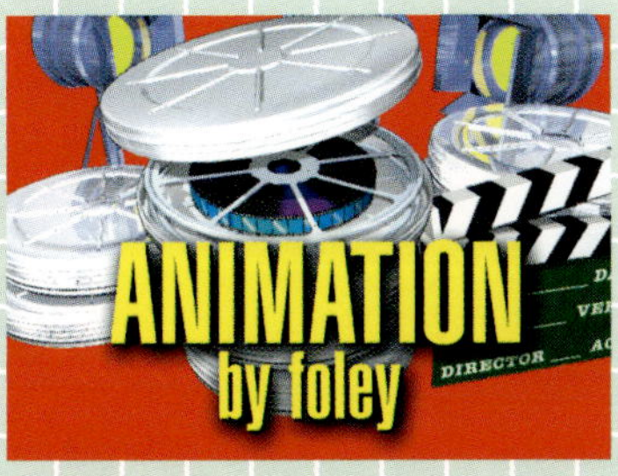

After this scene was created and rendered, the resulting PICT file was mapped to the sign (right).

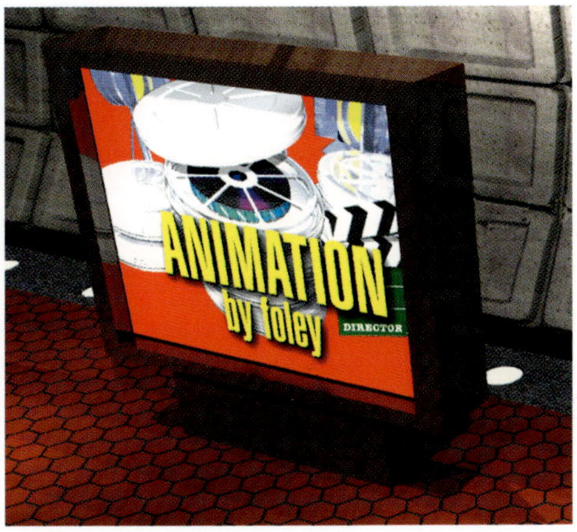

IF YOU DO NOT HAVE IT, MAKE IT

A great thing about having the ability to create photo-realistic images is that you can use the same set of skills to create an image that can then become a texture map. The image (left) is actually a third-generation map. The filmstrip and the directors board were mapped onto the surface to create the original image, which was then mapped onto the billboard image, which was then rendered again.

DECAL & MODEL MIXING

The strength of a model is often in the detail. Unfortunately, detail often uses large amounts of disk space, RAM and rendering time.

A good way to achieve a high degree of detail, without making a model that will give your Mac a coronary, is to create a decal that lends detail to non-essential parts of the model and marries them with true 3D models.

The example (right) consists of three models. The large, olive-green capacitor to the right, the red transistor to the left and the flat cube they both rest upon.

Making decals of this nature requires attention to a few details. The camera angle cannot be too low or the flatness of the decal begins to show. The circuit board here is just at the point where the shapes of the resistors begin to flatten out.

If your decal has shadows, try to position the light sources of your models to replicate the feel of the decal.

If you are going to move the object around in an animation, it is best to minimize the shadows in the decal, as they will not follow the shadows of the true 3D objects.

If you are building a model that will become a decal, set the light sources in the scene so they do not cast shadows, or place a single light source directly behind the camera.

If you do not want to create your own detail decal, many sources for detail decals are available on the market, including many CD-ROM photo disks. If you have a Kodak Photo CD compatible CD-ROM drive, you easily can build a library of detail textures using your own camera. Software packages exist which allow you to import images from your Photo CD into Photoshop so you can manipulate the image and save it as a PICT file for mapping.

PROCEDURAL MAPS

Most modeling programs support some type of computer-generated surface and color treatment. These are generally referred to as *procedural* or *volumetric maps* and surfaces which rely on mathematical algorithms rather than importing an image from an external file. They can range from a simple color applied to the surface of a model to a more complicated juxtaposition of hues dictated by a fractal pattern.

Procedural surfaces often have individual adjustment environments that allow for mimicking of real-world surfaces such as wood or stone. They also usually have enough surface variables to generate any number of surfaces, from glass, mirrors and paper to concrete, grass and clouds.

These procedural surfaces have notable benefits. Since they are computer-generated, they do not require the memory overhead of external image files. This keeps file sizes respectable and rendering time fast.

Patterns and grains generated by the computer are algorithm-based and not pixel-based. Your object can get very close to the camera without pixelation (where you can see individual pixels). The surfaces also are volumetric in nature, meaning they are applied to the whole object as well as *through* the whole object.

The drawback of procedural maps is that, unless they are meticulously handled, they do not always have a photo-realistic feel about them. An external image map can make a single cube look like a block wall. To achieve the same effect with procedural maps, you have to create the block color and apply it to an individual block, then replicate that block dozens of times to create a wall. Speed advantages take a beating in cases like these.

However, as part of the overall picture, procedural maps are of inestimable value. They give color and texture to all the little bits and pieces that can bring most scenes to life.

COMPUTER-GENERATED TEXTURES This entire scene (above), including the clouds in the background, was created using procedural surfaces. The canyon in the background is a fractal-generated model.

VOLUMETRIC, THROUGH AND THROUGH
One of the key features to procedural maps is that their surfaces are not only skin deep, like those applied by external texture maps. Break a procedurally mapped tree in half and you will find rings (if you designed it that way) or break open a stone block (left) and you will find more stone. If you mapped a rock texture straight to the front of the same stone, you would find streaks of the texture running through the interior cut-away.

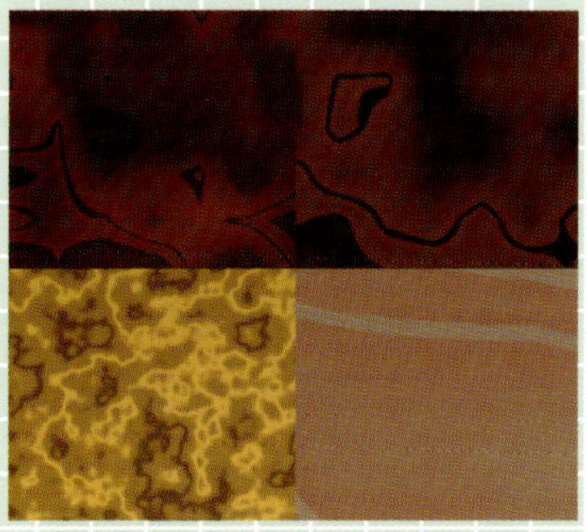

A variety of wood treatments

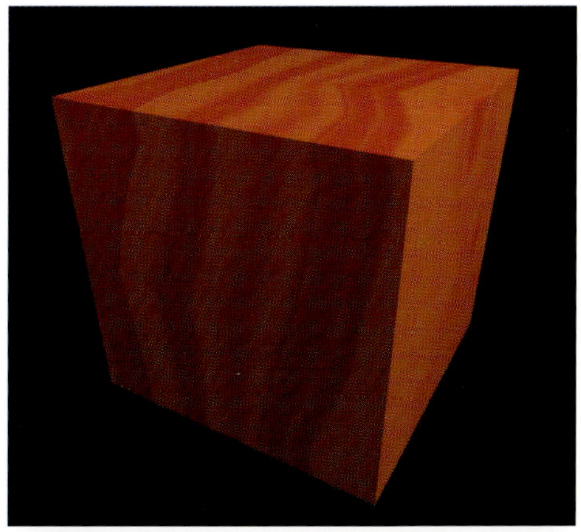

KNOCK ON WOOD

While it is hard to outdo Mother Nature, most modeling programs do a credible job by allowing the animator to control the rings and knurls of a real wood pattern. The best of these will allow the modeler to chop a volumetrically mapped cylinder in half and be able to count the rings inside. Like the stone procedural editing process, the final texture is determined by adjusting grain patterns between two user-definable colors.

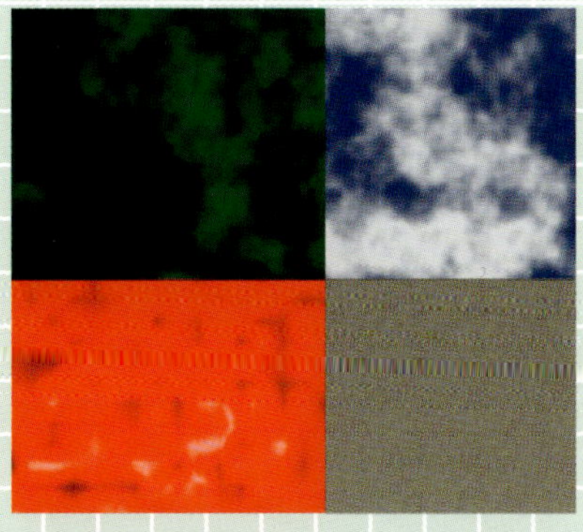

Jade to sandstone textures

CARVED IN STONE

Because of their volumetric nature, procedural maps work well for creating the often uneven surfaces of rock and stone. The computer uses its resources well in recreating grain in minerals which are often crystalline in nature. Reducing the highlights and reflection of a surface will give it a matte and natural finish while doing the opposite will give the rock surface the luster of a polished stone.

Mandelbrot (top) and Julie sets

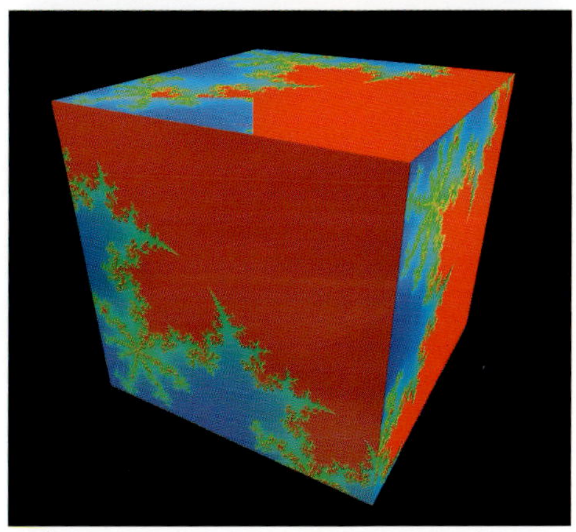

FRACTALS

Many modeling programs offer fractal-generated patterns to create procedural maps. Simply put, fractals are mathematical formulas which, if displayed graphically, seem to generate a never-ending pattern. If supported, fractals can generate both terrains and volumetric surfaces. Two of the most famous fractal formulas are the Mandelbrot set and the Julie set.

PROCEDURAL SURFACE TREATMENTS

SURFACE

Normal surface treatment responds to ambient and placed lights by showing tonal variation in its shading. Without any other treatment applied to the surface the object would appear flat or matte.

SPECULAR HIGHLIGHTS

The higher the settings are for specular highlight or ambient reflections, the more they tend to reflect hotspots from placed lights. The higher the specular lighting, the more shiny the object appears.

REFLECTIVENESS

Applying a reflective surface causes the object to mirror the world around it. In this case, a 40% reflection picks up the table color as well as the soft environment applied to the scene. Rendering time increases with this effect.

TRANSPARENT

Although a render hog, transparency can take a solid model and make it as clear as glass or translucent like wax paper. Anti-aliasing adds a good deal more to the rendering time as does additional lighting.

DEFRACTION

The defraction setting adjusts how the light rays deflect as they shine through an object that is transparent. A little bit tends to go a long way. Keep your defraction setting low if you want realism.

GLOW

Lots of things glow in the world. Light bulbs, LED numbers, exit signs and reindeer's noses. Glows flatten out an object quickly as it loses its surface shading.

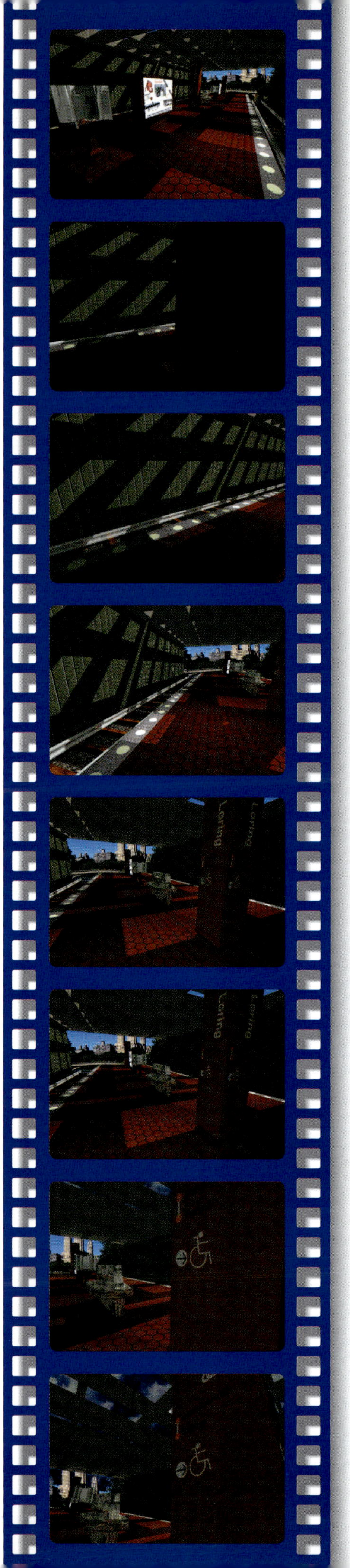

FOUND TEXTURES

Textures are everywhere. All of us are covered with them. The challenge is how you get them from the analogous world into the digital world. Fortunately, there are several solutions for achieving this.

One easy way is scanning. Color scanners give you a great deal of flexibility when importing a texture. The user can define, early in the game, the resolution of the texture. This is mandatory for sharp, clean texture maps. The biggest drawback is a flatbed scanner's limited depth of field. It is designed to scan mostly flat or near-flat things. Stand-mounted 3D scanners are more flexible and can easily capture textures of dimensional objects.

Another solution, that is less expensive and vastly more portable, is a film camera. By photographing your subject and having the resulting film transferred to a Kodak Photo CD you can use a Photo CD compatible CD-ROM drive to import almost any image or texture with clean, sharp resolution. The only drawback is the lack of immediate gratification–you have to wait for your CD photo disc to be processed.

One way to work around this, with less crisp results, is to import images from a camcorder or digital camera. Camcorders and analog still video cameras require a video input board or an AV Macintosh to capture the images. Digital cameras patch directly into the Mac, usually through the serial port. When shooting with these devices, fill the viewfinder with the image and plan on reducing the results at least 50% to sharpen the image.

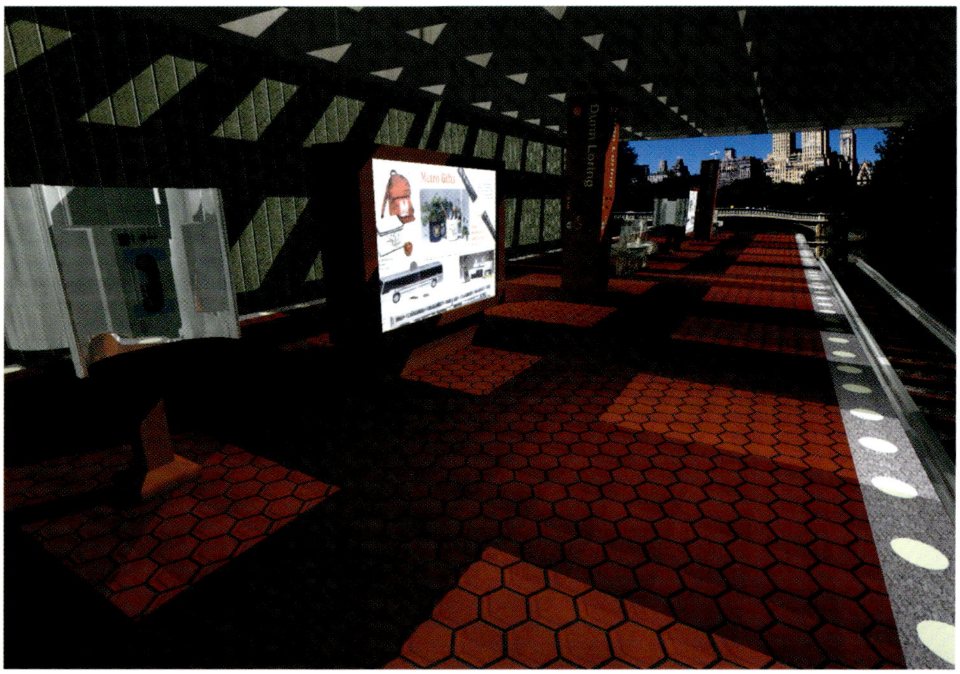

TEXTURE EXTRAVAGANZA All of the textures in this metro rail station scene (above) were either captured at the site, purchased as stock art, or scanned. The cityscape background is an image from a Photo CD-ROM, dropped into the scene's alpha channel.

Original capture

Image adjusted, filtered and tiled

VIDEO CAPTURES

Textures imported from the video world have the same constraints applied to them as images created for the video world. They have low resolution and tend to be a bit fuzzy. Capturing an image full screen and reducing it helps to sharpen its definition.

Photoshop filters, such as Despeckle, Blur and De-interlace, as well as image adjustments to correct saturation and contrast, can help tweak captures and remove scan lines. Since video images are different in brightness than your computer screen, you may want to adjust the color intensity as well.

150 dpi brochure scan

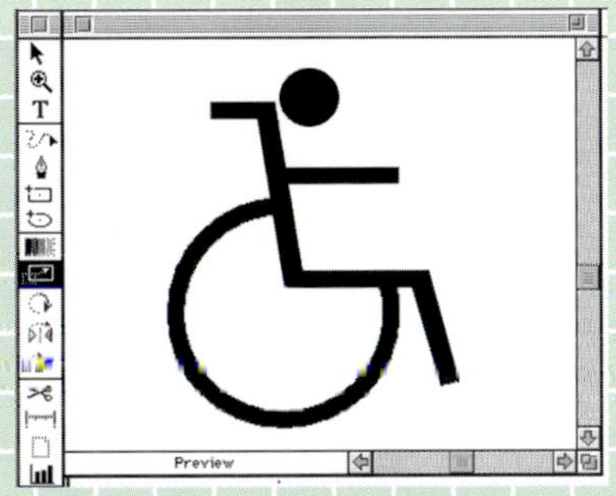

Digital file retrieved and saved as a PICT file.

Altered volcano rock from a Wraptures' CD, and rosewood from Specular's Replicas series.

SCANNED TEXTURES

"Garbage in, garbage out" applies directly to scanning. If you scan a texture, say 2" square at 72 dpi, and map it directly to a cube without tiling or reducing, you cannot plan to have the cube get any larger than 2" in your animation or it will become pixelated. Your screen is 72 dpi, so it can handle pretty low-resolution maps, but there is a limit. For best results, try to double the scanning resolution on texture maps if possible. Scanning the swatch above at 150 dpi will create a map twice the size. When you convert the file to 72 dpi for editing (some modeling programs do not handle high-resolution images well), your 2" square will be 4". When mapped to the same cube, the resolution will be much sharper.

DIGITAL TRANSFER

Art departments are becoming increasingly more digital–that benefits animators hunting for images to map. All 2D illustration programs support some format that can be imported into Photoshop. These include PICT, TIFF and EPS. For the programs that do not support exporting images, you can always take a snapshot of the screen. For instance, if for some reason you want to map an image of your favorite spreadsheet onto a model, you can capture it directly from the screen by entering Command-Shift-3 or using a third party software utility such as Capture.

PURCHASED TEXTURES

Falling short of all other possibilities, you can acquire found textures by using your credit card. You can either scan your card in and map the results to a model; or you can call your catalog computer software dealer and order textures on a disk. Some companies, such as Form and Function, sell tiled textures that are designed for the modeler/animator. Other disks, often on CD-ROMs because of their large file size, offer photographs of textures such as grass, rocks and clouds that can be mapped directly or easily tiled.

BORROWED TEXTURES

Using real wallpaper makes a convincing wall covering in your model. The directional lines and patterns that develop help make a scene believable. Creating your own wallpaper is a simple matter, since most have simple shapes and patterns that can easily be drawn.

One quick way to build a portfolio of wallpaper textures is to make a trip to your local hardware megastore or carpet and wallpaper showroom. Wallpaper displays usually have a small 4" sample for people to take home to see if the paper will match with their sofa. Pick up a few.

Usually a few inches of the sample will be enough; make sure you get enough so that the pattern begins to repeat itself.

Scan the sample

Create the tile

Apply to a surface

Scan the sample at 150-200 dpi. If the colors are light or pastel, and wallpapers often are soft in nature, you might want to boost up the intensity and contrast of the scan.

In Photoshop, create a tiled pattern by eliminating what you do not need and replicating what you do need in order to create a swatch that will tile cleanly on all four sides. Save the resulting file in PICT format for importing into your modeling or animation program.

CREATING SURFACES

The final step to model realism is applying surface treatments.

A detailed model with a great color map may look sharp, but in many cases the result may seem flat. A pair of jeans may be the same tone of blue all over, but they have a certain recognizable weave. A stucco wall may be the same throughout, but it has a distinct bumpy surface. The way to achieve these surfaces, as well as others such as reflectiveness and transparency, is to apply surface maps which work in tandem with color surfaces and texture maps.

Proper surface treatment can make the same shape–a cube–transform from a plastic hunk to a glass sheet, a concrete block or a mirror. Proper surface treatment adds that final edge to creating photo-realistic images.

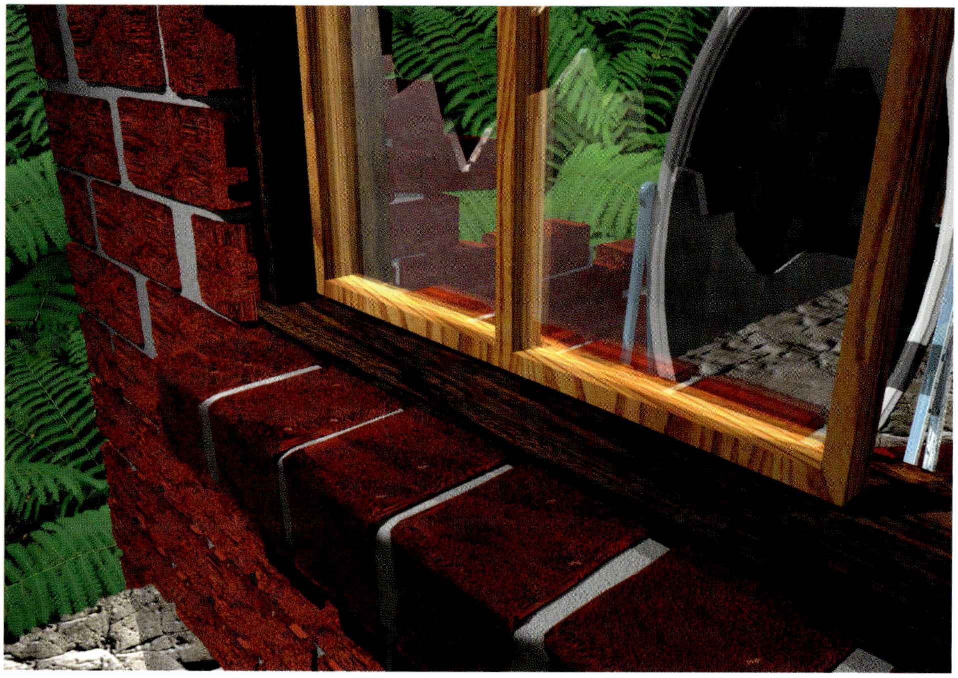

BUMP MAPS In addition to the color textures applied to a model, surface maps create the effect of raising or pushing back the surface plane. The three samples (below) were used in the image above. Creating bump maps can be done independently of the color maps or in tandem. The white areas push up while the black areas are pushing down, creating irregularities in the surface.

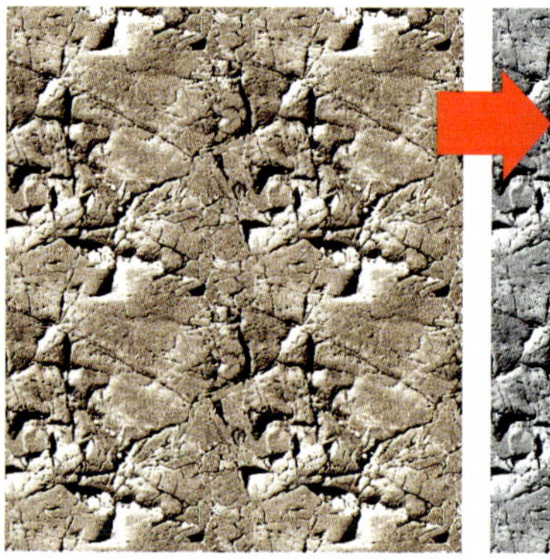

MAKE MATCHING BUMP MAPS
Color maps are often aided by matching bump maps that help accentuate the cracks and crevices. Commercially available textures often ship with associated bump maps. With handmade or scanned textures, it is easy to create a bump map.

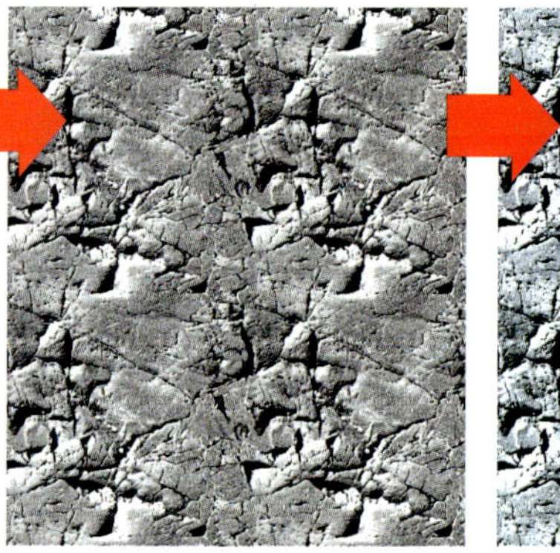

CONVERT TO GRAYSCALE
Although color images often can be used as bump maps, with the degree of effect depending on the contrast in the image, using a grayscale image will allow the user more control. Open the color texture file in Photoshop and convert the color file to a grayscale image.

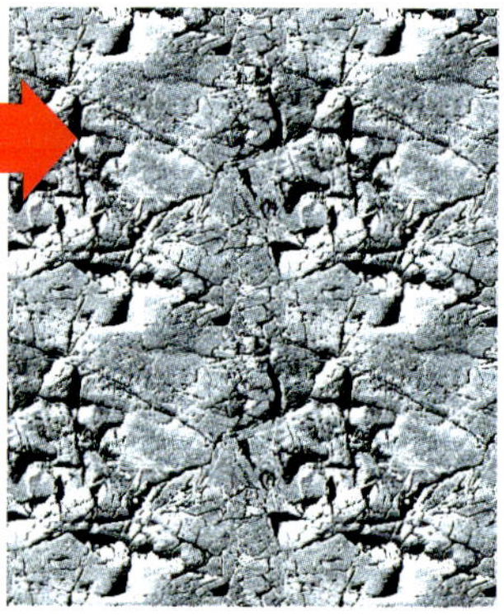

INCREASE THE CONTRAST
Increase the contrast to the point where the blacks are rich and the whites form crisp highlights (above). Do not go too far. You will begin to lose too much information. Export the image as PICT and import into your modeling document.

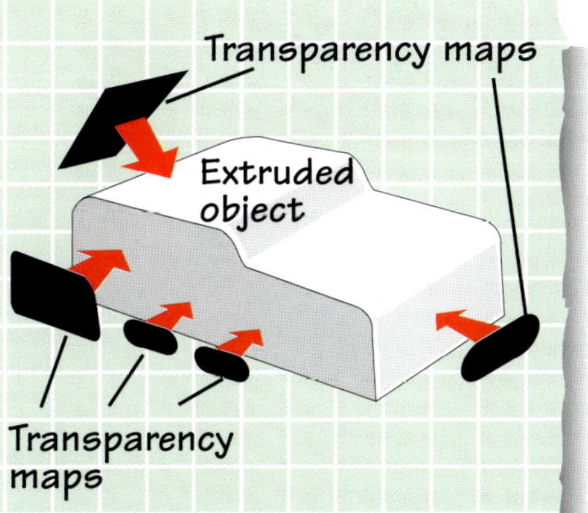

TRANSPARENCY MAPS

To poke holes for windows and create otherwise difficult shapes easily and cleanly, use transparency maps. In most programs that support transparency surfacing, apply a black map created in Photoshop in the shape of the window you want to make. Wherever you see black, there is a hole. In cases like the sailboat cabin (left) several sets of maps were used to poke windows from all sides of an extruded object. Note that the side portholes poked all the way through, so a second set was not needed on the other side.

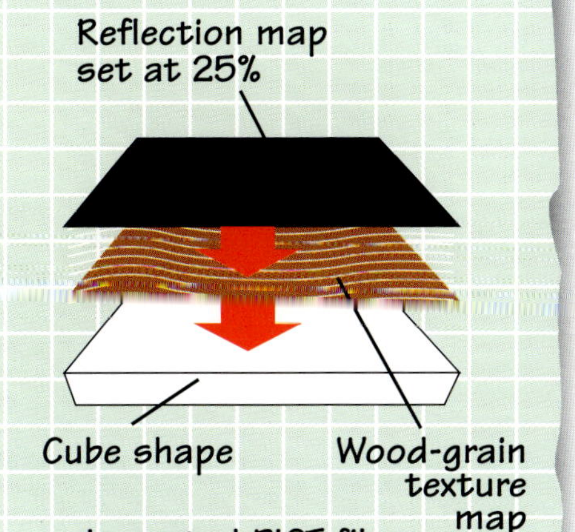

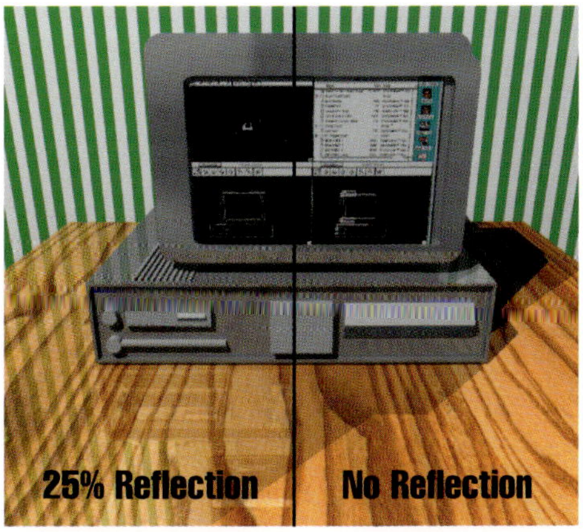

REFLECTION MAPS

Wood-grain texture maps can turn a cube into a table in a few easy steps. But left alone, the results can be a little flat. To add a couple of coats of furniture polish and bring the surface to life you can apply the computer version of furniture polish–a *reflection map*. You can apply the map to the whole surface by mapping a black square of that size or to selected areas by editing the map in Photoshop. Wherever there is black (or shades of gray), there will be a reflection. (As things get darker, they reflect more.) Differing percentages of reflection will change the amount the environment that reflects off the object. With 90% reflection most of the surface texture map would be obscured by the reflection of the objects and environment around it.

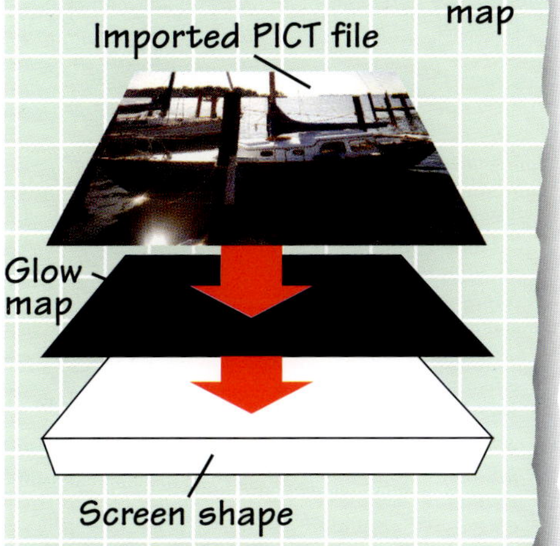

GLOW MAPS

Some objects in the real world emit their own light without reflecting light. Examples include the glow of a TV screen, neon lights and glowing signs. If an image, like one imitating a TV screen, is mapped directly to the surface with no surface treatment (left), the effect is flat. The addition of a glow map to the surface gives it the characteristics it needs to replicate what an image on the screen would look like and glow in a dark room just like the real thing.

APPLYING AND ADJUSTING SURFACE MAPS

Applying a surface map to an object can add a realistic edge to an image; or it can make the image a noisy, distracting mess. The key, as when using other surfacing techniques, is to know when to use them and to use them in moderation. Using a bump map at 100% may cause harsh pitting, as in the top example (far right). Limiting the bump to a smaller value is often more realistic. In some cases, the contrast on a texture map may be great enough to apply it as a bump map as well.

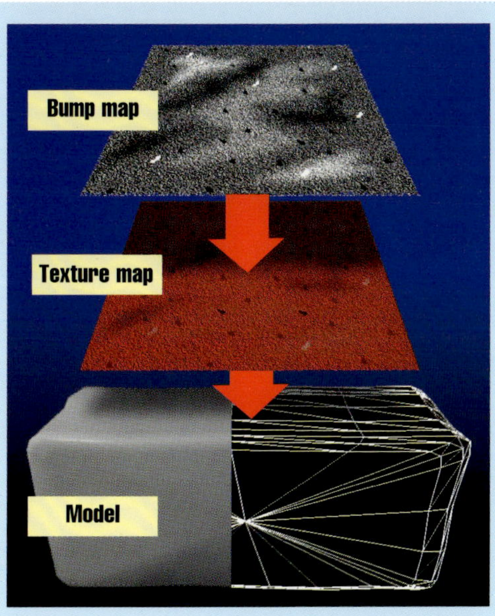

MAPS AND INKS

Creating texture maps is the first part of the process. Now the map must be applied to the surface of your model. Two variables define how your texture map will look: the type of mapping device and the style of ink effect.

The mapping device often is dictated by the shape of the object you are working with. As the forms you create begin to grow in sophistication and complexity, the choice of a mapping solution gets more complicated. If you are creating a planet surface, a spherical map seems like the obvious choice. But if you are creating a liver, you might choose between a wrap or spherical map. You must find out by trial and error.

Ink effects are more cut and dried. If you want your map to encompass the entire object opaquely, you can use use the copy ink. If you want a more subtle, integrated texture you can choose one of the blend inks.

When working with ink effects other than the copy, it is wise to plan ahead. Make sure you design your texture so it will work with the desired ink and any underlying textures.

USE INKS AND MAPS FOR ADDED REALISM Wood panels of the radio are a natural application of a straight map for a flat surface. The antenna and capacitors use cylinder maps. The speaker uses four circular transparency straight maps with a matte or reveal ink so just the circles poke through.

REVEAL INK

Design reveal inks with pure, white surfaces so the background drops out cleanly–as with this label.

COPY INK

In this mode, the whites remain solid and all elements of the map can be seen.

VARIOUS MAP TECHNIQUES

How you place your texture onto your shape is called *mapping*. While procedural maps affect the whole object, you must direct how imported textures will appear on the surface.

STRAIGHT

This mapping technique handles well the task of applying a texture map to a flat, or nearly flat surface. Shapes with curves and gentle undulations also take well to this mapping effect, but too much curvature might begin to distort the image being mapped. **USES:** Wall surfaces, table tops, machine facades, signs, clock faces, magazine covers, flooring.

CUBICAL

If an object needs mapping on all sides, cubic mapping might be the approach to take. Since objects come in such a variety of forms and textures, the sides may not always line up. Planning ahead to make the surface work with the form is important here, since the computer might tweak the edges a bit as it tries to figure out how to map your surface to your form. **USES:** Landscape elements, bricks, blocks and machine parts.

CYLINDRICAL

When you need to wrap a surface around a long, round object, such as a pencil, you will use this map effect. Cylindrical maps are usually defined as being able to wrap around all or part of an object. They are good for round objects, odd shapes and cubes. **USES:** Tree trunks and columns, as well as quick building facades and package designs.

SPHERICAL

This effect takes a flat texture map and maps it around the surface of a roughly spherical shape. The top and bottom pinch in, so carefully design your texture accordingly. This is much like a Mercator projection map, where Greenland appears much larger than it really is. Greenland will be reduced greatly in size by the time it wraps around the sphere. **USES:** Globes, planets, bedknobs, marbles and other kinds of spheres.

WRAP

This mapping technique takes your texture and, respecting its original dimensions as much as possible, wraps your flat map onto a round object or undulating surface. The treatment is much like taking a very flexible, rubbery bumper stick and plastering it on an object. **USES:** Stitching for athletic balls, aircraft windows and organic textures on organic shapes.

VARIOUS INK EFFECTS

Adjusting your ink effects gives you control on how your texture map appears on your surface.

COPY

With this effect, all colors, including white, lay as they were created on top of the surface on which they are applied. Useful for most hard-edge decal-type applications– texture maps whose images encompass the entire shape. Tiled textures run full to all sides and work fine with this effect. **USES:** Solid surface where the texture needs to be opaque, wood, metal and stone surfaces, decal-type textures.

MATTE

The matte ink works well when your texture map has an irregular outside shape, but you do not want the white tones on the inside to drop out. While white edges on the outside of the object become transparent, the integrity of the white surface on the inside is respected. **USES:** Packaging mock-ups, odd-shaped decal textures.

REVEAL

All whites drop out with this effect, including those inside the texture. This makes it perfect for handling elements such as type, where the trapped inside parts of the letters need to be transparent as well. If you have areas inside your art that you want to appear white, use a light shade of gray and it will appear solid. **USES:** Type treatments on the sides of packages, vehicles and machines. Graphic treatments where the image needs to appear painted on the side of an object.

BLEND

When trying to create an effect that needs to be subtle, just applying a texture map may be overkill. Using a blend allows the surface color or texture of the underlying layer to show through, giving the map a transparent effect. Since the overall treatment is similar to the copy effect, this is best used for images that fill up the entire texture area or that tile. **USES:** A smooth way to integrate a texture with an underlying surface such as a bump or ripple.

BLEND REVEAL

Combining aspects of both blend and reveal, this effect allows you to subtly and seamlessly integrate your texture map with an underlying surface. Like the reveal mode, all the white areas become transparent, allowing for a floating transparency effect. **USES:** Light gray type on a transparent surface would appear as etched glass. A floral pattern on a weave could become a curtain.

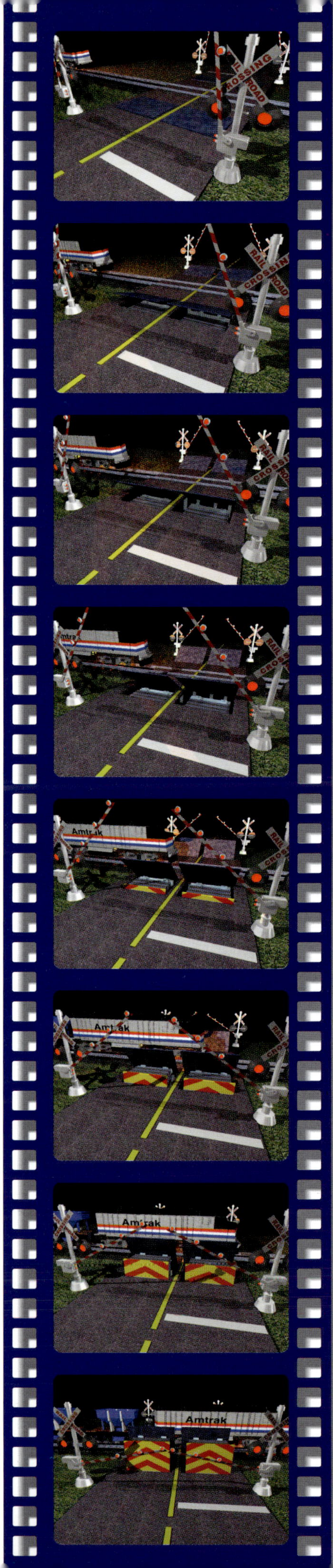

LINKING

Think of how joints in the human body connect the parts of the skeleton. This is analogous to how linking works with computer-generated objects.

Now think of your body as a 3D model you have created. It looks good–but you have to make it work dynamically. To make all the parts connect and move naturally, you have to link them properly.

Linking physically connects one object with another. You also can assign constraints on the angle an object can move, as well as the direction. For example, your elbow can move only 180° (for most of us) and can pivot on only one axis. So, in linking your body, you would connect your finger to your hand, your hand to your forearm, your forearm to your biceps, your biceps to your shoulder and your shoulder to your torso, which would become the base. Move the torso and everything else moves, but you can still move your finger or arm independent of what your foot or head is doing.

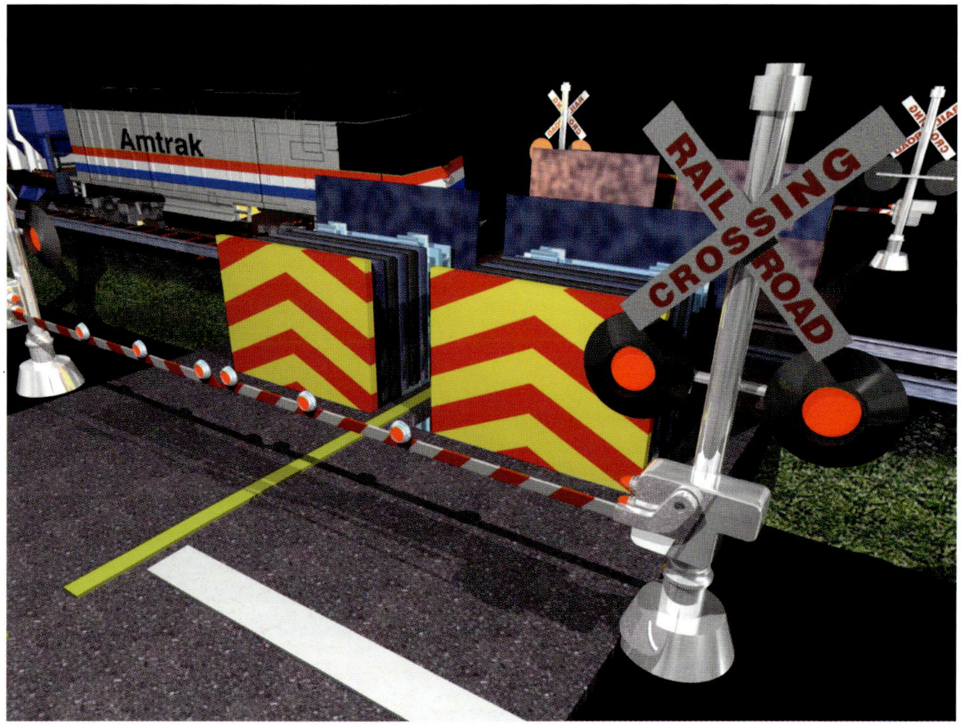

LINKING IT ALL TOGETHER The scene (above) has several links that mimic the design constraints of real objects. The train, linked to the rails, can only move in one direction and cannot pivot. The crossing bar pivots are locked to stay in one place, but can pivot on one axis (like your shoulder). Likewise, the doors on the barricade are assigned constraints of a minimum of 0° (flat on the ground) and 90° (wide open). With constraints assigned, an animation can take on real-life properties. The camera can be linked to objects as well. In this case, it pivots around an invisible cube in the center of the scene.

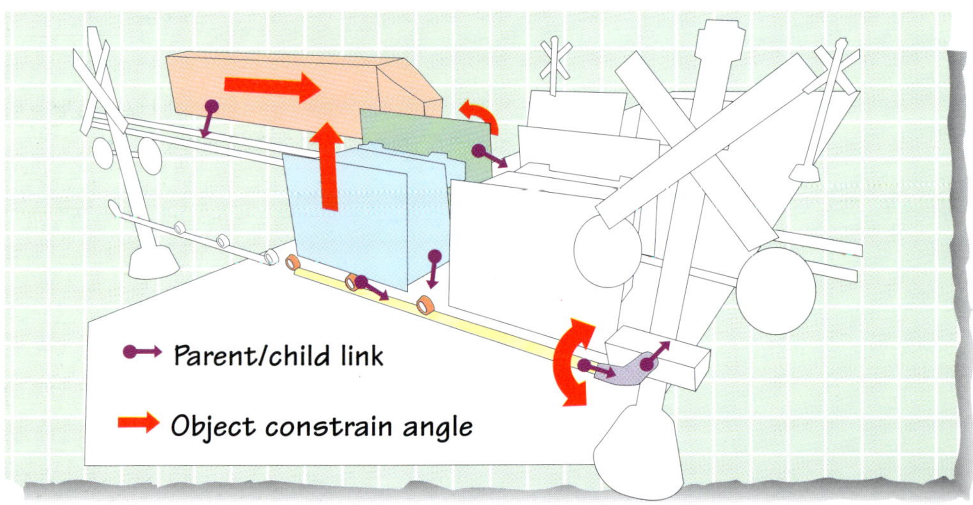

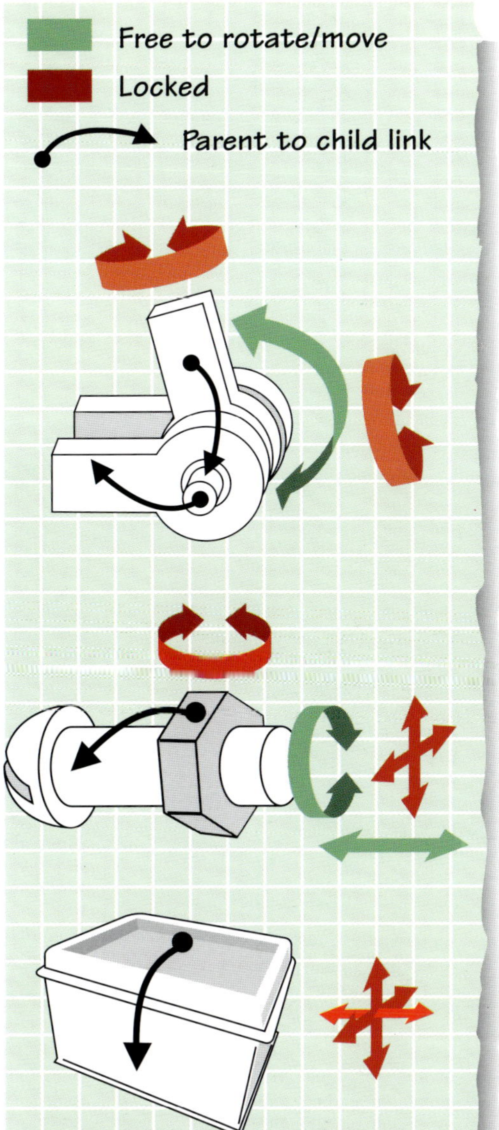

The top is linked to the base with all constraints turned on. Either object can be selected and moved, affecting the whole model.

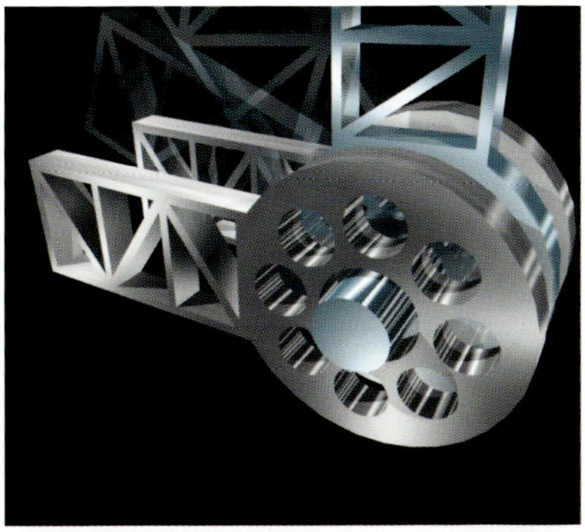

JOINT PIVOT

Door hinges, elbows and crane lifts operate from the simple principle of locking the center point of the moving object into the same place. Locking the orientation constraints it to a single axis. This allows the object to swing freely in one direction only. An object can pivot on its own axis, like a door hinge. The object also can be linked to a pivoting pin (left), which is then pivoted to make the object swing in the desired direction.

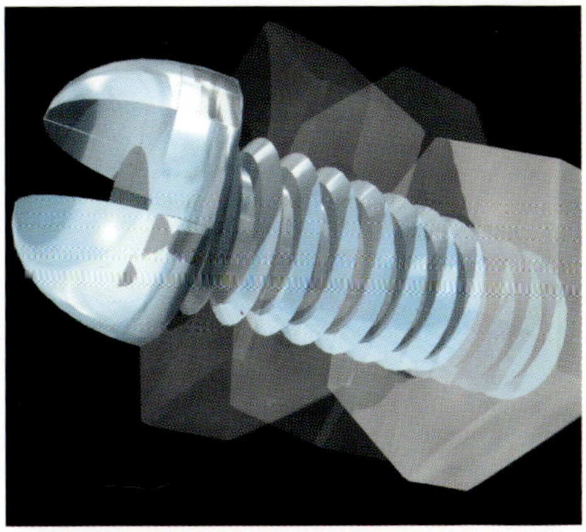

THE SLIDER

Like the train on the track, the nut (left) is constrained in position to slide up and down the bolt. It cannot go in any other direction. However, unlike the train, the orientation is freed on one axis so that the nut can rotate, simulating a nut tightening. Traveling distance can also be assigned to the nut so that it can slide all the way to the top of the bolt, but no farther. This helps in creating the realism of the object and keeps the two objects from meshing together.

LOCKED SOLID

Sometimes it can get confusing trying to remember what is linked to what and where the base of the object really is. In some circumstances, it is not important to have interactive links. You might want to have everything glued together so they cannot move. When links are locked or constrained in all positions and orientations, moving any part will move the whole object. An example of this is where the battery top (left) is locked solid to the base on the bottom. Moving either object moves them both.

INTERACTIVE AND INDEPENDENT LINKS

The Earth-Moon-Sun example (below right) shows how objects can be linked to each other, but still retain their own capabilities of movement within given constraints. The planets are designed to orbit on their own pivot points.

The challenge here is to have the moon orbit the Earth independent of the Earth's rotation. The solution is to use the sun as the base.

A cube (parent) is linked to the sun (grandparent). The Earth (child) is linked to the cube. The moon (child) is then linked to the cube. Now the cube can follow an orbit around the sun (taking the Earth and the moon with it), while the Earth is free to pivot around its axis, pivoting off of the cube. The moon, linked to the cube, can pivot around its own axis. At the same time the cube can pivot on its axis, which would swing the moon in orbit.

All of these movements can be orchestrated together; all is happening in harmony as the sequence plays out over time. Movements then can be edited independently or as a whole. For objects that have several pivoting or orbiting objects it is a simple matter to create an independent linking device, such as the cube used here, for each object.

LIGHTING

In an artificial 3D environment the modeler is responsible for setting up the lighting, much like a photographer would adjust the lights in a studio. A variety of tools and lights are available to add the proper highlights, accents and ambient lighting to a scene.

A focused spotlight can add drama and lead the viewer's eye to an object in the scene. Lights can be dispersed throughout the set to brighten shadowy areas or cast shadows to augment perceived depth.

As you add lights, keep in mind that this increases rendering time when ray tracing, as the computer has to calculate what the effect of each light will be on each object, as well as its reflections and defraction.

LIGHTING EXTRAVAGANZA Because of its strong but simple shapes and textures, Washington, D.C.'s, underground Metrorail is a perfect setting to replicate in a computer model. One of the most interesting aspects of the station is the hundreds of lights spread throughout. Some provide direct spotlighting, others a soft glow. This translates dramatically in a 3D model.

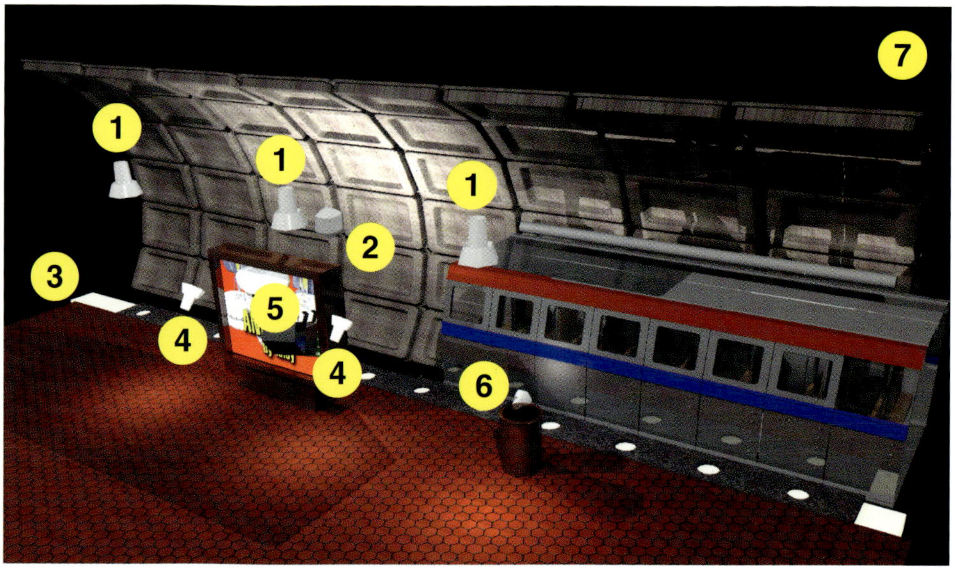

SHOW ME THE LIGHT Each light in the scene has its own mission. 1) Spotlights to mimic the inset lights on the platform. 2) A point light to cast a shadow of the billboard, adding some interest to the otherwise flat platform. 3) A glowing cube, stretched out the length of the scene and placed into an extruded object plugged with holes mimics the lights inset into the granite edge of the platform. 4) Two spotlights to toss a hot spot onto the back tunnel wall, just for effect. 5) A glow map on the billboard gives the sign luminance. 6) A single spotlight that shines through the windows of the train to cast a shadow. 7) Ambient light set to almost zero.

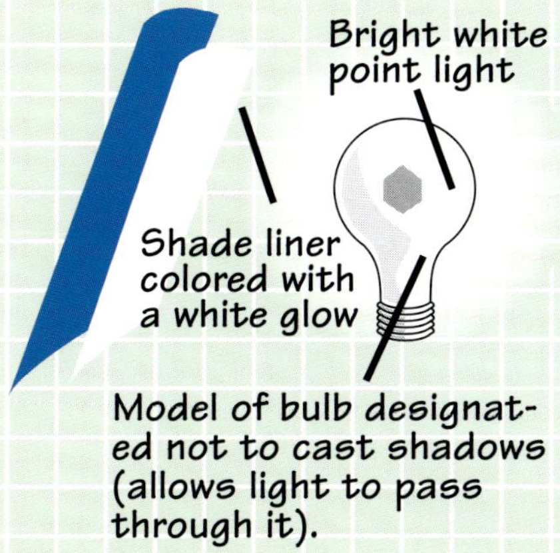

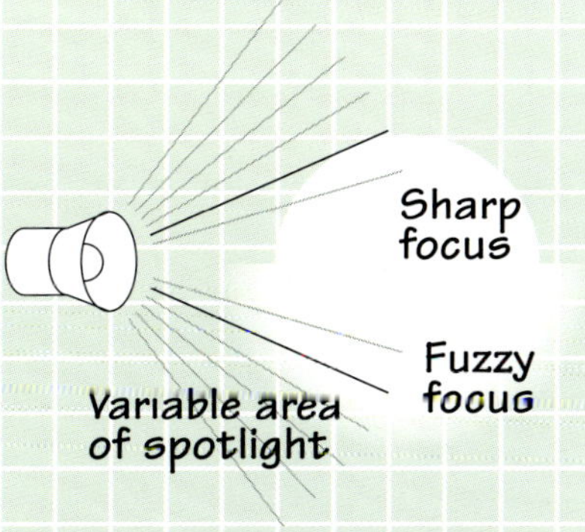

Ambient light can be given a color (below), such as the blue tint.

POINT LIGHTS

Imagine a bare light bulb controlled by a dimmer switch. Now you understand a point light. This is the most common source of light for most modeling situations because it is the most natural. Like all other light sources, point lights can be adjusted by light intensity as well as color. A bright light (left) is inside of the lamp, and another one is outside the viewing area to the upper right.

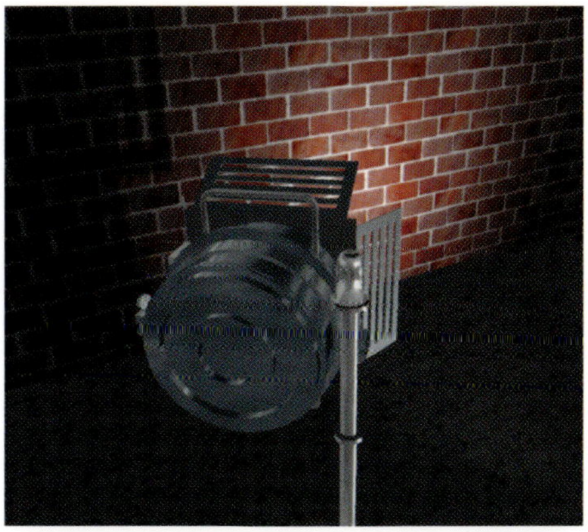

SPOTLIGHTS

Just like the one used in the high school play, the spotlight can throw a directional beam of light toward an object. The light's focus can be changed–creating either a hard circle of light or a soft illumination of an area. When animating, the spotlights can move just like any other object sweeping an area with a white or colored light. Edges can be adjusted in a range between fuzzy (left) and sharp, like the bright spotlights you see on Broadway.

AMBIENT LIGHT

This is the light you see when you wake up in the morning shortly before you turn on your bedroom light. It is a soft gentle light that seems to be everywhere, but does not cast a shadow. With no ambient light you have to count on point lights and spotlights to illuminate a scene, but the results might be less than natural. As you increase the amount of ambient light, the harshness of shadows soften and crevices lighten up or disappear. Ambient light can also be colored to give an overall hue to a scene. The examples (left) show composites of the same scene (far left) with different ambient light settings. The setting (near left) on the lower left is high and low on the upper right.

USING LIGHTS TO GUIDE THE VIEWER'S EYE

Positioning lights to cast interesting shadows or help bring an otherwise flat surface to life heightens the drama of an image. Adjusting lights and the shadows they create is often half the fun of setting up a scene.

Five light sources (right) create the scene. Three are as much key elements of the image as the models themselves. One light, positioned behind the window and the shades, casts the Venetian blind shadow across the wall.

Each blind is a separate extruded model allowing light to pass through it, just like it would in the real world. The thought behind using this element was to create leading lines from both the shadows and the blinds that would direct the viewer's eye inward.

Another harsh light is placed to the left of the scene. This is responsible for casting the shadow of the books onto the blinds.

A light directly above the scene casts a noon shadow from all the objects onto the desk.

Last, to add a final accent to the light that is sitting on the desk, a white glow color was used to color the orb. An invisible light source, placed just above the desk, creates a hot spot on the desktop, helping create a focal point for an otherwise cluttered image.

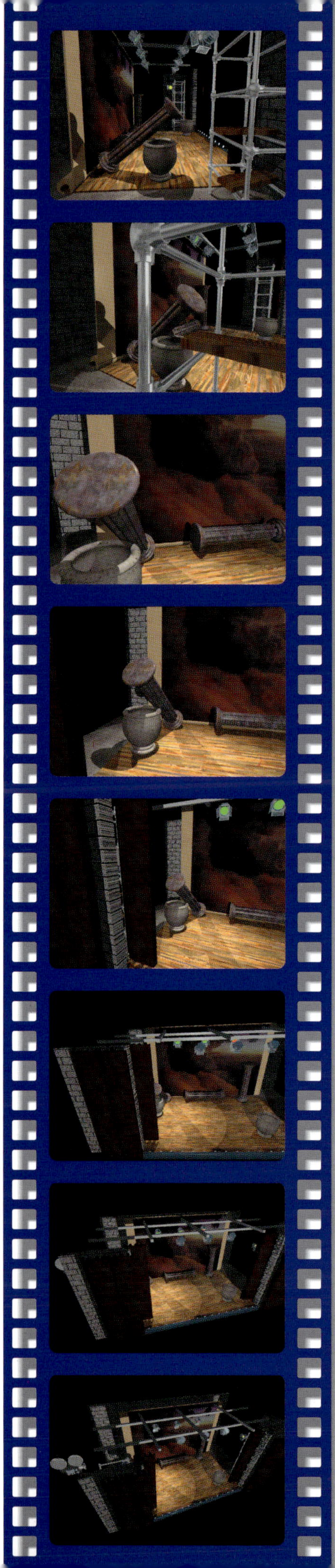

SETTING THE STAGE

After the modeling process is complete, the next step is to pull together all of the elements to create your scene. Your models will be the focal point of your scene, but less visible elements will impact your final render as well.

Setting up a scene is identical to a photographer setting up a studio shot. A photographer uses and adjusts a camera and lights.

Through the camera, you will view your final scene. Your choice of lenses will influence the drama of the shot. A wide-angle lens will pull and distort shapes and, if used properly, will create leading lines that will aid the viewer in focusing on the subject.

Each light needs to be placed with careful thought about highlight reflection and shadows.

If the photographer's studio is painted black, only the objects in the scene will show in reflective surfaces. If the studio is wallpapered with clown faces, these will show up on reflective surfaces. The photographer's choice of wallcovering is the same as your environment, and it can have great impact on your image.

THE SUBJECT In this case, the stage is the subject. Although there appears to be eight spotlights in this scene, they are just models with glow lights that contain no light sources. Three spotlights (yellow) and one point light to the far right provide illumination. The camera (red) is set at 30mm, a relatively wide angle lens. The environment, reflected mostly in the scaffolding and the spotlights, is a soft ball chrome.

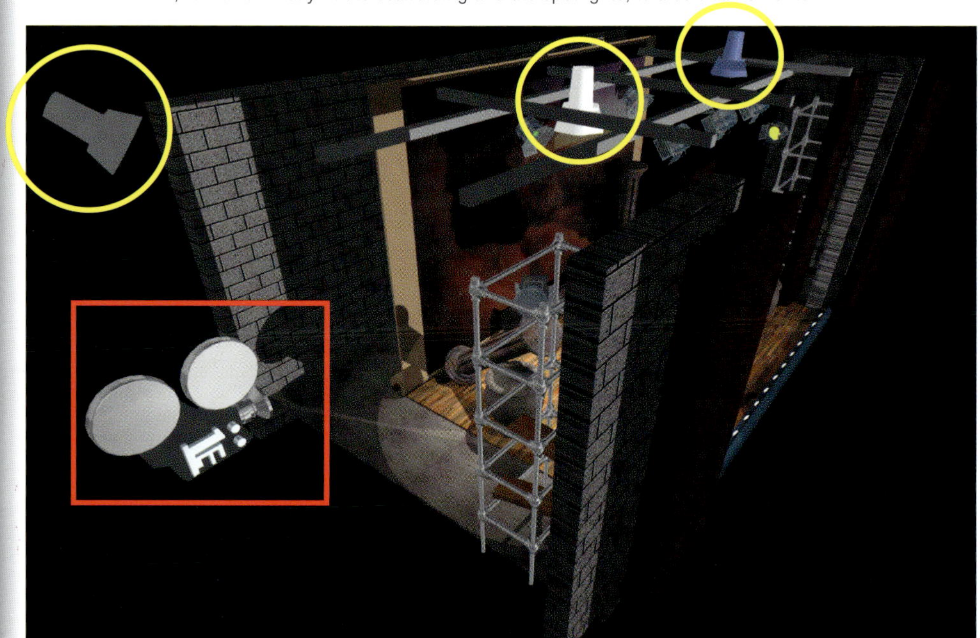

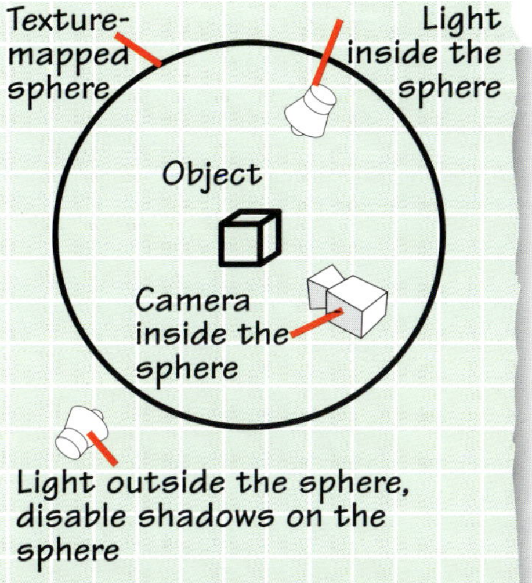

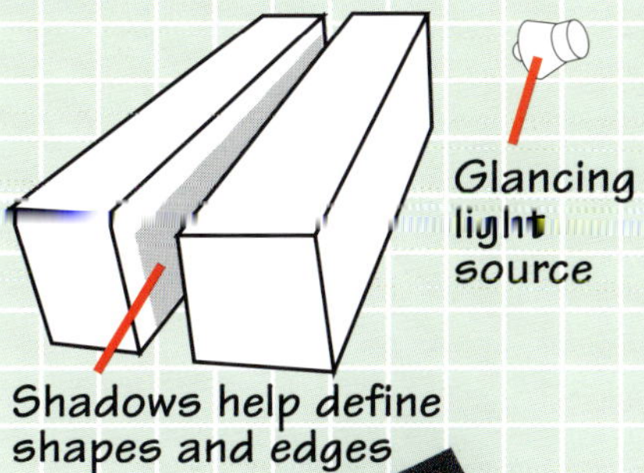

Scene with no fog

CREATE A GLOBAL STAGE

Not all stages need be flat planes where the action is played out. By placing your model inside a huge sphere, then assigning that sphere a texture, you can create some interesting effects. The motion of the airplane flying (left) for instance, can be faked by rotating the texture mapped sphere (cloud) and pivoting the plane like a teeter-totter. Light sources can either be inside the sphere or outside with shadows on the sphere object disabled. The same effect can work on cubes and tubes.

F-16 model by Viewpoint

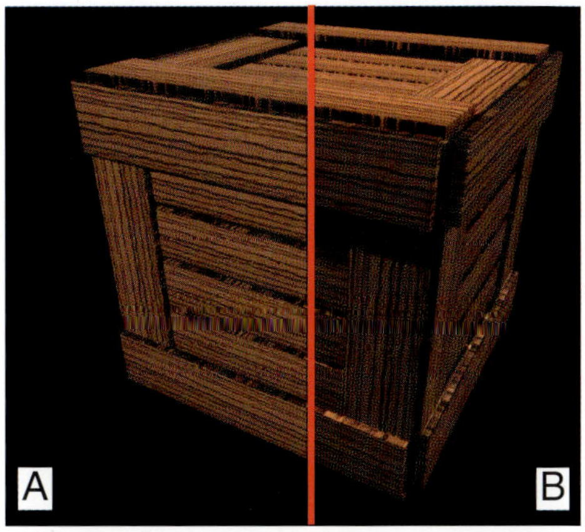

THINK CAREFULLY WHERE YOU PLACE LIGHTS

When establishing your scene, focus on the purpose of your light sources as much as you would any element in the model. Glancing lights help define some of the surfaces and sides of models and can be used in conjunction with overall light sources to avoid dark, shadowy scenes. Do not overdo the lights. Too many can be self-defeating and increase the rendering time. Colored glancing lights help define edges by adding a hue to sides and can be a powerful device when used in backlighting. Image A (left) was lit by a single light directly behind the camera. For image B, the right two glancing lights were used to help define the crate.

IT WAS A DARK AND FOGGY NIGHT...

Most modeling and rendering programs support fog-effects, which diffuse the image at user-definable steps as objects get further from the camera. Like other fun things in life, use this effect in moderation. Fog effects can be powerful tools in developing a scene's mood, but can also obliterate the hard work you put into your models (left). Planning ahead is the key here. Before you create your scene, calculate which objects will disappear into the fog and which ones will be playing center stage.

ADJUST THE LENS SETTING

When setting up your scene, choose a lens angle that is appropriate for the subject matter. A wide-angle lens will add more flare to any camera movement animation, but it also may distort your subject matter. A telephoto lens may aid in keeping your models from warping in proportion, but it will flatten out your viewing plane.

WIDE ANGLE, 12mm

Using a wide-angle lens adds a good deal of drama and interest to a setting. A low lens setting takes you into a scene.

NORMAL, 50mm

This is a mid-range lens which often lends itself to a more realistic setting, more like how we view the world.

TELEPHOTO, 120mm

A high lens setting tends to flatten out a scene, making it useful if your subject matter is spread across a large area, but still must be seen together.

CREATING THE ENVIRONMENT

Environments in the 3D world are confusing, ethereal things. They influence everything (which reflects light) in your scene. They are all-encompassing, yet you cannot see them. It is like the vampire myth in reverse. If you hold up a mirror, you can see the environment; otherwise, you cannot.

Environments should not be confused with background images that are placed or pasted behind a scene. Backgrounds are very real, tangible and precise images that stare right back at you from your scene. Environments are backgrounds' kindred spirits. Objects with some degree of reflectivity pick up on the environment's existence, permitting you to render a scene that feels like the image exists somewhere other than in a cold, dark computer world.

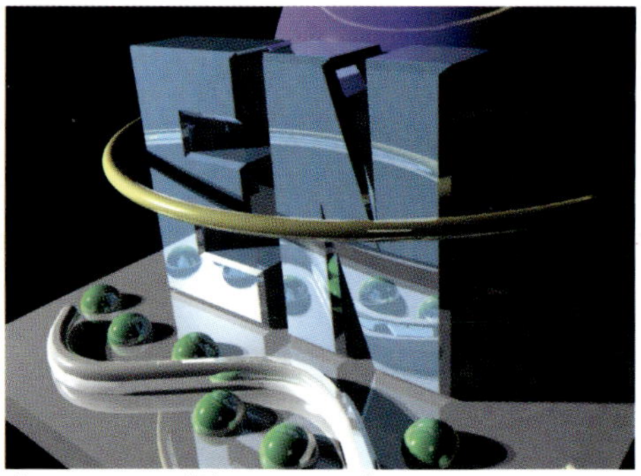

A scene with no environment map

Environments come in a variety of shape or form, each having a different effect on different shapes. You can create environments in any image creation program, much like you would a texture map. Since the effects are a little more ethereal than those textures mapped straight to a surface, environment maps are more forgiving in nature. The maps can create a seam in a reflection. If you create an environment map that fills the entire image area, make sure that it is tileable.

When setting up your stationery pad with your pre-set windows and procedural colors, include a few of your often-used environment maps to load when you open the document. Even if a scene does not have many reflections, it might add a nice polish to include an environment map.

Environment map used:

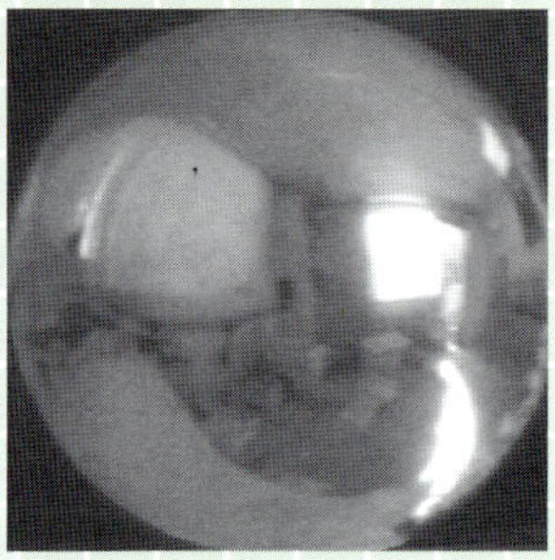

Soft chrome fish-eye view sphere

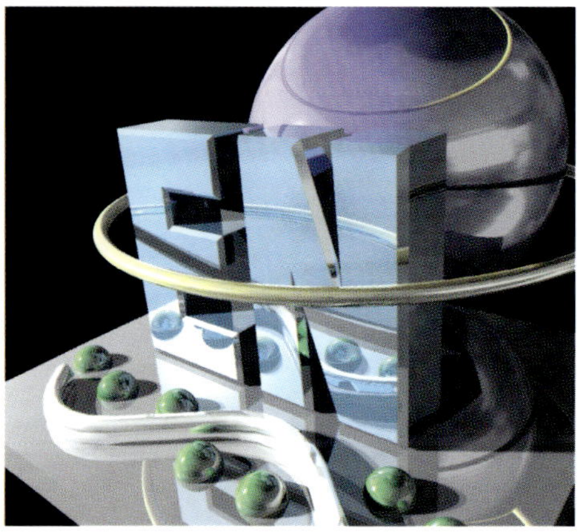

SOFT CHROME BALL

This map is great for adding a soft environment to rounded objects such as spheres or tubes. On flat planes and type the effect is muted, but still better than an environment without a map. To create a soft ball chrome: either start with a fish-eye lens photograph and digitize it, saving the results as a grayscale document; or convert a photograph to a fish eye feel by using Photoshop's Spherize filter.

Metallic chrome squiggle

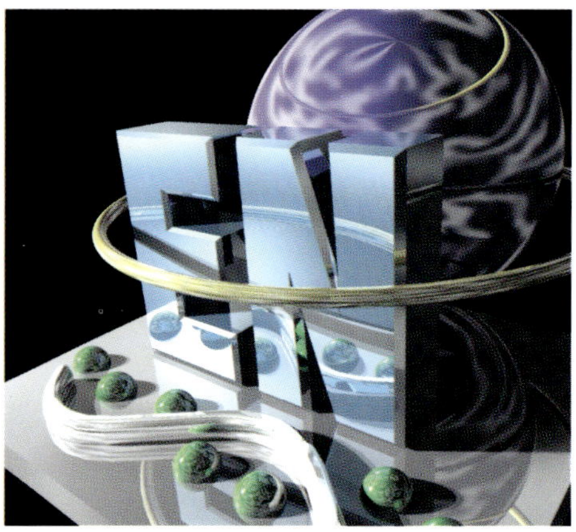

METALLIC SQUIGGLE

For a hard metallic sheen, a squiggled field works perfectly with scenes that are composed of flat surfaces, such as type or logos. Rounded surfaces tend to reflect environment maps in more detail. A metallic chrome environment map such as this one might add too much noise to spherical objects. Tiling is important with detailed maps like this one, so make sure that the edges will tile properly, or a very noticeable seam will pop up at unexpected moments.

Photograph that would reflect the true environment

PHOTOGRAPH

Nothing beats an environment map that accurately reflects the environment you are building your scene to replicate. In some cases even an early render of the scene can be used as an environment map to help reinforce a feel for the overall image.

4. ANIMATION

MOTION THEORY

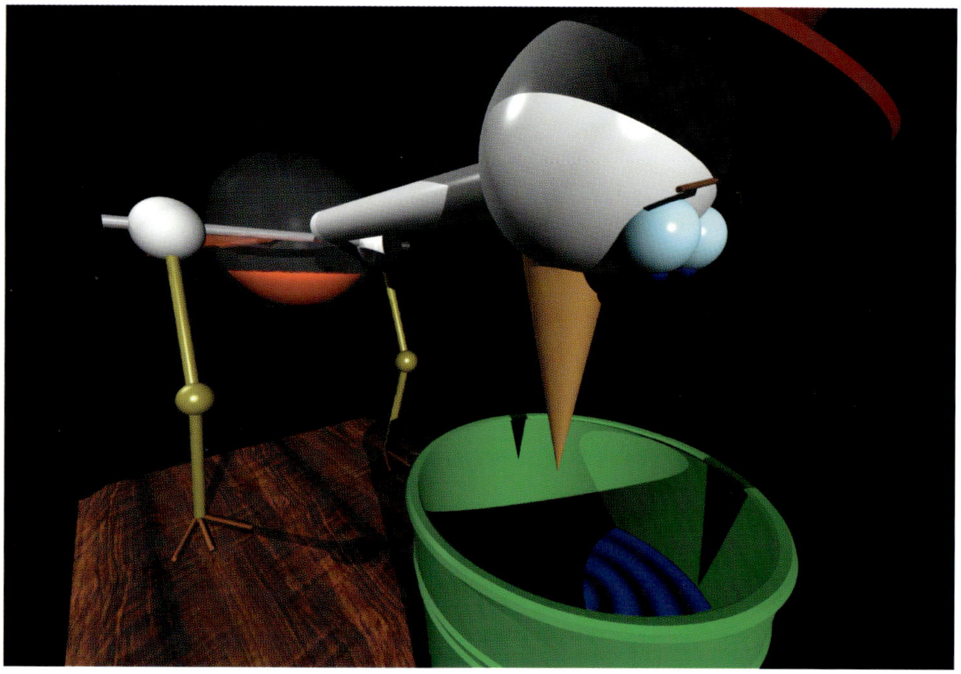

THIRSTY BIRD This simple model is excellent for demonstrating constrained motion on one axis. The bird's belly is linked to the pivot pole at the top of the legs, with only one axis allowed to pivot. The only two moving elements in this animation are the bird's belly and the camera.

Creating the illusion of motion is handled in much the same way in a variety of media–whether dealing with motion pictures, videotape or Saturday morning cartoons. The main objective is to get several still images to flash before the viewer's eyes and simulate motion. Instead of seeing 30 images strobing each second, our eyes see smooth motion.

The information is transmitted from your eye to your brain in a manner that accounts for the transitions from one image to the next. This illusion is brought to you by a phenomenon called *visual retention*.

A single image usually is referred to as a frame. The number of frames per second varies with the medium. Television standards (NTSC) demand 30 frames per second (FPS). More often than not, animators work within these parameters since they cover the TV/video world.

Another usage range is for computer screen playback. Since the media is your own, you set it at whatever your computer can handle. If you are designing an animation for an audience other than yourself, you will have to consider adjusting for them. This may mean shooting for the lowest common denominator of about 15 FPS.

On the other hand, the film industry runs at 24 FPS, but the resolution is much higher than the TV industry's resolution standards. For our purposes, we will base a second of animation on 30 frames.

To mimic time, the animator decides what actions will transpire at different times in the animation. This choreographing usually is done on a timeline that shows the actions of different objects over time.

The thirsty bird timeline (page 89) illustrates two movements. Both movements act separately from each other, but the results are recorded simultaneously in each frame.

The first and most obvious movement is that of the bird. Although the timeline lists the bird's face, beak, eyes and other parts, these objects do not move independently; they are connected to the bird's belly. As the bird's belly pivots, they move through space. In relation to the belly (which is their parent), they remain the same. Likewise, the bird's legs and the base also remain still.

The second motion, that of the camera, can take on all the motion attributes that any other object can. In this scene, the camera moves in close at the end to get a tight shot of thirsty bird's head.

The camera is not linked to any object,

although it could be. If animating a car chase, you might link the camera to the rear of the car so it follows behind the car. In the example with Mr. Bird, the camera is positioned as one would position it in a photography studio–separate from the object.

On the timeline, the changes that take place are called *events* or *key frames*. A great advantage of using computers in animation is that the computer can do the bulk of the work figuring how to get an object from point A to point B.

The animator positions an object at point A. Next, he finds a spot along the timeline reflecting the amount of time that should transpire, say during 30 frames (or one second) and re-positions the object at point B. The object's position in the 28 frames between points A and B will be calculated by the computer. This process is called *in-betweening* or *tweening*.

As the animation plays out over time, any number of objects can begin their movement. The duration of those movements can vary greatly.

A crucial element in creating believable animation is timing. The objects we bring to life in the computer's memory have no inherent finesse or grace. Each wink of an eye, each turn of a gear must be timed accurately if the motion is to be acceptable. The easiest way to set the duration of an object's motion is to copy it from real world situations.

A stopwatch is a very tangible way to introduce real world characteristics into the computer realm. A digital stopwatch is preferable, as you can transpose the numbers from a timed scene directly into the animation's timeline.

One example of how to time an element is the replication of a golf swing. In this action, very finite key events must be timed accurately if they are to be believable.

Have someone who knows the feel of a golf swing mimic the motion. Time each step as if you were setting the timeline of an animation. In this example, the golfer draws back the club–a motion which might take two seconds. Then the golfer swings–an action that might take one second. Between these two event marks there is a 30-frame gap. Since the club does not slow down when it hits the ball, the event mark for the club might not be noted. But for the ball, that

TIME CONCEPT

Most programs deal with time by assigning the different elements in a model their own channels in a timeline. Elements that do not move at all do not reflect any change in the line. Models that change position, attitude, color or size reflect those revisions in the timeline. Elements linked to a parent object, like the bird's neck is linked to the bird's belly, will follow the motion of the parent and not reflect its own change since its position to the parent remains constant.

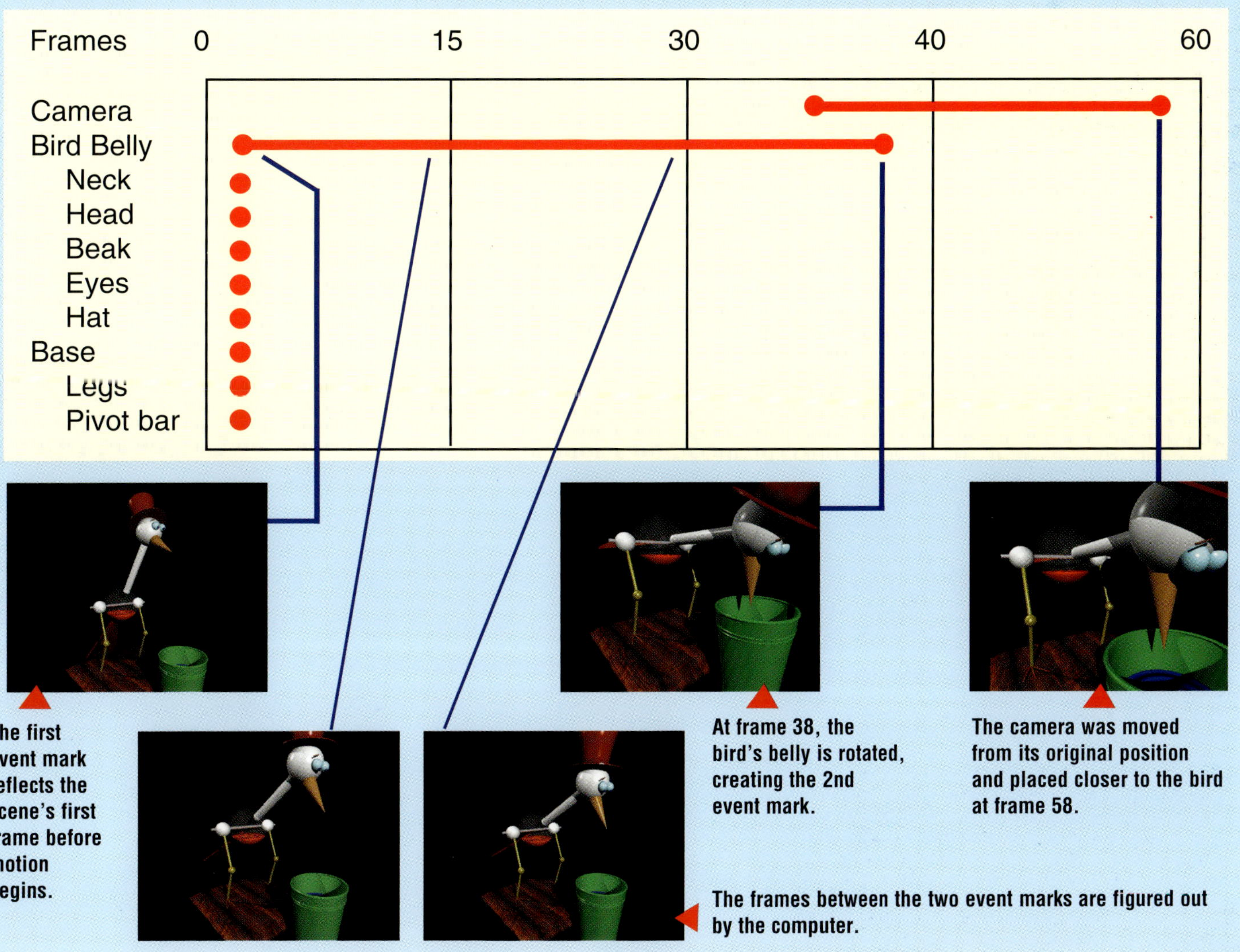

The first event mark reflects the scene's first frame before motion begins.

At frame 38, the bird's belly is rotated, creating the 2nd event mark.

The camera was moved from its original position and placed closer to the bird at frame 58.

The frames between the two event marks are figured out by the computer.

EVENT MARKS: PLACE HOLDERS IN TIME

Event marks make the moment. In an animation like the bouncing ball (below), the animator sets the key event marks (first ball, move down, move up...) and the computer figures out how to get the ball between the events.

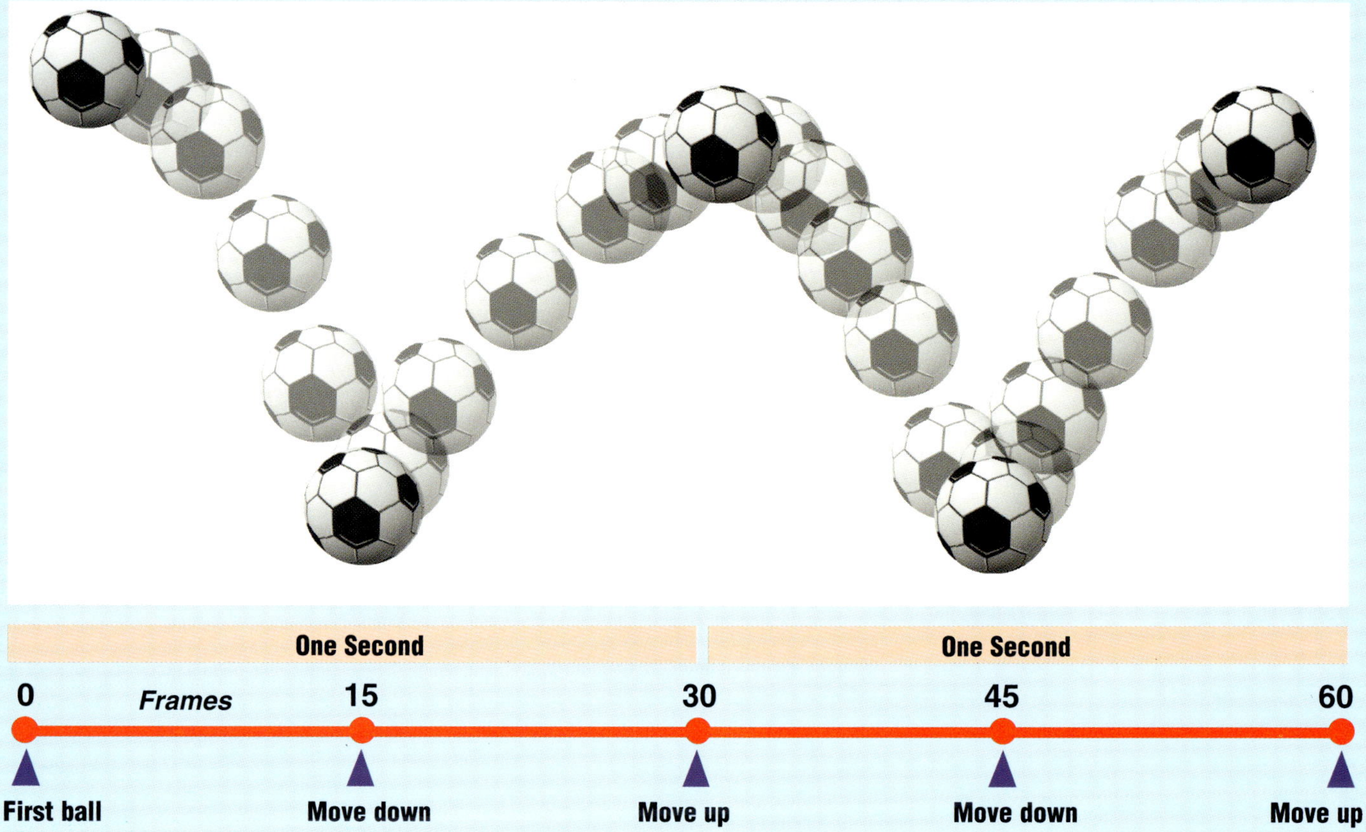

moment represents the first event mark as it begins its flight.

The speed with which an action varies during the motion also is crucial–almost as important as the timing. If you imagine all of the motions around you as points on a timeline, controlled by event marks, you will notice something about the object's speed in between the event marks. We would notice, in the case of our golfer, that the beginning and end of his stroke is slower than the middle part. This acceleration and deceleration of movement is usually referred to as *ease-in* and *ease-out*.

Almost all natural movements have some degree of ease-in and ease-out. Many mechanical actions do as well. A car rolling to a stop would decelerate–ease-out. Some single motions may contain a variation of speed. A hammer hitting a nail would be a good example of a motion that starts out slow (easing-in), builds up speed, then BAM! stops with no deceleration.

Most animation programs allow you to vary by percentage the amount of easing-in and out that an event mark can have. This is a vital tool in the creation of realistic animation. Movies created without the aid of acceleration and deceleration will have jarring, unnatural movements that can ruin an otherwise well-crafted production.

The smoothness with which an object enters and leaves an event mark also can be adjusted in a movie's timeline. This feature is usually known as *linear* or *nonlinear control*.

A linear event mark interprets an object's motion and direction literally. An object with

SEQUENCE EXAMPLE

In our golf stroke animation timeline, we begin with the club pulling back for 60 frames (or two seconds) until it reaches the second event mark. The swing begins at the second event mark and lasts for 30 frames (or one second). Contact with the ball is halfway through the swing when the ball then begins its journey.

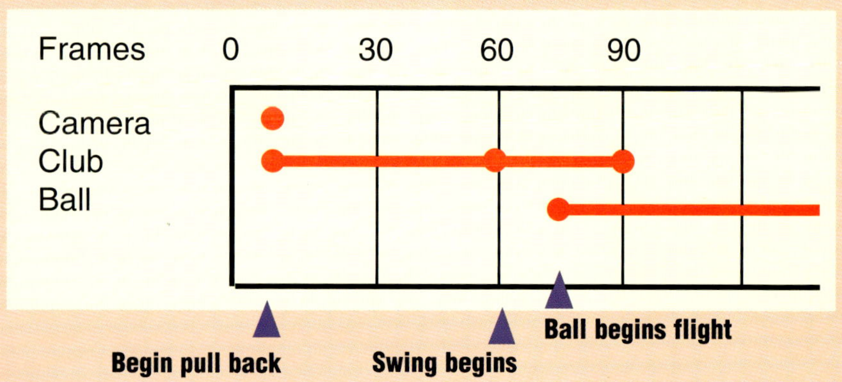

EASE-IN/EASE-OUT

Few real-world objects in motion start and stop suddenly. Usually, and almost always with natural objects, there is a certain acceleration and deceleration in motion. To accommodate this, most programs allow for ease-in and ease-out at event marks. For realistic animation, it is mandatory that the animator take advantage of these controls.

SMOOTHING OFF THE EDGES

The direction an object moves into and out of an event mark is as important as the speed. To avoid a harsh Point A to Point B to Point C linear approach to movement, controls are usually provided in the timeline to adjust the smoothness with which an object travels through an event mark.

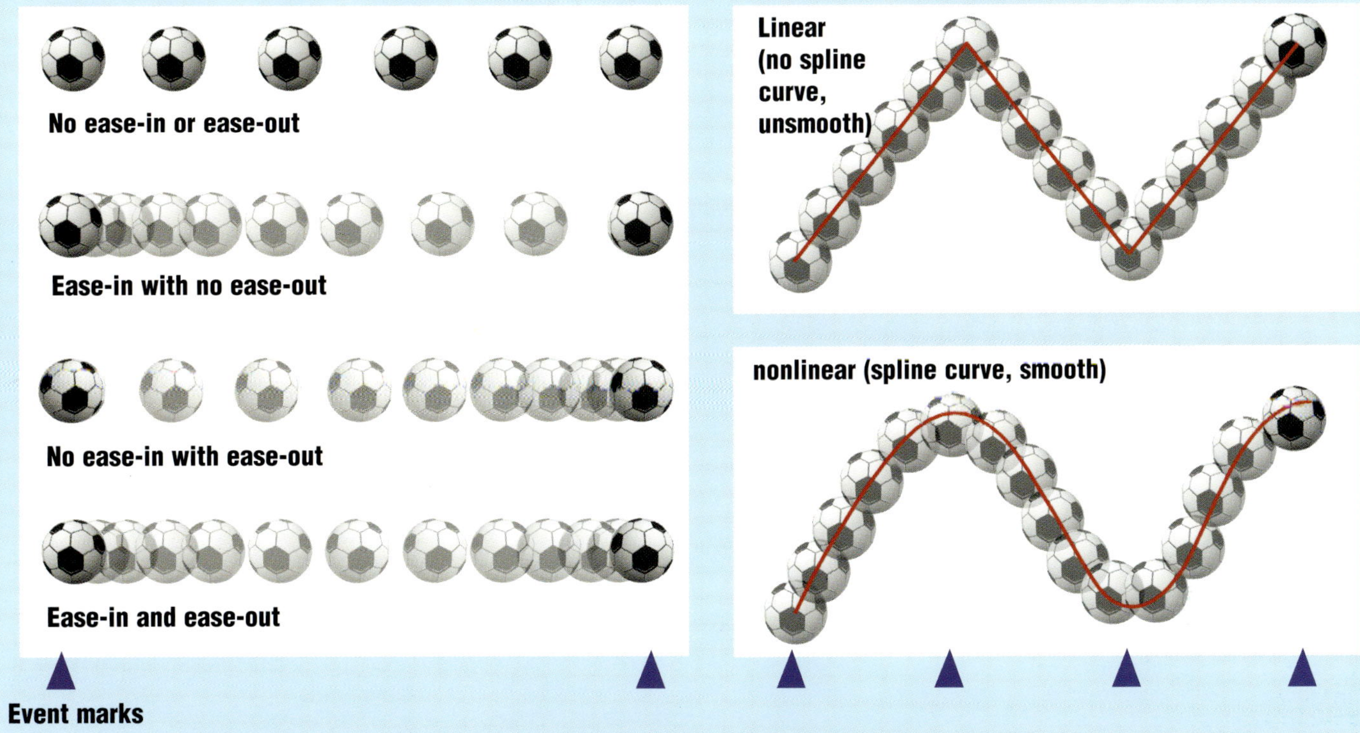

no smoothing or spline setting travels in a direct path between the event marks. This is fine if you are animating a bullet ricocheting.

Allowing the path of the object to be nonlinear (that is, a smooth, spline curve), takes off the harsh edges of the movement and rounds out the action. For example, if you are doing an animation of an airplane flying, a spline curve would allow the plane to gently roll between the event marks. The direction of the plane also would smoothly change in the direction of the motion path.

As you move an object around the screen and set event marks, you are inputting information that becomes the animation. All animation programs allow for a preview of the animation, usually in bounding box or wireframe view modes. This allows the animator to fine tune event marks or add new ones to help better define an action.

MOTION PATHS

Some programs offer a path which represents an object's actions. This powerful tool is called a *motion path* and allows for both accurate editing and instant feedback on an object's position.

The motion path represents the centerpoint of an object's position during the duration of the animation. Without having to preview, the animator can tell what an object is doing and can tweak event marks along the motion path to polish the animation.

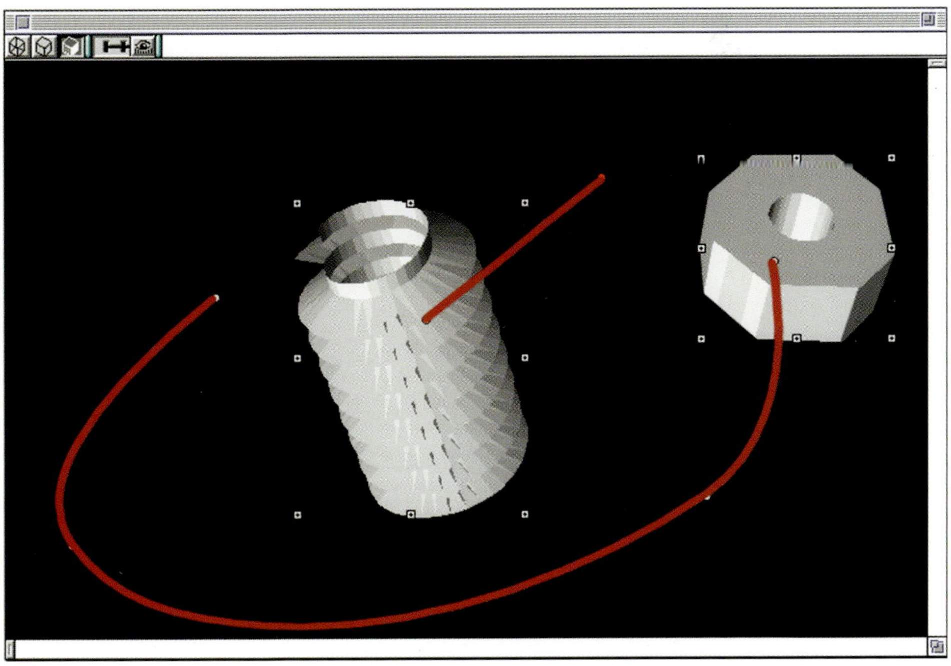

The motion paths (shown in red) in this StudioPro scene serve two purposes. They allow the animator to see and edit how motions will play out in the final animation. To edit, the user clicks on the line and repositions the animation's direction.

Animators that use programs that do not support motion paths can get some outside assistance in the creation of smooth motions. These artists can create a template in a 2D drawing program that serves as a guide for an object's motion. Although the template cannot be edited like a true motion path, it can be a useful tool in giving an animation control over its flow.

While creating the template, take advantage of the Bezier drawing tools offered by many drawing programs. These curve tools offer wonderful flowing paths that complement an object's motion.

The file then can be imported into a program as either a shape or a template. Bringing it in as an extruded shape allows for flexibility in repositioning, reshaping and rescaling the guide just as you would an object.

If the guide is saved in an image file format, such as PICT, and is then brought in as a template, the position and size are fixed. The advantage of using the template method is that it is just a template, and not a shape that would have to be deleted once the animation is ready to be rendered. Since the template centers itself in a fixed position, it should not be used as an afterthought when objects have already been positioned. Create the template and import it first, then build your animation around it.

CREATING A MOTION PATH TEMPLATE IN A 2D PROGRAM

If the modeling program you are using does not support motion paths, you can still take advantage of 2D drawing programs to help you orchestrate a smooth flowing animation.

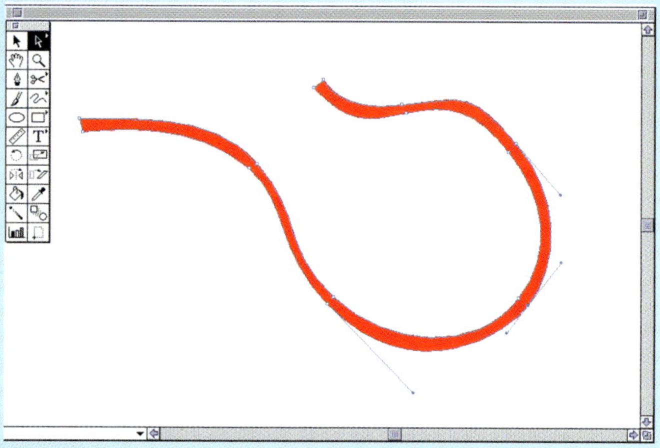

1) Start with a 2D drawing program such as Illustrator or Freehand. If you use one that has Bezier curve drawing tools, you can take advantage of the smooth sweeping paths they create. After creating the image, export it in a format that your 3D program will accept.

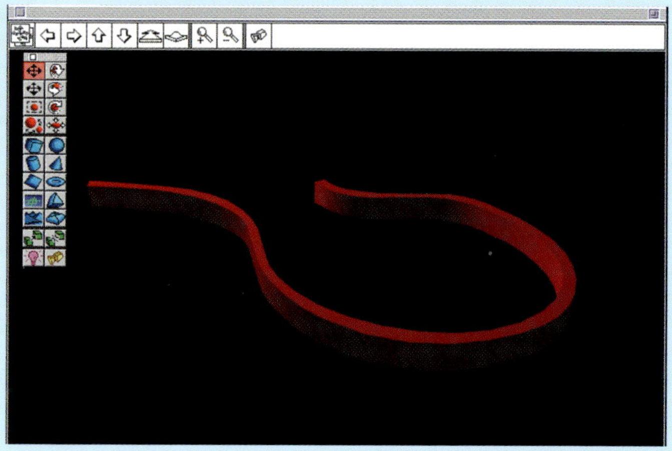

2) Bring the 2D shape in as an extruded object. The depth of the form is unimportant since you will just be using its overall shape. You might want to squeeze down the extrusion to keep it from being too distracting. This shape will serve as a guide.

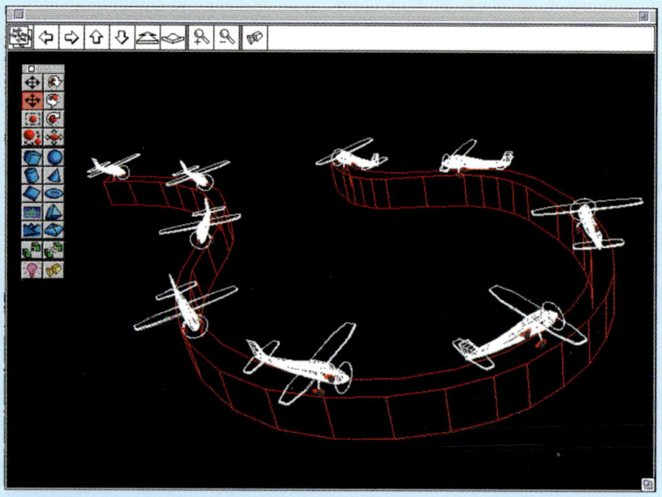

3) Place your model on the guide and advance to the next mark on the timeline. To automatically set a new event mark, move the model in both position and attitude. Repeat this process all along the guide path. The path helps to maintain a smooth and consistent motion.

4) When all the event marks are complete, delete the guide or make it invisible. Position your camera in the desired location (or move the camera throughout the animation, if desired) and render the file. The image above is a composite of an animation rendered with a cloud scene in the background and shows the path the single airplane took.

CREATING A CONTINUOUS MOTION

Most motions are complex and dynamic. While one object is doing something, another part of it may be involved in an entirely different activity. Working with an animation's sequencer, an animator can recreate complex and dynamic motions. In the Infini-D sequencer example (below) the blades of the helicopter spin independently from the aircraft's motion.

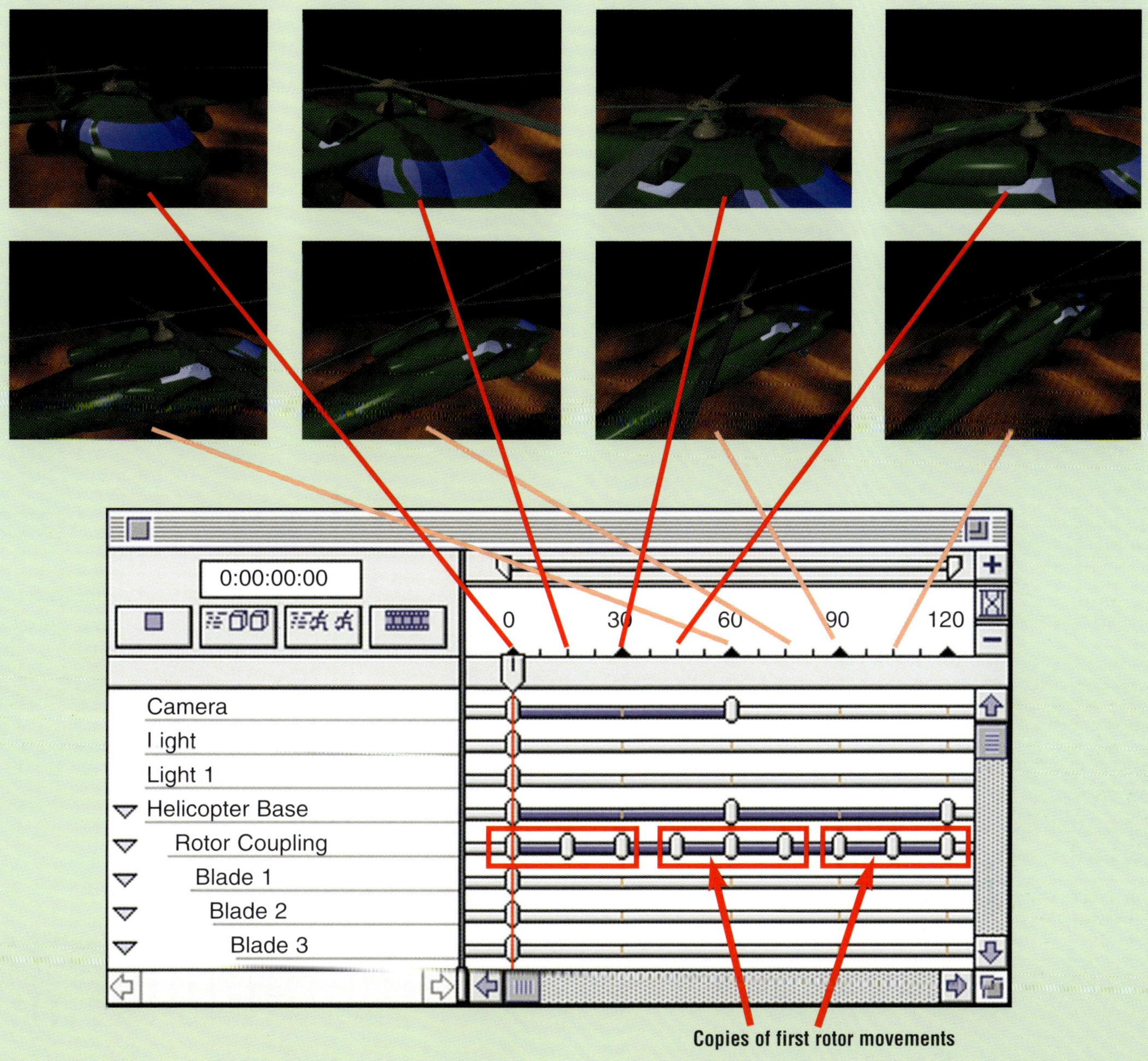

If you are compiling an animation with a continuous motion–like a planet spinning or a fan blade turning–you first set up the initial motion of the object, independent of other motions. An easy way to do this–and to make sure of an even spin rate–is to replicate the motion in the sequencer.

In the example (above), the first key frame was set at 0 (zero) and another at frame 15. At the frame 15 key frame point, the rotor coupling (where all the blades attached) was rotated 120°. Then another key frame was created at the frame 30 mark, and the rotor coupling was rotated another 120°.

With this done, the three new event marks were copied and dragged further down the sequencer so that the copy of the first event mark was at the 45 frame mark. Since it was a copy of the first event mark, the rotor coupling continues on its path to where it started, completing the circle. Do not use ease-in and -out marks on repeated rotations, or the spin will not be a constant speed and will have a jerky rotation to it.

Since the rotor coupling is linked to the helicopter base, it will continue to carry out its event marks regardless of what event marks the helicopter base is assigned. After setting the rotor spin (above), the key frames were then set for the helicopter, with the blades spinning along on their own.

The camera placement was also shifted, independent of both the helicopter and the rotor blades. Note that the blades themselves show no changes in the sequencer. They are linked to the rotor coupling and never change their attitude or position, they just follow the coupling because they are the children and the coupling is the parent.

SETTING UP THE RENDER

The model is built; textures have been applied and the animation is choreographed. Now it is time to set up the render. Since the computer is indifferent as to how your animation looks, you must tell the computer what final adjustments to make to create the final image.

The settings for a render usually involve two parameters. The first deals with guidelines the computer uses to turn your pile of math into pictures. The second determines the size, resolution and length of time to be rendered of the resulting file.

If you use an integrated modeling/animation package, you can adjust your render settings inside the program. If you use a separate animation program, like Electric Image or Three-D, you will make your adjustments in that program.

RENDER MODES

One of the most important rendering settings is the shading mode. Programs vary as to the names they give different modes. Infini-D, for instance, calls Phong shading "Shade Best" and Gouraud shading "Shade Fast." The shade setting tells the computer what algorithm to use to turn your data into images. The better the image quality, the longer it will take to render. If you need reflections and transparencies, you will need to ray trace the image. Electric Image is the exception, as it supports both of these features in the Phong shading mode. Some programs also may not support shadows on the lower settings, so it is important to understand what features are available in each of your software's shading modes.

Some programs can adjust the amount of final render detail by using settings that vary from coarse to fine. These programs will often use loose (coarse) or tight (fine) polygonal meshes to change the surface detail. As the quality increases, the number of polygons to be rendered increases, thus increasing rendering time.

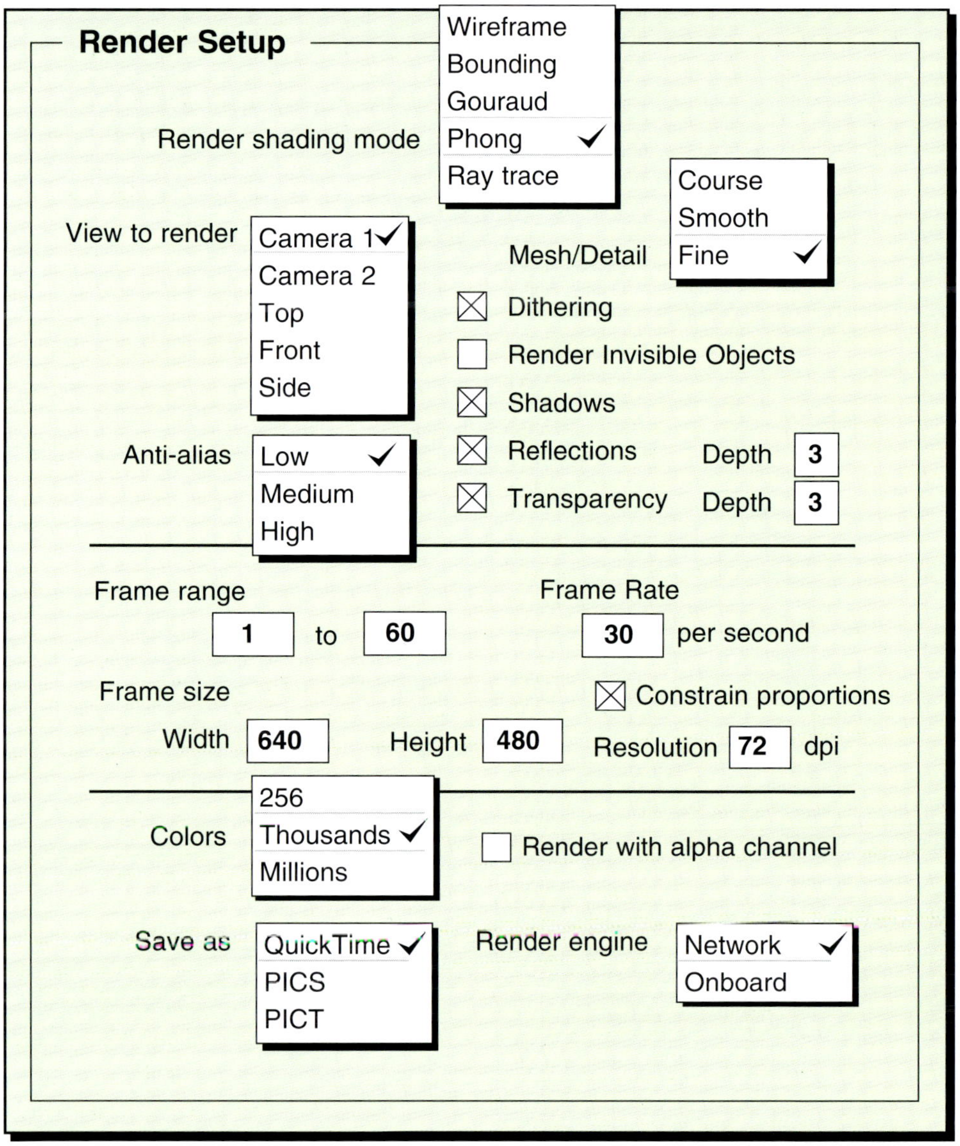

The overall quality of the image is determined by the settings chosen for the animation. The shade setting will have the most impact, as it determines which method of rendering to be used.

Information about the physical characteristics of the frame will affect the final render's image size, as well as the final resolution. The settings shown here reflect NTSC standard settings.

The final output format, as well as resolution, varies depending on your needs. PICT files for animation output render as single numbered PICT files. PICS and QuickTime are single files that contain the entire sequence.

This mock render setup dialog box shows many of the options that must be chosen before the animation file is rendered. Most of the options deal with the variety of quality settings animation programs have. Higher resolutions, tighter meshes, smoother rendering and better anti-aliasing all exact a toll in render time.

REFLECTIONS & TRANSPARENCIES

If using reflections or transparencies, you will be asked to specify a *recursion* or *depth setting*. For reflections, this means the number of times a reflection will bounce back and forth. For instance, if you had a mirror facing another mirror and you set your depth to three, in the final render you would see the image of the mirror reflected three times before it stops. The higher the setting, the longer the render. To cut back on ray tracing time, you should reduce this number to one, unless the reflection is of predominant importance.

For transparencies, the recursion or depth setting determines how many transparent objects you can look through before clear objects are no longer transparent. If you build a greenhouse model for example, with double-paned windows and in the final render you cannot see through the structure, you can either increase the depth to accommodate the total number of windows or decrease the number of windows you have used.

ANTI-ALIASING

Computer generated images have jagged, stair-stepped edges called *aliases*. When the computer computes the mathematical formula that results in an image, it does so with computer accuracy. Pixels on the edge of an object belong to either the object, another object or the background behind it. This very definite transition causes the stair-stepped edges. To remove these *jaggies*, an animator must either set up a file to anti-alias while it renders or run the final animation file through an anti aliasing program.

Rendering software handles anti-aliasing in different ways. Some programs use *super-sampling*. This involves rendering the file several times larger than the size of the final image. Information from the larger image is used to better define the edges.

Another anti-alias method is *averaging*. This technique usually is applied to an animation already rendered in QuickTime or PICS format. Since this technique deals with the render output, it does not use information from the original model. Each frame is analyzed and edges with high contrast, (which is often the case with jaggies) are blurred together to remove the stair-stepping. While this method is faster, the results tend to be less crisp and precise. Anti-aliasing takes time, but it is not a step to be overlooked. Rough drafts of animations can be rendered faster by toggling off anti-aliasing.

If rendering an animation is putting a serious time crunch on your system, which is likely if you are using a single computer for rendering, consider anti-aliasing only the scenes that remain still. Let the frames with fast moving, and thus less notable jaggies, remain aliased. Third party anti-alias programs such as JAG run comparatively fast and are better than not using any at all.

ANTI-ALIASING/SMOOTHING OFF THE EDGES

Computers tend to think in very defined terms. A pixel either has part of an image in it, or it does not. Period. This causes the edges of computer generated images to be jagged. Even though the jagged edge is usually limited to an object's edges, the effect can mar an otherwise perfect image. The solution to this is anti-aliasing. Anti aliasing blurs or blends the image edges together to get rid of the hard, jagged edge and is a very important setup when creating professional animations. All modeling and rendering programs offer some type of anti-alias support. Products like JAG can help take the edge off animation files that have been rendered.

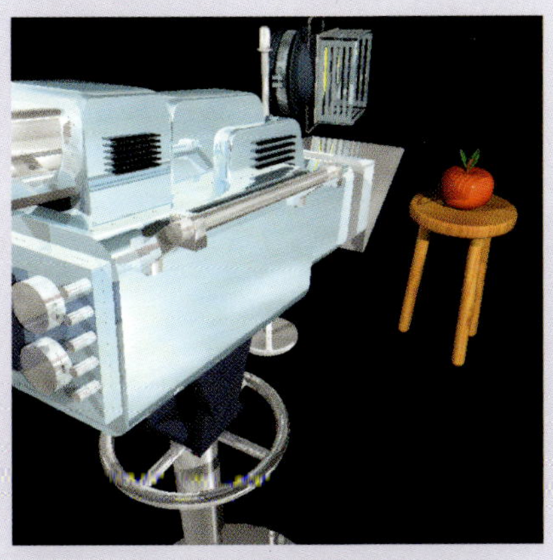

This image was rendered at 300 dpi with no anti-aliasing (above). Jaggies show up even more in low resolution, 72 dpi animation files since the stair-step edges tend to be one pixel wide.

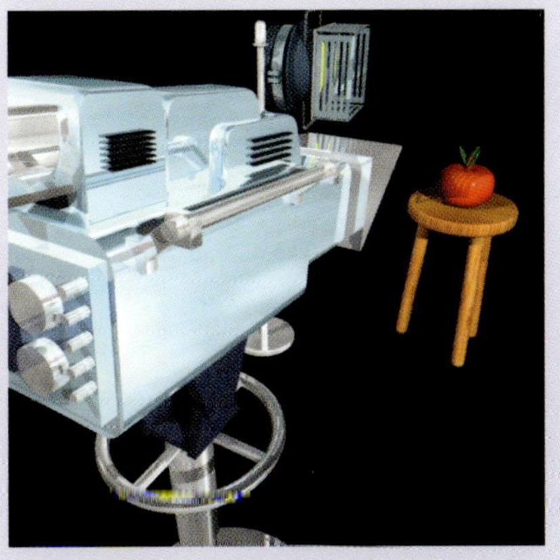

This image was rendered at 300 dpi with an anti-alias setting on high (above). This render used a process called *super-sampling* to smooth off the edges and clean up the image.

This close-up view with no anti-aliasing (above) demonstrates the stair-stepping effect.

A close-up view of the scene rendered with anti-aliased (above) shows the smoothed edges.

DITHERING

If you are rendering in any resolution less than millions of colors you may want to turn on the *dithering* option, if available. This will allow normally smooth graduated tones to simulate the graduation by dithering (tonal change using dots) instead of the banding that would occur without dithering. If you notice abrupt changes of colors on otherwise smooth objects, you may want to check and see if dithering was turned off.

FRAME VARIABLES

The size of the file is usually controlled

from inside the render setup as well. Most programs default to the window size that was set during the composition of the animation, but seeing the size again in the final render setup is a convenient way to check on it before you render. Most programs also allow you to constrain the dimensions so they are always proportional. Use this feature when you want to run a test file to see how your animation works. Reducing one dimension changes the second so that the height/width ratio remains the same.

If you want to render a test of your animation–which is always a good idea–you can do this from your render setup dialog box. Assuming your animation is for video, your dimensions are 640x480 pixels. With the *Constrain Proportions* feature selected, you can change the width to 320 and the height will change to 240 automatically. For a test window, use the lowest possible solid render setting. *Wireframe* and *bounding box* give you a feel for the object's motions and timing, but do not allow you to see how different objects interact.

The frame range to be rendered also can be altered here. A useful function for this feature is patch repairing an animation file. If you find a few frames with an error in your animation–whether your fault or the computer's–re-render the offending frames without having to process the whole file again. Integrate the resulting frames together in your editing program.

The frame rate selection depends on your final output. Usually the default for this setting is 30 FPS, the video standard. If you designed your animation on a time-based timeline (as opposed to frame count), and are creating a QuickTime movie for playback in a kiosk, you may choose a lower frame rate to accommodate your computer processor's speed without affecting your animation's playback rate.

RESOLUTION

The *resolution* of a frame determines how many *dots per inch* (dpi) will be in a single line of the image. For video animation conforming to NTSC standards, the dpi will be 72. The same goes for animation that is to be played back on a computer screen. If you want to output a single frame for print uses, you would choose a higher dpi setting.

Newsprint images commonly use 160 dpi, magazines 220, and books–such as most of these images–are rendered at 300.

DITHERING THE IMAGE

Dithering removes abrupt banding in low-resolution renders. Banding may be a benefit in helping to more accurately represent subtle tonal change, but it also may add to the overall noise of an image. Dithering is best done on a case-by-case basis.

This scene was rendered in thousands of colors with dithering turned on. Note the smooth tonal change on flat surfaces.

Banding occurs in the output of the same image rendered in thousands of colors where dithering is turned off.

The same scene rendered with 256 colors with dithering turned on. Dithering helps avoid banding, but causes the image to be much more "grainy."

This scene was also rendered in 256 colors, but with dithering off. The banding is much more predominant, but the image is a good deal cleaner.

COLOR DEPTH

Animation color depth also is determined while setting up a render. The final output will often determine the color depth needed.

For video, where file size is not too critical a factor, the most popular choice is 24-bit or millions of color. If rendering with an *alpha channel*, you will need to do the render in millions. (An alpha channel is a channel, in addition to the red, green and blue channels, that contains masking information. Many programs denote the color depth as 32-bit or millions+ when using an alpha channel.) If this is the case, but the final animation needs to be at a lower resolution, change the bit depth of the animation after editing the file.

If you are creating a large animation and your purposes tend to be more industrial-level, rendering in 16-bit, or thousands of colors, creates a smaller file size and more manageable animation files. You might render in 16-bit even if your final product will be an 8-bit, 256-color production. During the editing process, you can always dither down your animation file with acceptable results. If you start at 256 colors, it is impossible to go up the scale. If you plan to take your file directly from the render output and incorporate it in a computer screen based production that will always run in 256-color mode, 8-bit mode will do the job. You also may use this to output animation files for tests.

When rendering and viewing animations in millions of colors, you are taking advantage of the full range of colors on the computer's color palette. With this full palette almost any color combination is possible, but you pay the price in both file size and screen redraw speed. Using a 256-color palette decreases your option in color combinations dramatically, but the file size is much smaller and the animations play much faster in real-time.

A partial solution to obtaining the best of both worlds exists. If you create your animations in millions of colors, chances are you are not using all of the colors. In designing your animation–if you plan carefully–you can reduce the number of colors needed for your animation, even if you render it in 24- or 16-bit. After rendering the file, process it through a program like DeBabelizer to change the depth to 256 colors. The program will create an optimized palette which contains only the colors used and averages out the others. If your animation did not contain the full rainbow of colors, the quality of the scene will not be too different from the original.

OUTPUT FORMATS

The file format you render your image in is largely dependent on what you plan to do with your files. While there are a variety of still image formats to choose from, such as PICT and TIFF, animations are almost always rendered as PICS or QuickTime files.

PICS is a "what-you-see-is-what-you-get" format. Every frame rendered is represented by a single frame in the PICS file. There is no compression setting so the image is as clean as possible.

The individual PICT files contained in a PICS document are stored sequentially in the file's resource fork. Due to a system limitation, the size of a resource fork is kept to 16mb and files cannot exceed it. Programs that support PICS segment the file automatically as the file renders. Usually the animator can adjust the size of the PICS segment.

Since there is no compression with PICS, this format is not intended to be a final product. PICS files can be imported into virtually all editing programs.

QuickTime is equally portable and also has the advantage of being able to be played back directly after a render. Speed and quality of the playback depend largely on the user's system. Variables such as RAM, hard drive speed, video acceleration and the presence of hardware compression/decompression boards will influence playback.

If the animation is destined for further editing, the animator should use the highest quality setting available in the QuickTime options dialog box. Lower settings will remove information that cannot be replaced. If a lower compression setting is needed, the final output from the editing program can be adjusted to suit the user's needs.

QuickTime movies rendered in small screen sizes can play back in real-time on most computers. As the screen size and the quality setting increase, more power is needed to pump the data through the computer.

When designing a QuickTime movie, the animator must take into consideration the type of computer the final user will use to play the file. If the final product is to be placed on videotape, the concern is not so pressing, as long as the hardware to play the file back for the final recording is available. This will be covered more extensively in the "Output" chapter, but when the animator is making these adjustments for the render, the final product also must be considered.

With all the render options chosen, it is time to start the render.

Rendering time depends on two variables: the complexity of the model and its associated texture files and the options chosen during the render set up. You can count on a long render if you have a full-screen scene

COLOR-DEPTH SETTINGS

Whether an animator chooses to render an animation in millions (24-bit), thousands (16-bit) or 256 (8-bit) colors depends on the quality he or she desires in the final product. The better the quality, the larger the file size and the slower the playback rate on most computers.

MILLIONS (24-, 32-bit)

REASONS TO USE: High-quality images that would be demanded by most broadcast uses. If you are rendering with an alpha channel, you will have to do it in 24-bit (the extra 8 bits for the channel makes the file a 32-bit image).
REASONS TO AVOID: Huge files that will play back slowly without hardware assistance.

THOUSANDS (16-bit)

REASONS TO USE: Good-quality images without all the overhead of 24-bit images.
REASONS TO AVOID: Files still tend to be large. Some banding in tonal changes begins to occur, but this can be handled smoothly by dithering. Still requires some hardware assistance to play back smoothly.

256 (8-bit)

REASONS TO USE: With less data in each pixel, creates small files which play back quickly. Small windows can be easily played back, even on mid-range computers.
REASONS TO AVOID: The amount of dithering it takes to convert a photorealistic scene to 256 colors can be distracting to the point of ugliness.

ANIMATION FORMATS

Although animation files can be saved as a series of individual files, animators almost always will save their rendered files as either PICS or QuickTime. Each has its advantages.

PICS

PICS is a no-frills format that simply saves each frame rendered as a separate PICT image sequentially ordered inside a single document. There is a system limitation of 16mb of information that can be stored inside a document's resource fork. Since the PICS formats keeps its images inside the resource fork, a single PICS file cannot be larger than 16mb. To overcome this, most programs that output PICS files segment the files so that they are smaller than the allowed size. 32-bit PICS files are saved in RGB (red, green, blue) format with an alpha channel being the fourth channel.

QUICKTIME

QuickTime output requires the presence of the QuickTime extension in the System's Extension folder. The file combines image files...

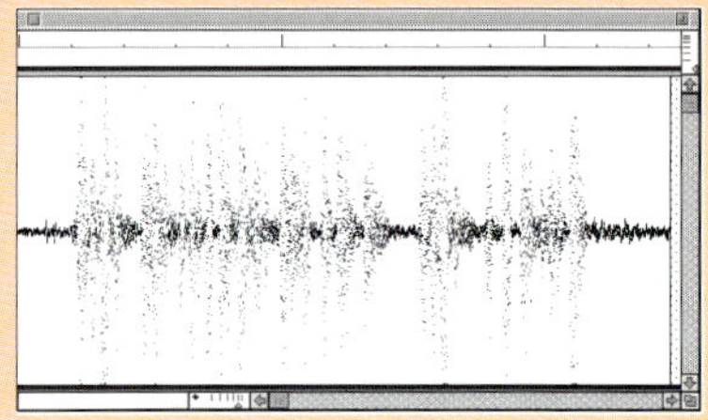

...with sound files. Sound can be imported from pre-digitized clip files or recorded through a sound digitizer. Some animation programs have built-in sound support.

The QuickTime file combines both image and sound in a single synchronized document. When saving as QuickTime, you are given options for window size, color depth and compression.

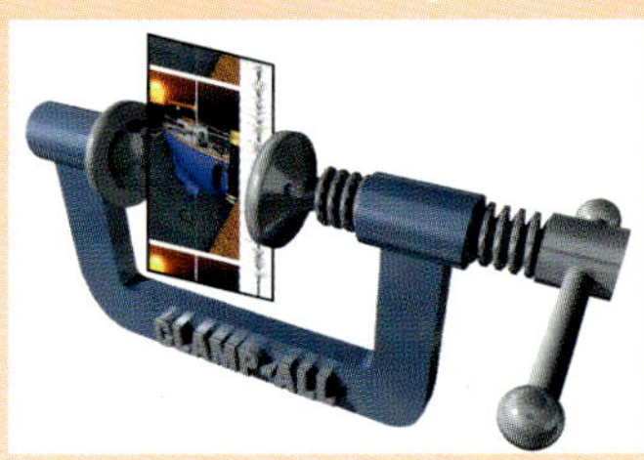

Compression takes place as the file is rendered and written to the disk. The highest-quality setting leaves the image intact, and the file size large. A low-quality setting instructs the QuickTime compressor to discard information to make the file smaller.

Sailboat QuickTime

with hundreds of objects (a simple object like a bike wheel can have about three dozen objects), a few transparency maps, some 20mb texture maps and three or four reflective surfaces all set to ray trace with high anti-aliasing on a single Mac—even a PowerPC. With this setup, a single frame might take the better part of a day.

On the other hand, if you create an image of an airplane that fills a quarter of the screen, and you render it with an alpha channel for editing on a cloud background using Phong shading and low anti-aliasing, you could render 100 frames overnight on a single Mac.

NETWORK RENDERING

If you plan on complex renders, then consider network rendering. Most rendering packages offer some sort of network process-sharing scheme. Even if they do not, you can always copy your file to other Macs and render out separate frame sequences. Mailing them to friends with idle Macs or using e-mail is perfect for this. If a network of Macs is available, you will profit from the speed that Ethernet affords you.

Another way to speed up rendering time is to take advantage of dedicated hardware processing boards like Radius Rockets or YARC (Yet Another Ruddy Co-Processor) boards.

Rockets are network friendly and act like individual Macintoshes. You need to load RAM on them like you would any Macintosh, so plan on buying at least 16mb of RAM for each board.

A YARC's speed depends on being tied directly to the motherboard of a host Mac. If you are using YARCs, plan to dedicate a slot for each one. YARCs are very fast and come with their own RAM. A smart recycling maneuver is to find an old Mac IIfx with six slots and fill five slots with YARC boards. You can free up a sixth slot if you use Timbuktu to control the files instead of installing a video board to drive a monitor. Make sure the IIfx has at least 32mb of RAM if you are planning to render even slightly complicated files. The support of the different rendering programs varies, even from version to version, so make sure the rendering software you want to use is supported by the YARC boards.

5. EDITING

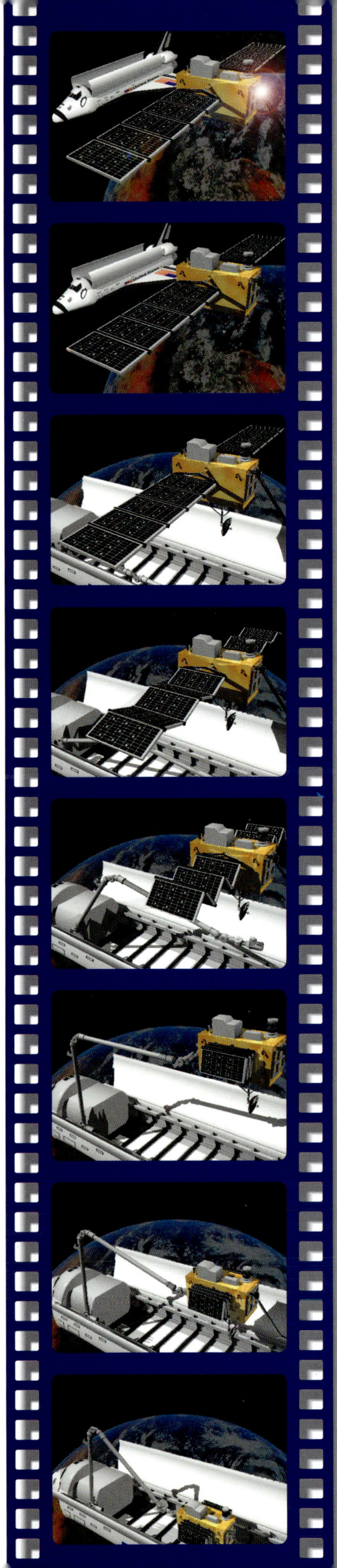

EDITING THEORY

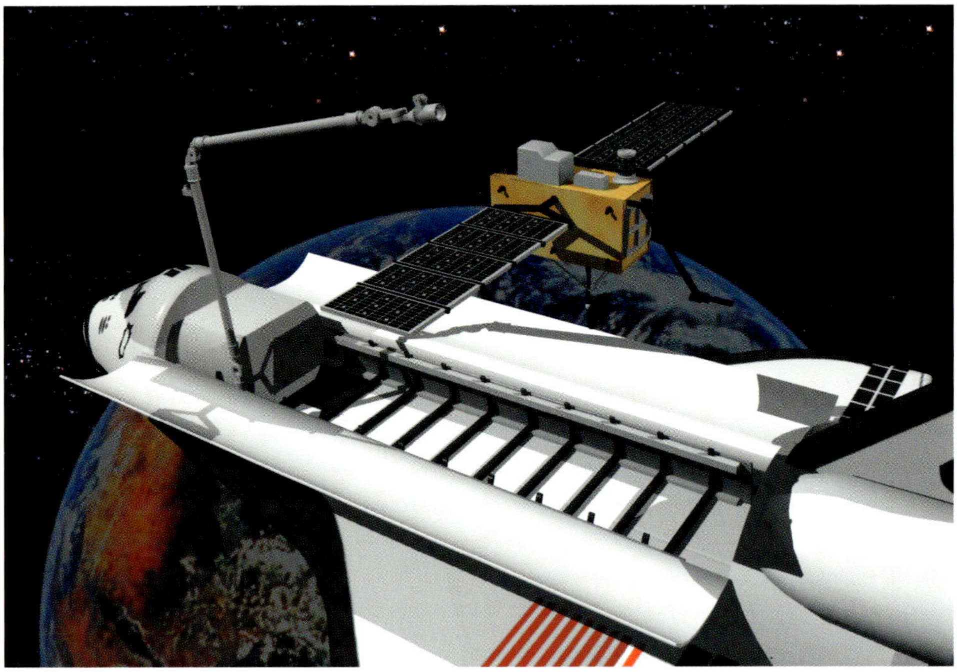

COMPOSITE EDITING In this animation three completely separate elements are joined together in an editing program. The background helps set the mood, the Earth image moves slightly in 2D to accentuate the motion and the shuttle's 3D animation file plays on top of the two other elements.

Abracadabra!–and, with no magic involved–it is time to pull all your work together. Your model building and rendering product leaves the 3D realm and enters the 2D editing arena. This editing process serves two purposes.

The first purpose is to compile the elements together–compositing rendered 3D files on top of backgrounds or adding special effects and titles. The second purpose is to edit completed animation segments together to form a narrative.

Watch a TV program or movie and pay attention to how the show was edited. You will never see an entire project being shot from one static camera. The scenes tend to be a constantly moving montage of different angles, lenses and viewpoints–all married together to create a believable story line. Computer editing programs give you tools to accomplish this editing.

You also can take advantage of the editing environment, even if your rendered file is the only one to be edited. Pauses can be added; unwanted elements can be deleted; and titles and special effects can be incorporated.

Although the interfaces for editing programs vary, the general concept underlying them is similar to the timeline concept used in animation programs.

Your final rendered output may be exactly what you need. In this case, editing programs may simply give you production support if you choose to change the scale of the animation or alter its color depth.

KEEPING TRACK

Computer editing systems all use two dimensions, with time represented horizontally and elements stacked vertically. The main difference is in the the number of tracks.

A-B ROLL SYSTEM

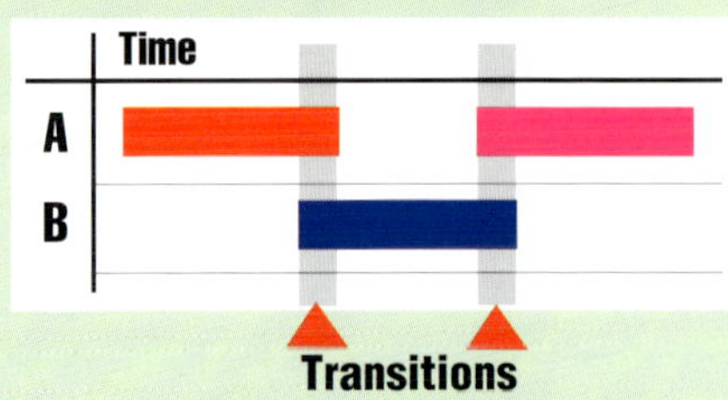

MULTI-TRACK SYSTEM

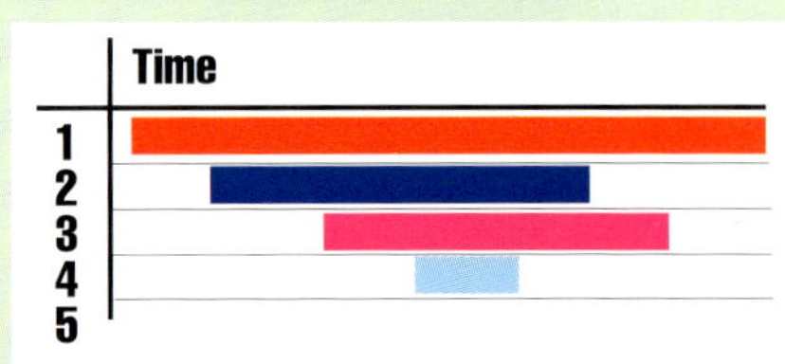

Editing programs also can be used to splice together animations. Most programs offer the animator many professional effects when cutting from one scene to another. While some transitions–like page turns or checkerboards–may be fun, a direct cut or fast dissolve usually results in a most professional transitions.

Some editing packages such as Premiere or Media 100 try to mimic the feel of traditional analog editing stations by giving the user an A-B roll interface. If you were editing on video decks, you would use at least three decks. For example, decks A and B would be the source decks where the original video plays and the third deck would record. Decks A and B would be patched to the recording (third) deck by a device called an *effects switcher*, which can perform transitional effects–like dissolves–as the video on deck A switches to the video on deck B. Imitating this system in a software interface provides a simple analogy that video professionals can quickly understand, but it was originally designed for video editing purposes and lacks some of the dynamics needed for animation.

Creating animations in layers gives you more control over the final product. Elements can be added or removed quickly without having to render the entire sequence a second time. The need for animators to work in layers means they need some place to pull their layers together. Programs like After Effects and Director give the animation editor a place to record several tracks of animation all at the same time.

EDITING THE PARTS TOGETHER

It is possible to create animations with all the elements intact, so the rendered output is final, but in doing so, you lose some control over the final production. For example, many of the elements (below) are separate. The Earth, stars and shuttle are three different elements. If the animator decides to remove the Earth, or put in more dramatic stars, it can be done easily in the edit stage. If the background was created in the original render and you changed something, the whole animation would have to be re-rendered.

The original shuttle animation file was rendered on a black field, using a straight alpha channel.

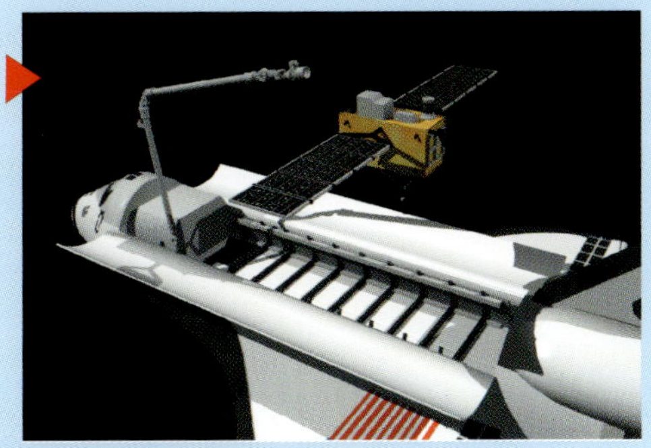

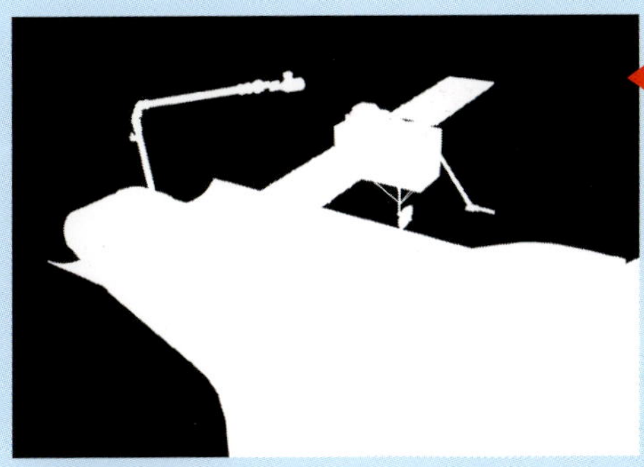

The alpha channel acts as a virtual cookie cutter, creating a file that will later be used to select just the image area and not the black background.

A 640x480 PICT file of stars was imported into the editing program to act as a static background

The Earth image also was brought in as a PICT file. It will move slowly across the screen as a 2D animation.

The final animation incorporates all of these objects to create a seamless image. Anti-aliasing information for the shuttle is stored in the alpha channel, so when it is composited in the scene the edges blend into the background.

EDITING WITH MACROMEDIA DIRECTOR

Macromedia Director is a multi-purpose editing program. You can import PICS, PICT and QuickTime files for manipulation.

Animators take advantage of Director's editing capabilities by importing animations such as PICS. Each frame in the animation is represented as a *cell* in Director's *score*. This control lets you easily dictate what happens to each element of the animation. Further control is added by allowing you to open up each imported frame with an integrated bitmap editor.

Director's strength is the variety of ways it can work with finished animations. Files can be output for playback as Quick-Time; but the program's true power is what you can do with the animation before you quit the program.

Without leaving Director, you can edit together an animation; export it as an animation file; and bring it back into the program to incorporate it as part of an interactive production. The final project can be exported as a self-contained interactive program for any number of multimedia purposes.

Director also offers wonderful device control, allowing the user to control industrial- and broadcast-level devices. Controlling external devices is important for recording animations on laser disks or videotape decks.

When working with Director, you can choreograph all of the elements in the score and see the results on the *stage*. If you are dealing with full-screen animations, a two-screen system setup is desirable. Set preferences for your stage to play on Screen 2–ideally an NTSC monitor–while you work with the program's other palettes on your regular computer screen. This method gives you instant feedback on your animation's color balance.

One of Director's biggest faults is its lack of alpha channel support. To overcome this, you can render your animation on black and import it into your Director movie. Since white areas drop out when using the program's background "transparent ink" (similar in concept to "reveal ink" used in modeling), you will want to switch the white tones in your scene to a slight gray using Director's "Switch Color" command. After that step is completed, use the same technique to switch the black background to white–which makes it transparent.

If your animation falls on a dark background, this effect works well. On light backgrounds, you will see a fuzzy edge because the animation was anti-aliased on a black field. Rendering the file on a white background presents the same difficulty if your background is dark. Until Director supports

You can import sounds into Director or you can use the Mac's built-in microphone to record sounds directly in the program.

Timing can easily be adjusted to pause a frame for any length of time.

Transitions such as dissolve and wipes can be applied to effect the introduction of elements in one cell to the next.

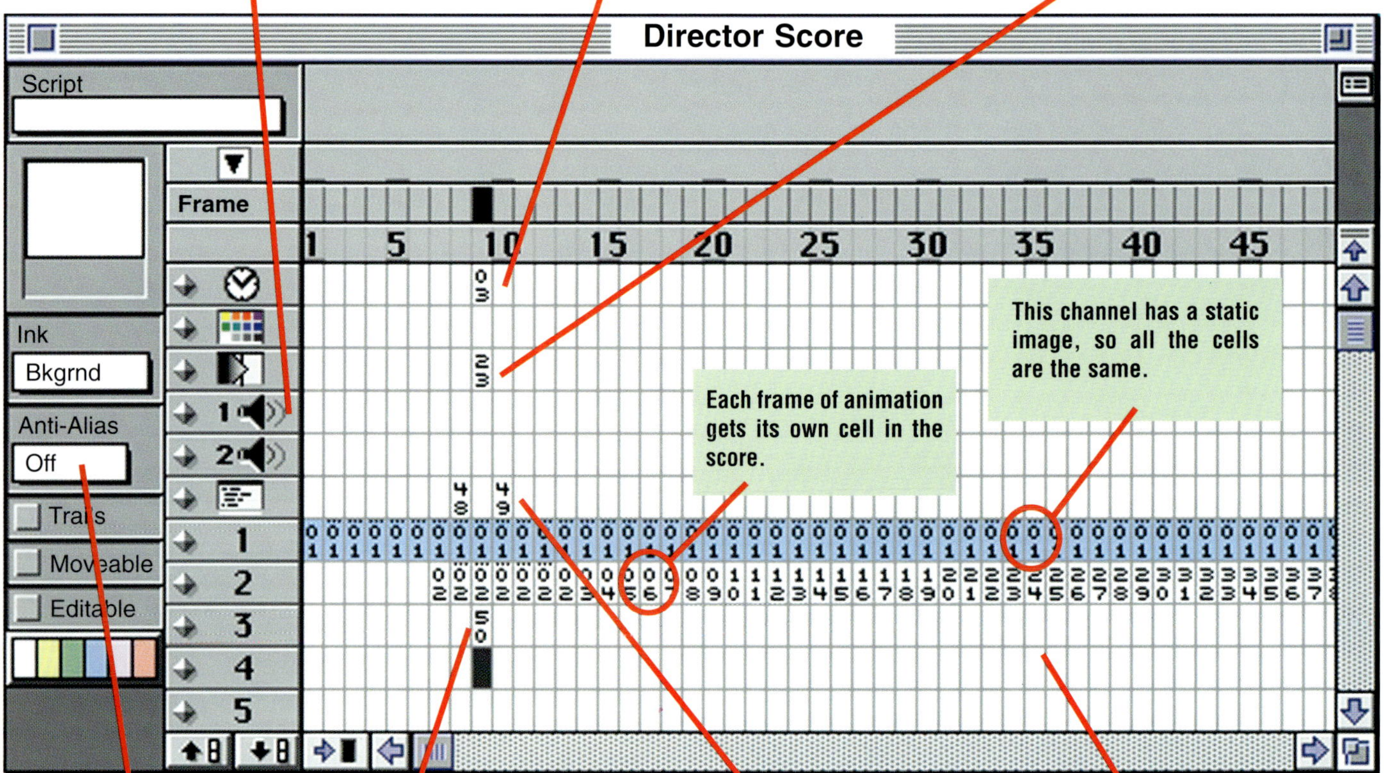

On-board anti-aliasing is available, but it tends to be fuzzy. Type tools also are available, but type is inferior to that created in Photoshop.

Channel layers can be shuffled as needed, with the lower channel being the foreground layer.

Scripting allows for precise device and interactive control.

Director has 48 channels for layering both static and animation elements.

EDITING PICS IN MACROMEDIA DIRECTOR

If Director has the features you need in an editing program, you will have to live with its lack of alpha channel compositing. The technique below demonstrates one way to bring in a PICS file for multi-track layering. The whole process can be streamlined by creating a function key that does all of the outlined functions and then advances to the next frame.

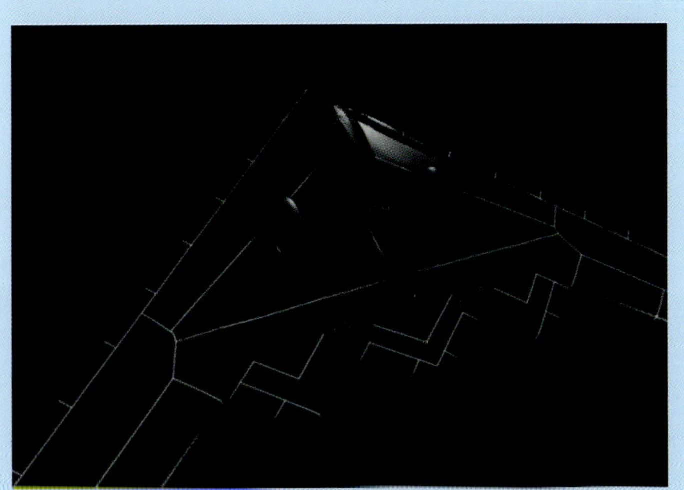

1) Render the animation on a black field. With anti-aliasing turned on, your edges will blend to black. If your background is light you may want to render on a white field.

2) Import the PICS file into Director. Since you will be using the background "transparent ink"–which makes white transparent–you will want to switch the whites in the Stealth bomber to a light grey.

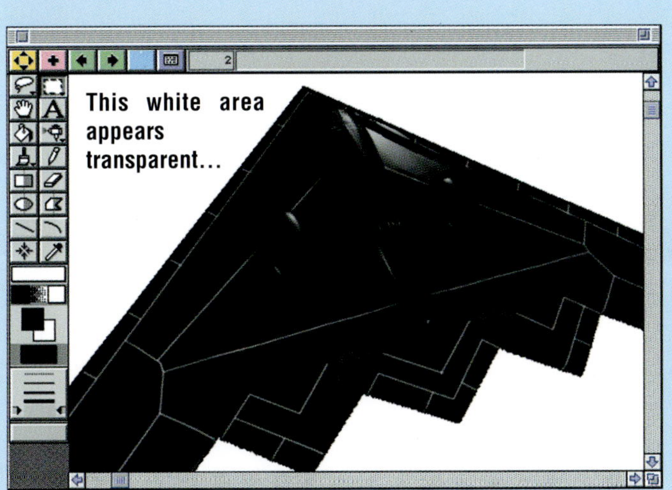

3) Switch black to white. If your animation has 100% black tones you may need to use the white paint bucket tool to fill selected areas to drop out.

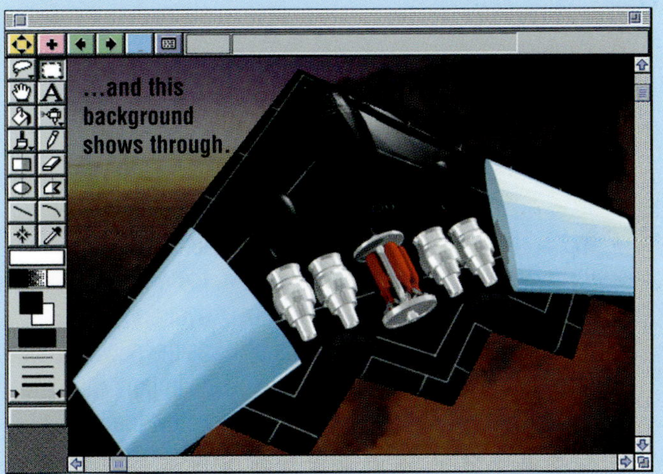

4) The final version shows a composited frame using three Director channels: the background on the first channel, the aircraft on the second and the internal parts on the third.

alpha channels, this is a quality concern that the animator will have to weigh against the convenience of using the program.

Since Director allots a single image to each cell and 48 cells can be stacked on top of each other, complex compositing can be achieved. For animators interested in adding information, such as labels, arrows and highlight boxes, this amount of control can be a great aid.

Director also can animate still 2D images over time–but in a limited manner that does not allow for motion-path editing or object rotation. You can import a panoramic scene, such as a star field or a mountain range, and move it in the background to complement the motion of your imported 3D file.

Individual cells also can have varying degrees of transparency, so if you cannot spare the time to render complex transparency images, you might be able to fake the effect in Director. The transparency feature, called *sprite blend*, also can be used as a transitional device by softly blending on and off full-screen frames over time. The on-board dissolve is really a pixelated, grainy transition which is not professional-looking. Many of the transitions available in editing programs are fun to play with, but some are distracting and unprofessional. When starting out, try to stick to clean edits using smooth fade transitions or direct cuts. Try to avoid using splashy transitions just because you have them.

Most of the ink effects available also serve little purpose, but you might want to experiment with them to produce special effects. If you have an animation like an explosion created on a black background, you can run the file on top of your animation using the lightest ink effect and the black background will disappear, leaving only the lighter tones of the explosion.

CREATING INTERACTIVE DIRECTOR FILES

Director shines when it comes to assembling interactive productions. The sky is the limit as to the number of creative multimedia products that can be created using Director. Animations can be incorporated easily into Director files and brought to life by clicking on user-defined and user-created buttons.

The first step in making an interactive production is creating the interface. A common design might involve a window or area for the animation to play in, buttons for the user to navigate with and a background for the whole production.

You can use the same tools and skills in creating the interface that you used while working with animations. Rendered PICT still frames of models depicting control panels are easy to create in 3D. Buttons and windows that would appear flat if created only in Photoshop take on life as a 3D model, with light accents and shadows giving a realistic feel of depth.

Since your multimedia production is going to play back from a computer and possibly a CD-ROM, do not make your animation window too big. Unless the final product will play back from a system with hardware compression/decompression, you want to render and play your animations at around 50% of full screen–320x240 pixels.

On high-end Macs, animations play back smoothly at 50% size in 16-bit mode. If you are not sure who the user will be, dither the animation to 256 colors before importing.

If you work in another editing program after you finish your original animation render, you may be adding a soundtrack. If not–and you want one–you can import a sound file into Director and instruct it to play at the same time the animation runs.

With your interface image and your QuickTime movie prepared, you are ready to assemble your production.

If you know what screen the file will run on, tailor it to that specific size. If not, build it around a standard 13" screen. This choice can be found in the File/Preferences selection. It is a good idea to set the screen to always play in the center of the monitor and to make the monitor's depth level conform to the movie's setting, and not the current user's setting. These options also can be found in Director's "Preferences."

Import your file into Director by selecting Cast/Cast to Time to place the file. Using "Cast To Time" will always center the new cast member on the stage. This feature will be useful later as you make adjustments to your interface. If you introduce recessed buttons at a later time, for instance, your new file will line up exactly with the old file, avoiding unwanted shifts in the art elements as the new cast member is introduced.

Import the QuickTime movie in the cell below the interface background. If you made your render size the same size as your playback window you should have no difficulty moving the QuickTime movie on your stage and into the proper position. Just click and drag on it.

Now you need to introduce an element to act as a button. Click on the cell below the cast member and import the background interface again. Use "Cast To Time" to position it in the cell you selected earlier. This will guarantee that the elements will be lined up exactly. Next, open up the Paint window (Command-5) and, using the Selection Marquee, select and delete all the image except the desired button. You now have a button that can be assigned a script.

All the elements in the Director cast can be assigned *Lingo* scripts. Lingo is Director's native scripting code that gives the user interactive control over what the movie is doing. For example, if the button has a script written for it that simply says "beep," the computer will beep when the user clicks the button. If the script for the button says, "go to frame 4," the movie playback head will jump to frame 4 of the score when the user clicks the button.

In Director, you want this example to run the animation when the user clicks on a button. To create this script, highlight the button in the Cast Member window. At the top of the window are icons for controlling the cast members. Click on the script icon (it looks like a sheet of paper with writing on it). Notice the program has already done some scripting for you by putting "on mouseup" and "end mouseup" in the Script window.

CREATING THE INTERFACE

Use the same skills and tools you have developed for 3D animations for creating realistic, dramatic interactive environments.

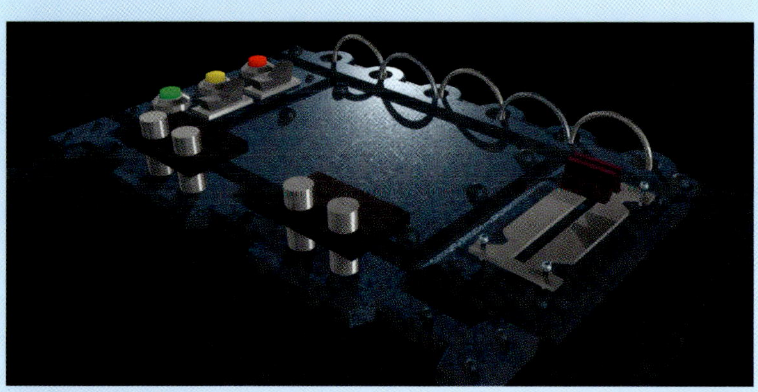

Half the fun of making an interactive product is developing the interface. Use glancing lights to keep the image from being flat.

The final output can be rendered to fit your playback screen's size. Most common is the 13" monitor, which is 640 by 480 pixels. The final image is rendered at 72 dpi, a computer screen's resolution.

The insertion bar will blink between the two statements, waiting for you to type in a command. Type "go to frame 4"–or whichever frame the movie was placed. Hit the Enter key to compile the new script. Once in frame 4, Director will play the animation or any sounds in that frame, as well as display new PICT elements (recessed or highlighted buttons).

When the finished Director movie is played, clicking on the button you created will make the playback head go to the indicated frame and play your animation. Keeping the QuickTime files in the same folder as the Director movie will assure that the program does not lose its link to the animation files.

When you have completed your Director file, you can create a self-contained file from the document that will not require the Director application to be installed for your animation to play. First, Choose File/Save And Compact to optimize the document. Then select File/Create Projector to create the self-contained file. You still will have to include the QuickTime animation file in the same folder, but all your work will be imbedded in a tight little package easy for a user to play.

INCORPORATING ANIMATIONS IN AN INTERACTIVE DIRECTOR MOVIE

By bringing in animations saved as QuickTime files, Director users can create self-contained interactive movies that can play back on anyone's system without having to run Director.

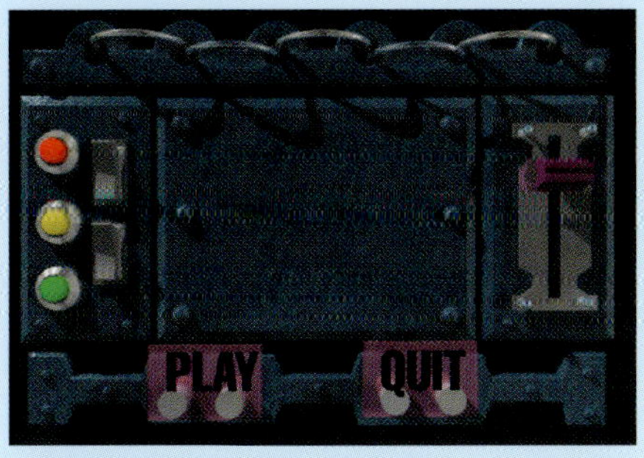

1) Create the interface. You can build 3D models and render still images to mimic dramatic controls and panels.

2) Import the QuickTime file and the still interface file. Also bring in any sounds you want to add.

3) Import the interface image again and put it on top of the existing image. Then delete everything but the button. This will create a button.

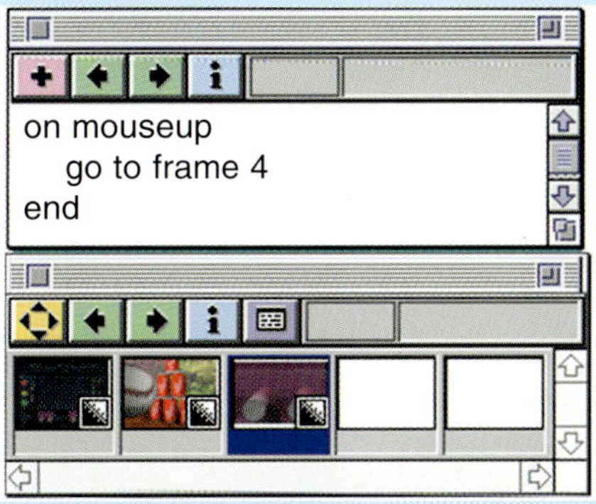

4) Write the lingo command for the button cast member. When you click on the button, the computer will follow the command.

5) Use the Save And Compact command to optimize the file and then use the Create Projector command to create the final file.

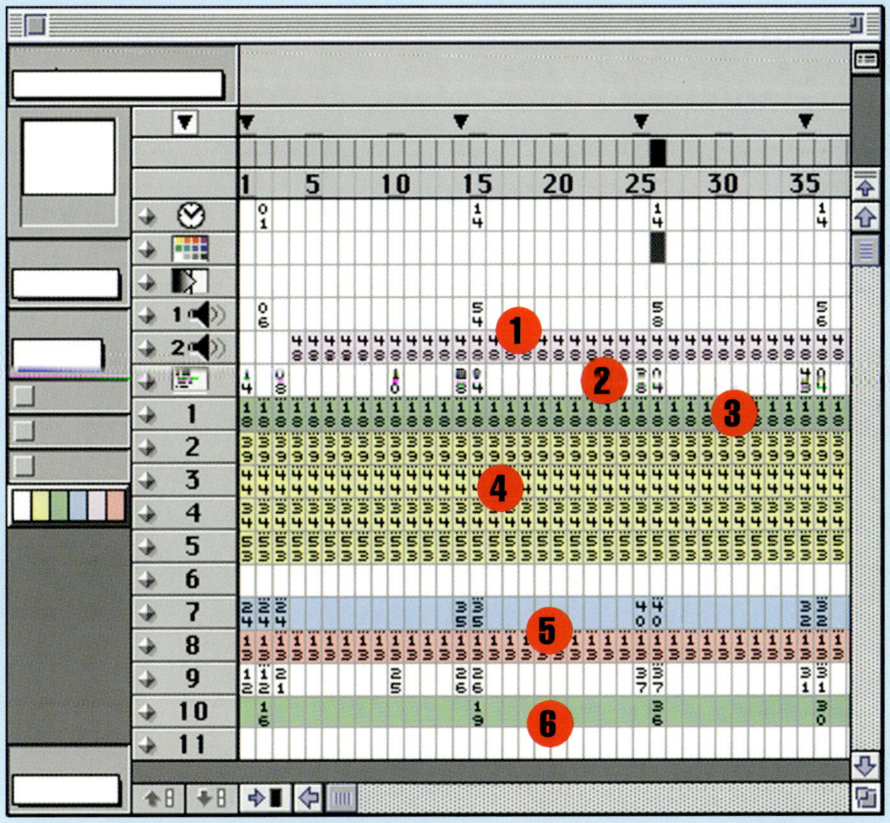

Interactive projects take advantage of Director's multi-track layers. In a complex multimedia project (above), the cast members in the score can perform a number of functions such as: 1) soundtracks, 2) lingo scripts, 3) background, 4) buttons with attached script, 5) animation previews that appear while the animation file loads into RAM, 6) the actual animation QuickTime file.

EDITING WITH ADOBE AFTER EFFECTS

Adobe After Effects provides animators with one of the most complete software-based animation editing environments available. The program imports QuickTime and PICT files and supports Photoshop import plug-ins. If you are planning to work with After Effects, set your animation to render as a QuickTime file using the animation compressor and the highest-quality setting. If you try to import a PICS file, After Effects will ask you if you want to "Convert." This will change the file to a QuickTime import on-the-fly. This is fine if the file is already in PICS format, but if you are rendering the animation yourself, you have more control saving it as QuickTime with your settings.

If you are including an alpha channel, use the Millions+ color depth setting (32-bit). If you are including still image files, such as text, you can also bring in the alpha channel information. When you import a QuickTime file with an alpha channel, the import is transparent. When you bring in a still file, After Effects presents an Interpret Footage dialog box asking you how you want the alpha channel interpreted. Under most circumstances you will want to import it as a straight alpha channel. A *straight alpha channel* incorporates a separate (fourth) channel to handle transparency and masking information. Applications that output as a *pre-multiplied alpha channel* change the value in each of the three (R,G,B) channels without adding a fourth channel.

Imported files are stored in the Project window. Still images as well as animation files are kept here while the movie is assembled. The Composition window is the stage that shows the final product. When an imported item from the Project window is introduced to the Composition window, it shows up in the Time Layout window. The Time Layout window works similarly to all the other sequencers and timelines we have seen. The layers stack up vertically on the left side of the window while time in seconds or frames displays horizontally. Unlike Director, the layer on the top of the pile is in the foreground. The last one is usually the background. You can shuffle layers as needed.

If your animation is going to be compos-

Animations are edited in a Composition window which allows the user to bring together PICT and QuickTime files (sources) and composite them over time.

Layer switches are used to toggle on or off features available for each layer as well as implement features such as motion blur.

Time can be set to seconds or frames. If needed, you can zoom into the timeline to edit the composition a single frame at a time.

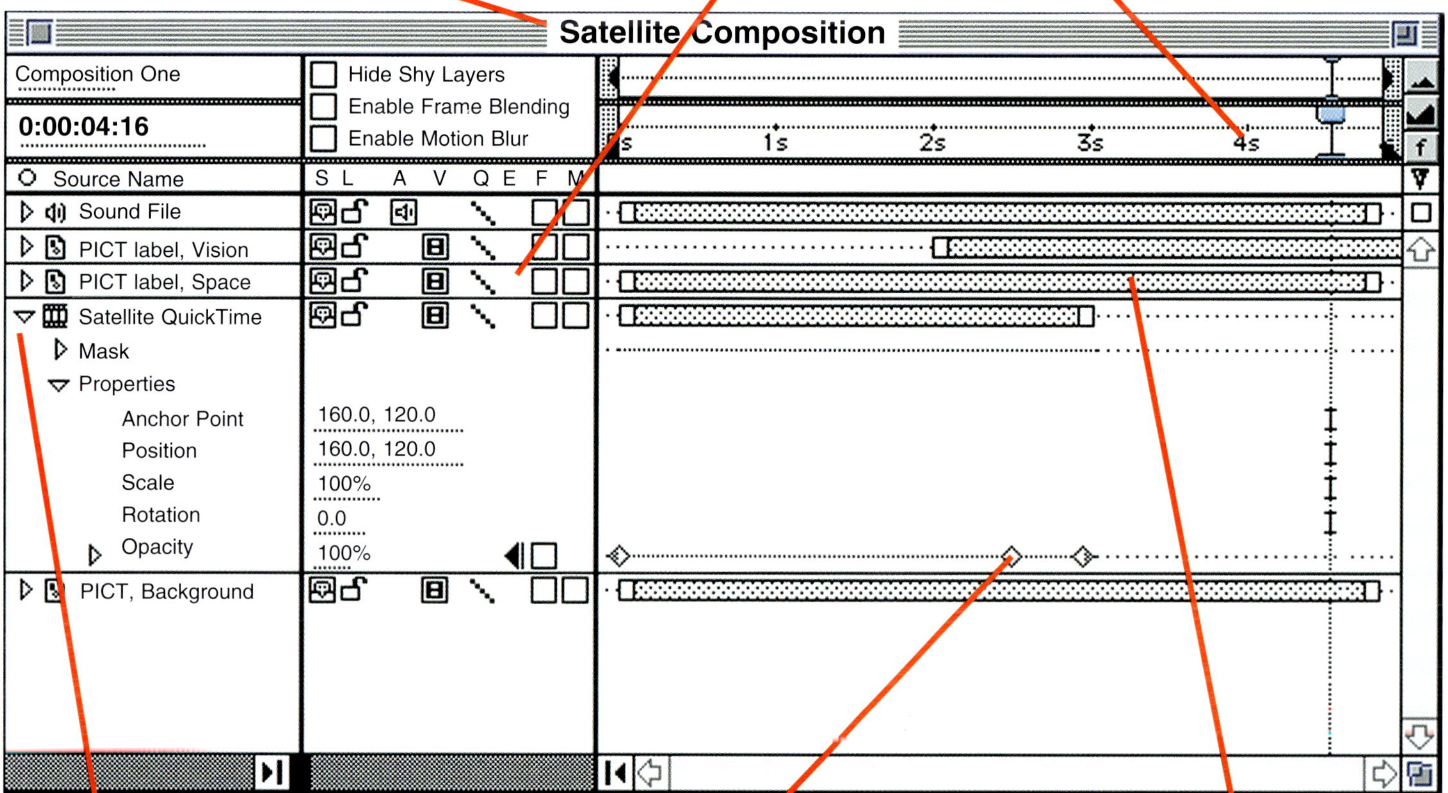

The source files are displayed in the left column. Using the Macintosh Finder metaphor, users can click on an arrow to display detailed information on each file.

Using precise key frame animation techniques, users can make adjustments to an element's position, scale, rotation or opacity over time.

Each layer of the animation is represented by a layer bar. Animation elements can be trimmed in size to fit precisely. Still elements can be set for the length of their duration on the screen.

INTRODUCING 3D AND 2D ELEMENTS INTO ADOBE AFTER EFFECTS

Three factors make Adobe After Effects a solid working environment for animators: alpha channel support, unlimited layering and flexible key frame animation for 2D elements. The animation (below) shows how some of these features can be used. It is based on the timeline from the preceding page.

1) An oversized background is created. The final window size will be 320x240, so a 640x480 star background was created and saved as a PICT file.

After Effects composition workspace gives the user the ability to influence elements not visible in the final stage window. Light lines represent bounding boxes that show the location of elements in the animation. Using these, the animator can change an element's position, rotation and scale before the item enters the scene. This is useful in scenes where text rolls in from out of the screen's boundaries (above). The text was positioned before it came onto the screen using the bounding boxes off stage.

2) The background is imported full size, so only a portion of it can be seen. Then using key frame animation, it is shifted in position over the six seconds of the animation.

3) The rendered QuickTime file is imported with its alpha channel. The file was rendered with the highest-quality settings even if the final output will be lower.

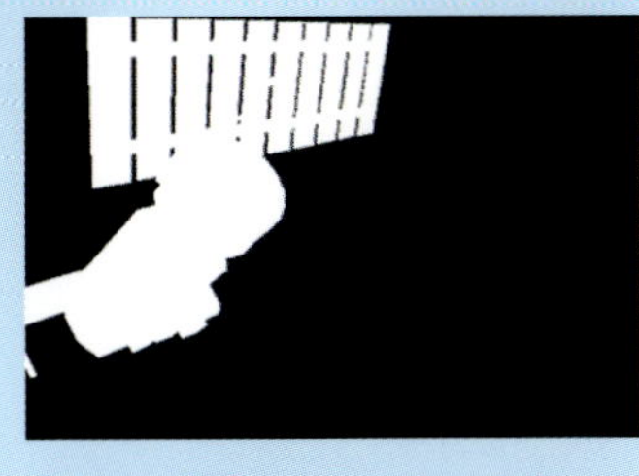

4) You will not see the alpha channel when you import, but if you want to check it, you can hold down your Command and Option keys while clicking on the window proportion indicator.

5) You can drag the imported file into the Composition window, but positioning will be by eye only. For exact positioning, click on the item in the Project window and do a Command-/ keystroke.

6) Text elements, such as this space label, can be animated over time by adjusting position, scale or rotation.

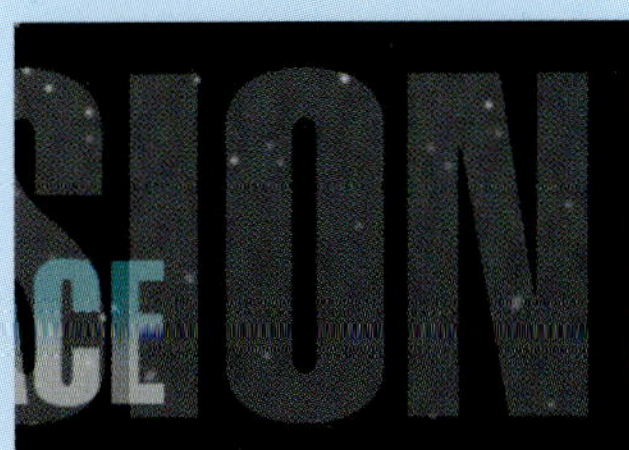

7) An unlimited number of layers, depending on your RAM and disk space, can be added to the file.

ited on a background using an alpha channel, drag the background from the Project window to the Composition window. To move the animation file, you could drag it as well, but it might be better to use the Command-/ keystroke to place the file. This insures precise placement so frames placed later will line up exactly.

After Effects allows for an unlimited number of layers. Each layer can contain a still image file–a background–or an animation file. Although still image files come in static, they do not have to stay static. After Effects has powerful key frame-based animation features that allow the user to scale, rotate, move or change opacity over time.

Motion control is one of the program's best assets. Any element, including an imported 3D file, can be introduced into a layer and be assigned a fully-editable motion path. Bezier path tools give you an incredible amount of precise control over the motion of an object. The software allows for highly accurate (sub-pixel) positioning, which translates to smoother, more professional motion.

Special effects also may be applied to the animation. These range from the familiar filters–Gaussian Blur and Spherize–to more sophisticated effects such as Motion Blur which helps take the edge off of quickly moving objects. Effects can be used on individual layers allowing the background to blur out so the focus of the screen is an animated element in the foreground. The effects use the same key frame system that manipulates object position, rotation and scale.

When the final movie is done, it is rendered. Rendering in After Effects amounts to processing each frame with the effects applied to it, similar to running a filter in Photoshop. If you have a ton of filters, layers and effects, the render could take hours.

High-end animators will be interested in this editing program's ability to field render (for field render, see page 120). This process writes a frame for each odd and even layer of a video signal. The result is the smoothest possible animation. However, to achieve this effect, an animation frame must be written for each field. This means that you have to render 60 frames (30 even numbered and 30

SETTING 2D OBJECTS IN MOTION

Even in a complex 3D animation there are times you will need to animate a 2D object. If you do not have time to render an animation, sometimes creating a single frame of a 3D object and moving it across the screen will do the trick. After Effects is the leader of the pack when it comes to 2D motion control. Bezier tools give control to the object's position while scale, rotation and opacity can be adjusted. By moving the time frame indicator and making needed adjustments, you create key frames. These can be edited and adjusted as needed.

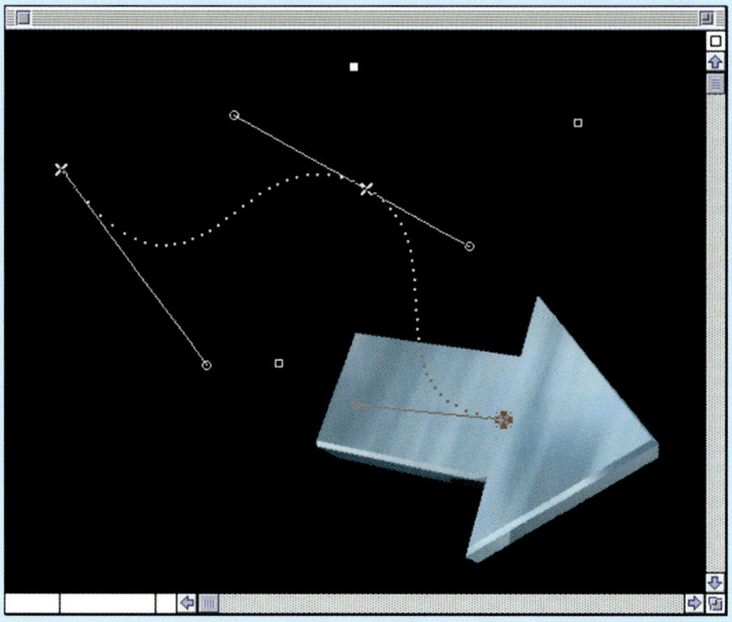

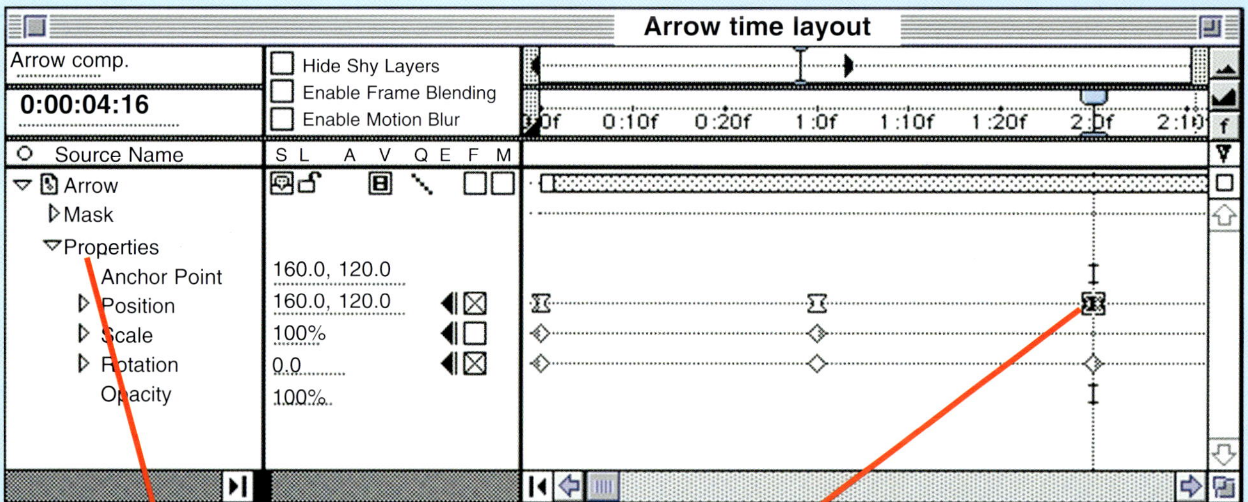

Using a System 7-type interface, variables can be adjusted on each element in the timeline. Variables can be typed in or created interactively using manipulation tools.

Each mark on the timeline reflects a point in which a variable was adjusted. As time passes, left to right, the events play out as the animator created them.

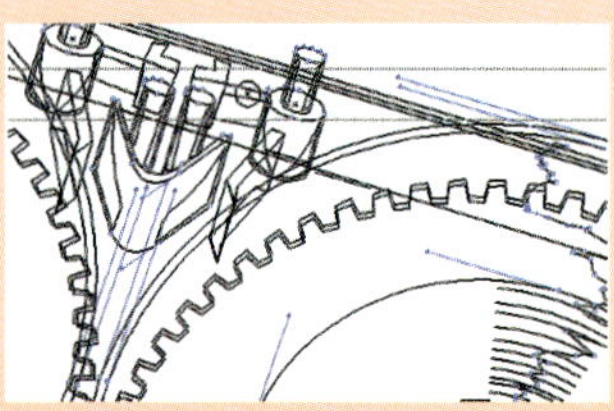

Bezier paths in blue affect the tangents of the Illustrator paths in black.

WHAT IS A BEZIER, ANYWAY?

Postscript drawing programs have them, modeling software is better with them, Photoshop path tools work miracles with them and After Effects can edit motion paths with them. But what are they? Beziers are convenient graphical tools that allow users to precisely edit paths by adjusting the tangent of an arc, usually by clicking and dragging on handles. The ability to adjust the tangent of an arc gives the user a great amount of control whether the path will be used for editing motion paths, creating selection or defining fill areas.

odd numbered) for a one second NTSC animation instead of 30 frames. Theoretically, rendering time should not take twice as long, since you would need to render only every other line in each frame, but that would be assuming your 3D rendering software supported field rendering. At this time, none of the 3D rendering packages mentioned here support this feature. If you plan to render 60 field animations, double up your render files by telling the rendering software that you want the file to output 60 FPS.

After Effects has a nice way of nesting animation files. This means that you can take an entire production in process, even before the output has been rendered, and reintroduce it to the time layout as an individual element. By doing this you can apply masks and filters to the entire production giving the animation an incredible amount of production control without ever leaving the program. An entire edited animation with multiple layers could be re-introduced into an animation as a window that is flown around the screen using the Basic 3D effect, so the animation is taking place inside the window while it is moving around.

USING FILTERS FOR PIZAZZ AND PRODUCTION

Editing programs such as After Effects and Premiere allow the animator to apply filter effects to the finished movie. These filters–many of which can be applied over time–can add spice to an otherwise flat image or provide valuable production tools, such as converting the animation into an NTSC safe document or removing unwanted flicker.

The Spherize filter could be used over time to show a bulging effect, only the pipe layer is influenced.

The untouched composite. This example uses three layers: the grass and sky photo in the background, the land chunk and the pipes. The land and the pipes were imported into After Effects with their alpha channels for clean compositing.

To help focus the attention on the subject, "Levels" were changed to increase the brightness of the land chunk and darken the background.

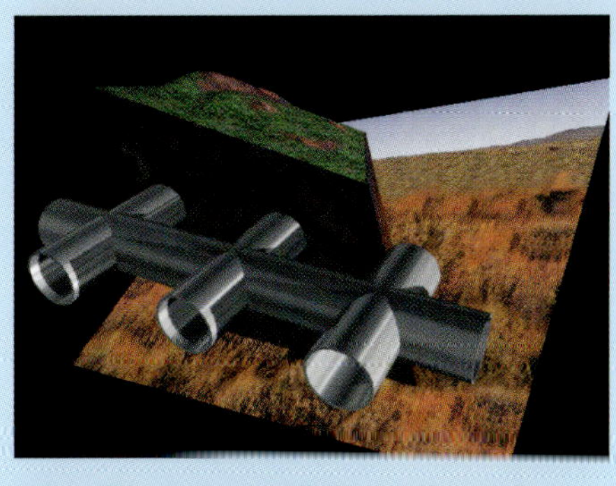

After Effects Basic 3D filter allows simple 3D animation over time, in this case background elements animate off the screen leaving the pipe.

Even artistic effects, such as brush strokes, can be used. Photoshop filters can also be applied in the same manner.

All of the image's color ranges, hues and values can be manipulated on a selected layer without affecting the rest of the scene.

Although you normally would not use an Emboss filter on a photorealistic image, the results can add some punch to text and logo elements.

Blur filters can be applied in over time to simulate the change of focus. In this case it brings attention to the foreground element.

EDITING WITH ADOBE PREMIERE

Adobe Premiere is one of the most popular general purpose video-editing packages on the market. Its interface suggests an easy transition for video editors familiar with a traditional A-B roll editing format while providing some important tools for the animator.

The program accepts several different types of formats, including the predominant QuickTime and PICS formats. Regardless of your final output quality, you will want to save the 3D animation file that you are going to edit in Premiere with its highest-quality settings. If you want to composite your animation with other animations or place it on a background, make sure you render the 3D output with a straight alpha channel.

Once you import your animation file into Premiere, it is stored in a Project Bin. Double clicking on the file while it is in the Bin allows you to trim the animation before introducing it to the construction timeline or add and subtract duration time from static elements. Animation and still elements are introduced into the Construction window timeline by dragging them from one window to the next. Where you put animation files will determine how you can manipulate them.

Premiere's most basic setup involves a two-track system, A and B, with a transitional track between that controls visual effects on the main stage as the edit switches from one track to another. A-B roll editing is fine for putting together video clips, but lacks versatility when compositing animations. This is where the superimposition tracks come into play.

The program's default setting has a single superimpose track that comes to the screen, but as many as 97 can be added for complex layering. The superimpose track is the only one that can isolate your animation elements using the alpha channel, so this is where to drag your animation for editing. Use the A and B channels for your backgrounds. You can use the transition track to change your backgrounds on the fly while your animation plays on top of them.

Unlike bringing an animation with an

Premiere's editing interface attempts to mimic the world of analog editing, primarily with A and B source tracks that use the transition track in between to create a crossover effect.

Animations using alpha channels are edited in a superimpose track. By using the Add Track command in the project window, an animator can create up to 97 separate superimpose tracks.

The transition track gives the user a device to hop between the A-B tracks. Clean dissolves are possible as well as 3D page turns.

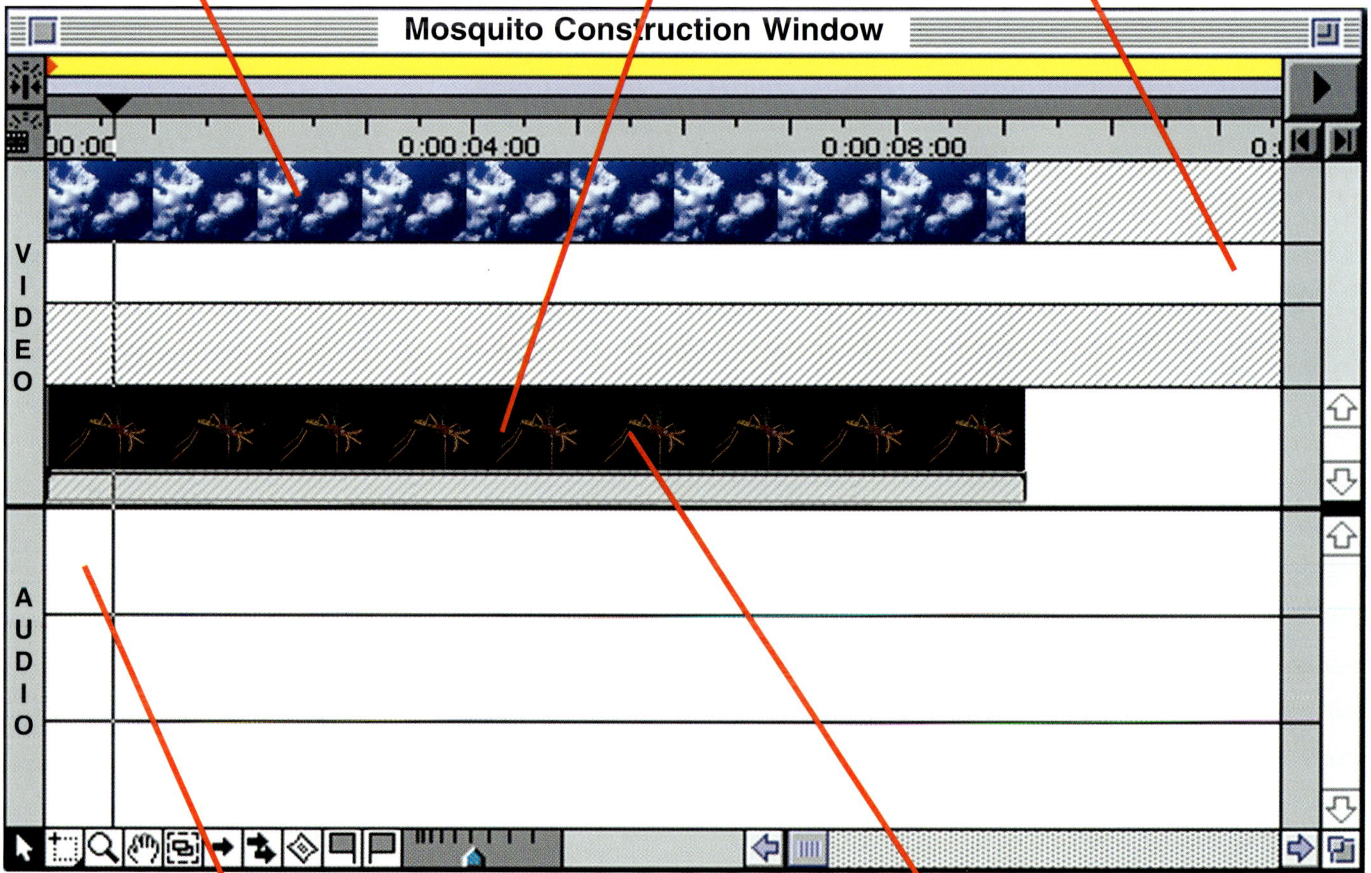

The program allows for sound editing and synchronization control superior to most other editing programs.

Premiere uses small replicas of imported files as a visual placeholder for the editor to construct the movie.

IMPORTING AND EDITING ANIMATION FILES IN ADOBE PREMIERE

Both QuickTime and PICS animation files can be imported into Premiere as well as still PICT files that can be used as static backgrounds. Premiere excels in marrying sound with animation, so you might consider importing your sound files as well.

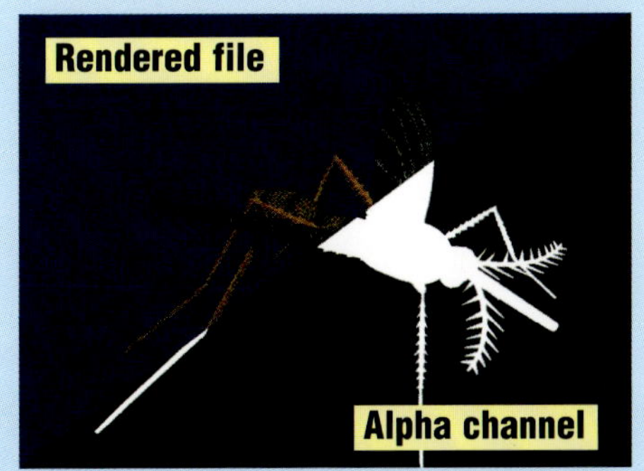

1) Save your render with an alpha channel. QuickTime, PICS and numbered PICT and Targa (an IBM format) formats import.

The alpha channel information will allow the image to smoothly blend with the background. You can add tracks to increase the number of layers you can composite.

2) Import the background. Premiere imports Illustrator, Photoshop, PICT, Photo CD and Targa still images.

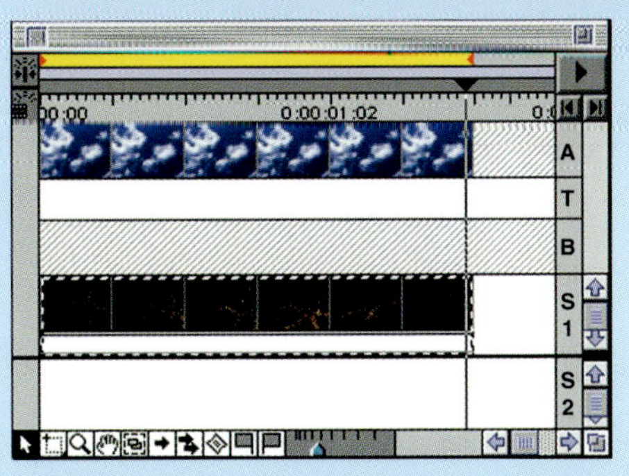

3) Import the files (Command-I) placing the animation file into the construction window on the superimpose track.

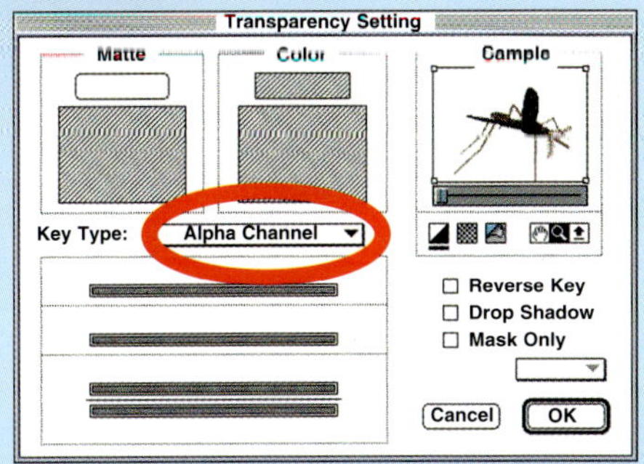

4) With the track selected, go to Transparency under the Clip menu. Choose alpha channel in the options.

alpha channel into After Effects, the existence of the alpha channel does not automatically composite your animation. You must tell the program what you want it to do. Select the animation file in the superimpose track. The selection marquee will circle it, letting you know which track you are affecting. Choose Clip/Transparency. In the middle of the dialog box you will be given a choice of keying methods–choose Alpha Channel. You will see the results in the sample screen in the top right corner of the dialog box. If you do not see it, you may not have put an alpha channel on the animation file. Click OK to go back to your Construction window. You will not see the results immediately in the Preview window. Instead you will see your background with a big X on it. You must choose Project/Preview to see the effect.

Premiere may not have the sophisticated object movement and key frame capabilities of After Effects, and it may lack the ability to control external devices or author interactive productions like Director, but it is a strong performer in its own right at a reasonable price considering the many things it does do well in the video-editing arena.

Since Premiere is primarily a video-editing system, you can take advantage of its video-editing tools to combine real-world video with animation. Place digitized video on tracks A or B and run your animation files on the superimpose tracks.

Premiere also accepts most Photoshop filters, allowing them to be applied to animations over time.

Premiere saves primarily as QuickTime, but numbered PICTS (a series of PICT files numbered sequentially) and FilmStrip files are also available. If you are going to bring your animation into a non-Mac environment, numbered PICTS may give you the flexibility you need. FilmStrip format creates a file that can be opened in Photoshop as a single file with all of the frames in the movie in one BIG chunk. This gives you the option to do single-frame editing on a file. It is possible to import your animation into Premiere, export it as a FilmStrip and clean it up in Photoshop, then re-import it back into Premiere for final compositing. If you try this procedure, alpha channel information will be preserved.

Field rendering for video is supported as well. Although the NTSC standard plays 30 FPS, the frames are interlaced, meaning they display all the odd lines on the TV screen in the first frame, and then the even ones. A field rendered movie actually has 60 fields. This will give you the smoothest possible playback for your animation, assuming you have available hardware devices compatible for field rendered output.

EDITING WITH ADOBE PHOTOSHOP

Adobe Photoshop, as an editing tool associated with the flat world of 2D images, also plays a vital role in animation. The two key areas where 2D image editing rules supreme are texture creation for surface maps and as a crucial editing tool for 2D elements such as titles, art elements and backgrounds.

Although most bitmap-based image-editing programs can handle the job, Photoshop is usually the animator's choice. Not only does the well-designed interface and wide variety of tools make creating image maps a snap, but the array of filters available from third-party vendors makes the process almost automatic. At a minimum, you should include among your image arsenal Aldus' Gallery Effects, Xaos Tools' Paint Alchemy and H.S.C. Software's Kai's Power Tools.

When applying some of these filters to a flat color field you might want to add a little noise to the area to give the filter something to act on–the Noise filter included with Photoshop does a good job. With no noise added, the Emboss filter used on a flat color makes no change in the field, since there is nothing to emboss. A gray area with noise, however, becomes a concrete texture or a green becomes Astroturf.

Some filters provide video production features as well. The De-interlace filter can help remove scan lines from video frames that have been digitized and brought into Photoshop. The Blur filter can be applied to thin horizontal lines and noisy areas to help remove annoying flicker when recorded to video tape. The NTSC filter creates an image that is NTSC safe–meaning it takes color ranges that fall out of the video world's gamut and adjusts them to within acceptable levels.

After the 3D animation file has been rendered, everything is flat. This is where Photoshop can work its magic. Photoshop-created 2D objects can be brought seamlessly into animations with the aid of an alpha channel. Backgrounds can be created at a size to fit the final production or they can be oversized and moved behind the animation to simulate camera pans. Art elements such as labels, text, type balloons and icons can be created in Photoshop and imported into editing programs such as Premiere, Director and After Effects.

Photoshop's Text tool is usually far superior to text tools available in editing programs. Text elements can be saved with an alpha channel which guarantees a smooth, professional anti-aliased appearance.

Photoshop can also provide an access to image input tools. Hardware devices such as scanners and digital cameras often ship with Photoshop drivers that can control the import of images into the computer.

Another helpful feature of the program is the ability to save paths created with the Path palette as Adobe Illustrator paths. This means that when creating a texture map for a specific object in Photoshop, you can export the path. The path is actually an EPS file which can be opened up as a shape in programs that support EPS shape import. This allows your texture to be exactly the same shape as your object.

CREATING A 2D ELEMENT AND ITS ALPHA CHANNEL

Animators will often need to import 2D elements such as icons and labels into their productions. Photoshop is not only an excellent tool for creating these elements, but it also can create needed alpha channels to make the import seamless.

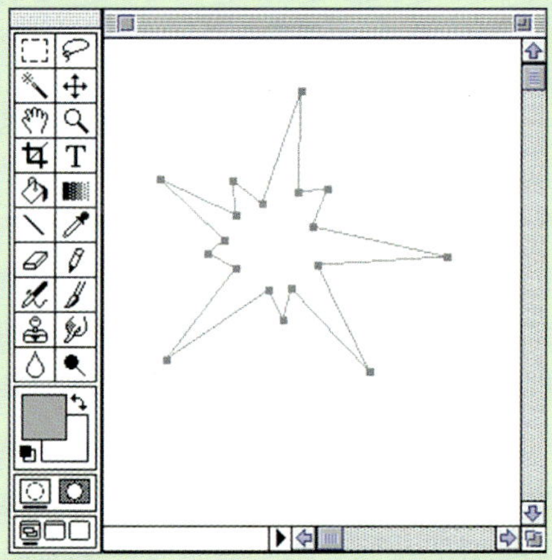

1) Create the element. If you can, save the paths used to draw the item. Text created can use the "Save As Path" command.

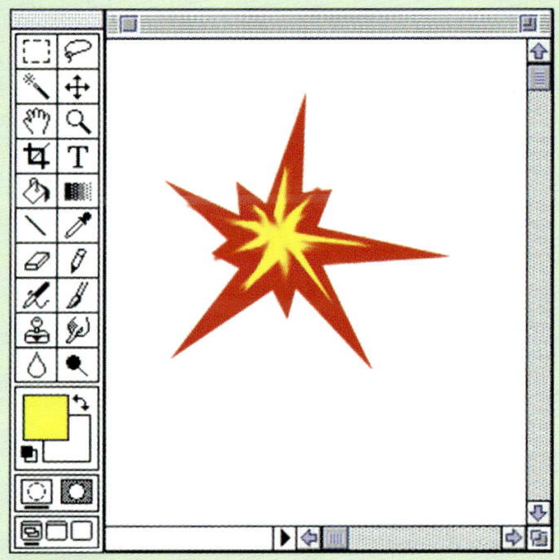

2) Draw the internal parts of the icon or color the text as needed. Blends or filters can be applied.

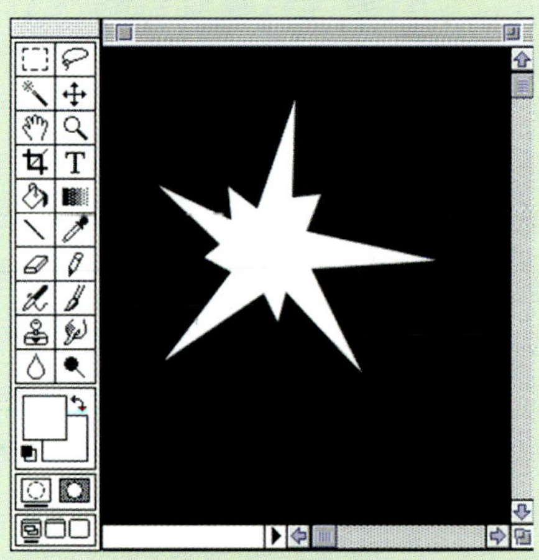

3) Use the "Save Selection" command. When you do, an alpha channel is automatically created. Save the file as a 32-bit PICT file.

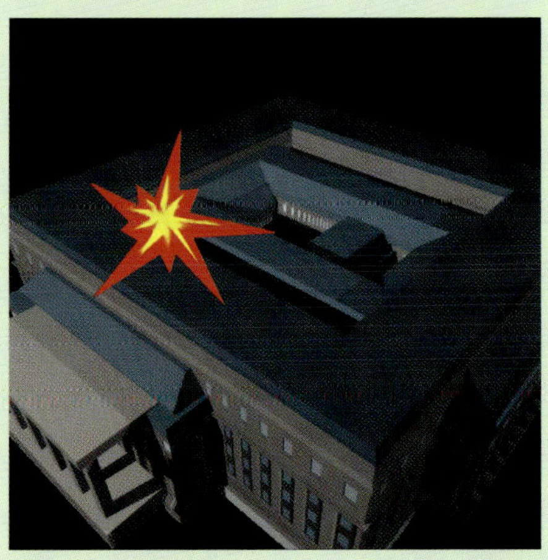

4) Import the image into an editing program that supports alpha channels, such as Premiere or After Effects.

USING ADOBE PHOTOSHOP TO EDIT SURFACE TEXTURES

Having photorealistic surface textures, such as wood or stone surfaces can certainly add to an object's realism, but creating your own surfaces in an image-editing program also can add impact. Third-party filter packages can aid dramatically in making quick, painless textures. All the textures in the skin section below were created in less than five minutes.

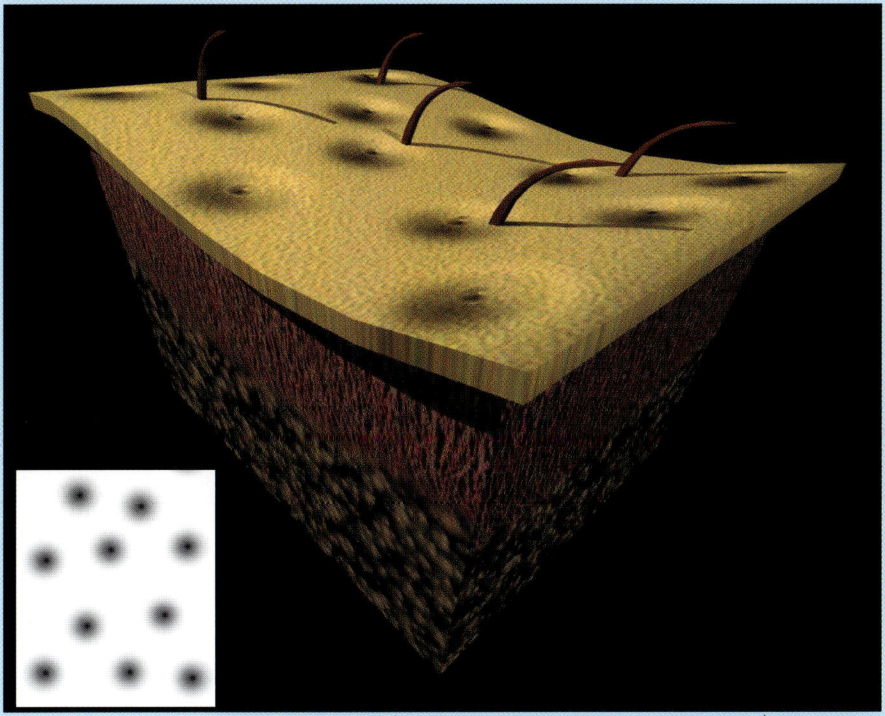

The skin section (above) uses three texture maps, each edited in Photoshop using widely available filters. A bump map (insert, lower left) was used to create the dimple in the skin's surface.

CREATING THE MUSCLE TISSUE COLOR

1) Fill the screen with the a color representing the general hue of the object.

2) Use the Noise filter to add some texture to the filled area.

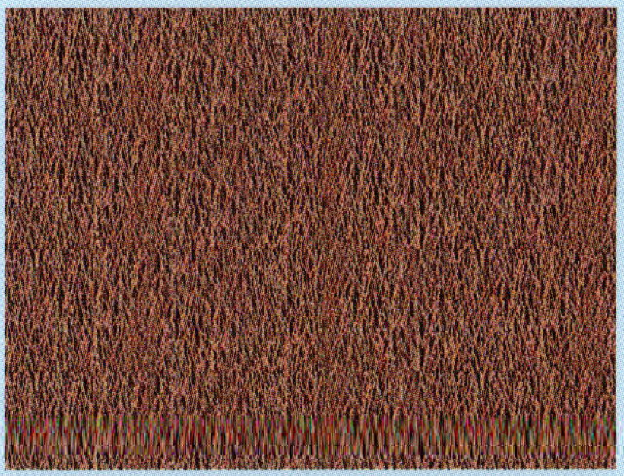

3) Use Xaos Tool Paint Alchemy Thread filter to give the muscle tissue texture.

CREATING THE FAT TISSUE LAYER

1) Fill the screen with the a color representing the general hue of the object.

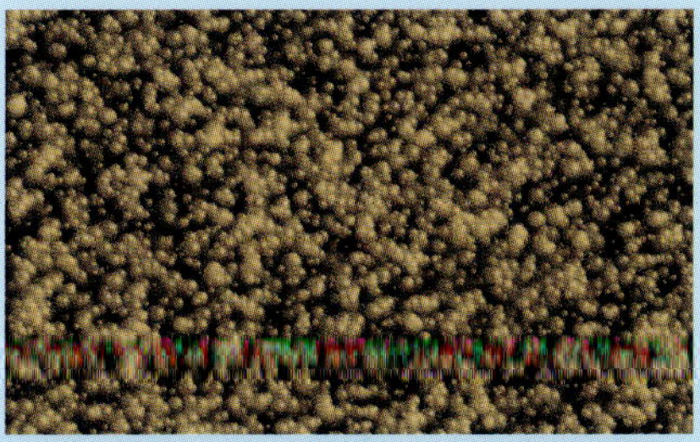

2) Use Xaos Tool Paint Alchemy Opaque Bubbles filter to create the fat tissue texture.

CREATING THE SKIN SURFACE

1) Fill the screen with the a color representing the general hue of the object.

2) Use the Noise filter to add some texture to the filled area.

3) Use GE Gallery Effects Emboss filter to add depth to the noise, giving an organic bumpy feel.

EDITING WITH MORPHS & DISTORTIONS

One of the first things an animator does after ripping off the shrink wrap from the package of a morphing program like Gryphon Software Corporation's Morph or The Valis Group's Movieflo is to transform digital images of friends and family into assorted barnyard animals and other oddities. While the morphing or distorting tools have a great WOW! factor, they can be put to serious production use after you have finished with the parlor tricks.

An animator is often confronted with the difficulty of creating an object or motion that seems impossible to model. Among these challenges are replicating scenes like mud slides or bursting arteries. Morphing reveals its true power creating fluid subjects like these.

A morphing program's magic mostly consists of its ability to shift pixels from point A to point B and to blend images from one scene to another. By combining these two effects, you can make one image transform into another.

All morphing programs start by asking you to define the parameters of the first image and specify where you would like that information to end up when the morph finishes. For example, if you are morphing a cat to a dog, you would tell the program to take the area around one animal's eye and morph it to the other animal's eye. You would do the same with ears, mouth and nose as well as the general outline of the creature. Character morphs seem more natural and believable if both subjects are facing the same direction. Images are more polished if the motion of one morph is carried through to the next.

Animations can use the same morphing functions to show how an object changes over time. While it is a simple matter to make a model that looks like a vein–and you might even be able to use your animation tools to make it bulge–making the vein burst would be a challenge. If you alter the final frame with a photo-editing program you can morph between the rendered frame and the photo-edited one, giving you an animated effect that might have been impossible to build in a 3D animation program.

Programs that specialize in distortion such as Elastic Reality's Elastic Reality, or The Valis Group's Metaflo or PixelPutty also serve a similar purpose. These programs take an existing image, usually a PICT or TIFF file, and let the user warp and distort the image with their changes being able to be recorded over time.

MORPHING IMAGES

Morphing tools can be an important addition to an animator's toolbox. Not only can they perform the usual tricks of morphing friends and relatives into obscure objects, but they can create fluid motion difficult to do with 3D motion.

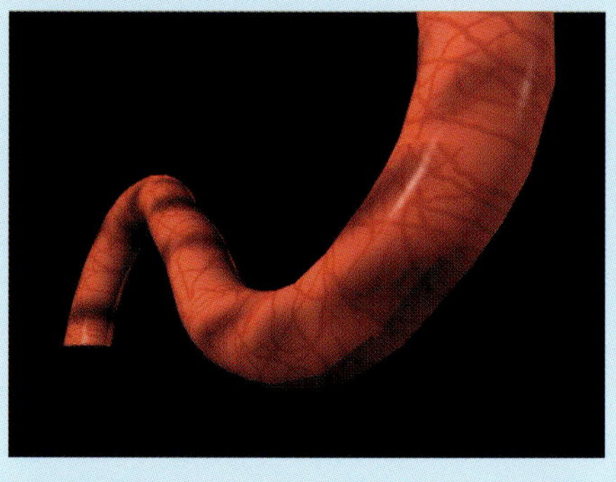

1) Create the initial image. The unaltered rendered output from a 3D animation program is used (above).

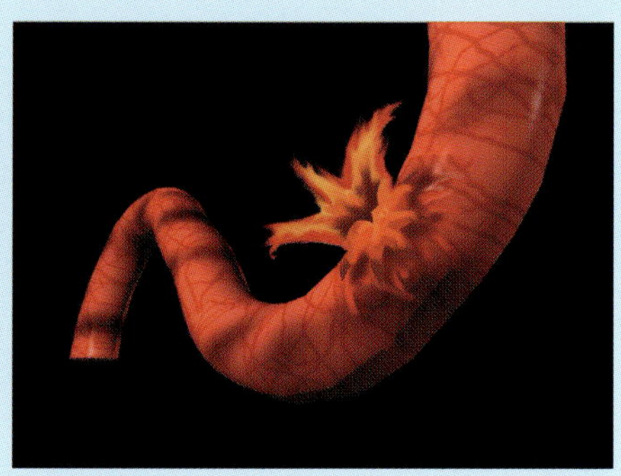

2) Alter a copy of the image using a photo-manipulation tool such as Photoshop.

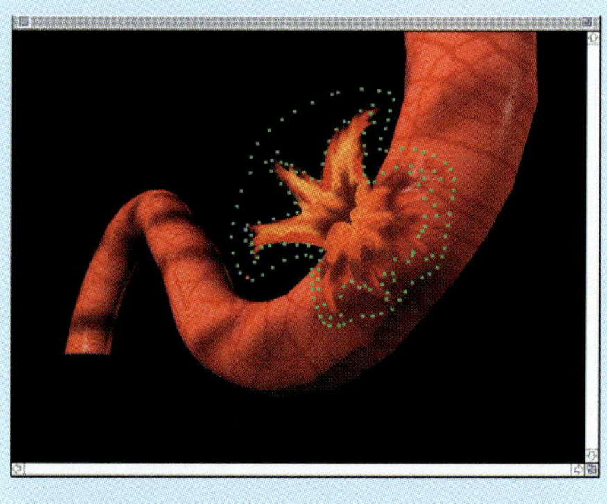

3) Import the image into the morphing program and define the final points first–this helps you specify the parameters. Note the points drawn around the outside of the changed area.

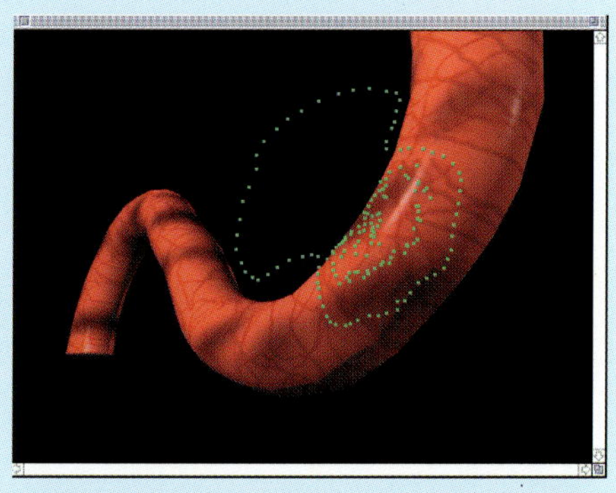

4) Reposition the morph points on the starting frame leaving the outside points alone. This will help lock the rest of the image so it does not shift during the morph.

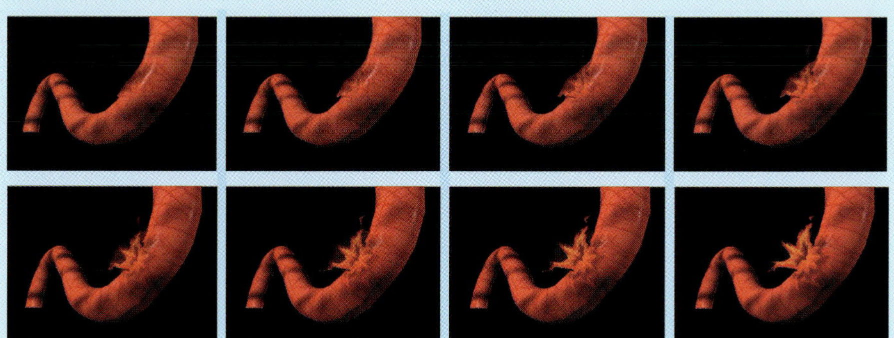

5) The final output can usually be output as QuickTime, PICS or numbered PICT files and then imported into an editing program.

6. OUTPUT

PLAYING THE ANIMATION

DIGITAL TOOLS/ANALOG OUTPUT When the time comes for digital information to enter the video world, it takes a combination of hardware control combined with video encoding. An introduction clip for a Virginia production company (above) is an example.

Showtime! Time to view the fruits of your labor. A variety of editing methods exist to complete a final animation project.

In most cases, the end product will be either a computer- or video-based display. In computer-based display, the results remain digital, while with video output, the animation leaves the computer world and becomes an analog signal.

Digital output relies on the computer's power to display the animation. Even if your final product is an automated display system–like a kiosk–a computer is controlling the animation.

By going the digital route, you have to consider who the end user will be. If the final product will be used for in-house training and will always run off the same computer, you can configure that machine's RAM, speed and compression to optimize playback. If your end user will be running your animations from a CD-ROM on who-knows-what kind of machine, you may have to take the lowest-common denominator approach to guarantee proper playback.

Analog (video-based) playback is less confining since the final output is recorded to videotape. The animation always plays back at the full speed and anyone with a VCR can view your work.

If you go the analog route, the next decision is whether to get your animation to tape via *frame recording* or *real-time playback*. With frame recording, you need special hardware that records animation to tape a single frame at a time. With real-time recording, you rely on hardware compression/decompression boards that pump the video through the computer fast enough to display 30 frames a second.

Before going any further, you must realize that computer video is substantially different from video output, so transcoding hardware may be needed. Some Macintosh models include AV (audio/video) output cards built-in. Other models require either dedicated video boards to output the video signal or scan-encoding boxes which convert the computer's non-interlaced video signal to the correct interlaced scan rate.

Before the animation models are built, you should determine what the mode for the final output will be. Knowing this will help you determine the window size for your modeling program and the color tone for textures and light adjustments. Animations that are viewed on computers are substantially darker than those output on video. While building models, it is important to keep this in mind since dark shadowy areas in animations may turn black for the computer but will look fine on a TV set.

Some of these lighting adjustments can be made after the animation has been created by filtering it through a program like DeBabelizer. For quality's sake, it is best to get the color right in the first place.

Once again, file size is important. Video standards for NTSC require a specific window size very close to 640 pixels wide by 480 pixels deep. This is also the same size for a 13" computer screen–but what you see is not always what you get. Even with the 640x480 window size, a portion of the edges of the animation will be cropped off–about 1/2 inch on all sides. The area within the uncropped region is called *graphic safe*, and this must be planned for while the model and animation are being constructed.

If your final product will be on CD-ROM, the window size is based on how smoothly you can get your animation to play. The larger the window, the more information the computer has to move off the CD-ROM and onto the screen. QuickTime playback is unforgiving–it considers time more important than images and will remove frames that are not keeping up with the pace. The result can be choppy playback.

Color depth is another concern. Should you assume that everyone who views your animation has video support which can display millions of colors or should you create the production in 256 colors and sacrifice quality?

Digital does not always have to be synonymous with computer-only output. The growing trend in the video world is toward digital recording and storage, such as D1 and D2 tapes. At the moment, no viable digital end-user devices exist for recording computer-generated animations. Since we are already in the digital world, the crossover should be quick and painless as new products become available.

DIGITAL VS. ANALOG

Editing systems all use the same conceptual scale, with time represented horizontally and elements stacked vertically. The main difference is in the the number of tracks.

Although some aspects, such as window size, intensity of lighting and color value will be different for digital or analog playback, production of the two output methods is almost identical.

	DIGITAL	ANALOG
USES	CD-ROM Kiosk for information/sales Presentations Interactivity Games	Broadcast Video post production Video training tapes Video entertainment (movies, TV) 3D and effects for video
FINAL PRODUCT	Viewed on computer screen, animation file playback controlled by the computer, often interactively by the user.	Viewed on television screen, animation playback controlled by tape deck.
PROS	Interactive, nonlinear control over animation, image definition crisp. Output can be ported into many programs for as various purposes.	Full-speed, full-color playback without concerns about user devices. High-quality broadcast images possible.
CONS	Full-screen, full-speed playback requires expensive hardware. Small window sizes needed for smooth playback on most computers. Large file sizes.	Linear format cannot be played back on computer equipment once recorded to tape.
REQUIREMENTS	Most digital files are saved for QuickTime output and imported into interactive programs such as HyperCard, SuperCard or Director. Users can also play the QuickTime file by simply opening it with the free Apple-supplied utility, MoviePlayer.	Real-time playback requires video conversion/compression board that both converts the signal to video and pumps the images fast enough for full-screen playback. Single frame recording requires frame-accurate video deck, a hardware or software deck controller and a video output board.

DIGITAL ANIMATION OUTPUT

If your animation project is intended solely for computer playback, the chances are you have all the hardware needed sitting in front of you. Any Macintosh that can run Quick-Time can play your animation file. The quality of the playback will be determined by the speed of the computer, hard drive and video display, as well as the amount of RAM.

First and foremost is the existence of QuickTime in the System's Extension folder. QuickTime is Apple software that allows for the transportability and playback of QuickTime movies, complete with sound, within different programs. Make sure you have the latest version, since leaps in quality exist between different versions. If you do not have QuickTime loaded properly the computer will not be able to save in the QuickTime format when you are rendering an animation file or trying to save an edited movie.

When QuickTime plays back a movie, its main concern is keeping time, not with displaying all the frames in an animation. If an animation is six seconds long, the QuickTime movie will play back in six seconds. If the computer cannot keep up with that pace, it simply skips frames to catch up to where it needs to be. The result can be jerky or stuttering playback.

To create an animation that plays back in its best capacity, it is important to know the limitations of the host computer. If your file will be played back on a Macintosh in a kiosk, base your maximum quality output on that single machine, altering the window size, color depth and compression setting for the best possible output. You also may consider using an add-on board such as Radius' VideoVision Studio. Although you may not need the board's video output capabilities, its compression/decompression hardware accelerator allows you to play an animation at full speed on a 13" computer monitor. Another possible choice is to use a third-party accelerated video board. The slowest possible video display is usually the built-in video available on most models. Some computers' video RAM, like the IIci, uses the Mac's main RAM for display, slowing the computer down even more.

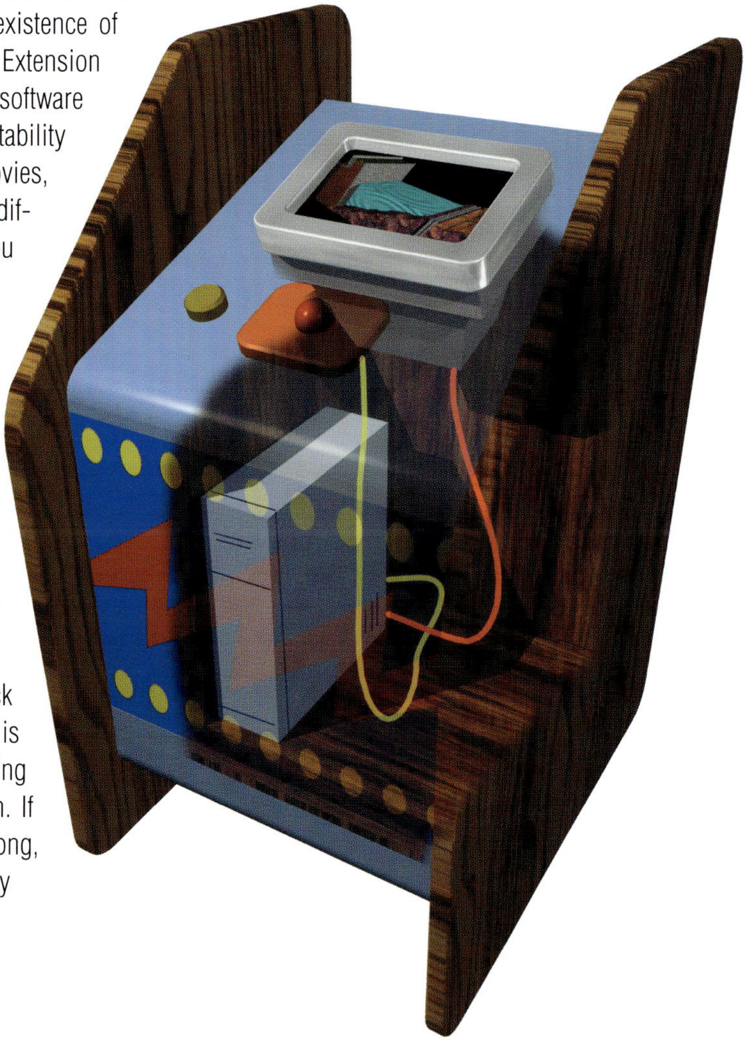

Look inside a kiosk and you will find a computer at its heart. The same rules that apply to forcing animations through your desktop computer are present here as well. In this example, the computer uses a trackball as the user control device.

On the other hand, if you are creating an animation that will be distributed on a CD-ROM, you will have to base your adjustments on the least-common denominator situation, clearly defining the limitations to the end user. When you buy any software, it is clearly labeled on the packaging with the minimum requirements for system software, RAM amount and possibly the computer model.

In many cases planning for the lowest-common denominator will mean designing around a 256-color depth, with a small window (25-50% full-screen size) and medium to medium-low QuickTime quality settings for compression.

You can output your render at 256 colors and let the rendering software handle the dithering for you, or you can use DeBabelizer . With DeBabelizer, you can open up an animation render created at a higher-quality color depth such as 16- or 32-bit and create a customized color palette. The program allows you to output a 256k file that maintains the dominant colors used in the animation, and, if properly designed, little image degradation will be seen. If your animation uses only a few color ranges, you may not see any difference at all. If you created a spaceship animation that contained mostly blue hues, then the palette will contain mostly blues. If your animation has a rainbow of colors in it, then you may not see any quality improvement when the image is dithered down, since the palette still would try to represent the colors in the image.

RAM is one of the most important factors in quality playback. If your animation can load entirely into RAM, the playback will be much smoother. This is pretty straightforward to figure out. If the animation takes 5mb, the program running it uses 2mb and your system uses 2mb, you will need 9mb to run the animation completely in RAM. This is not always possible, especially if the disk is being distributed to unknown parties. If your computer is running an animation and it makes a disk access before that segment could be loaded into RAM, you can count on it skipping frames. To take advantage of the RAM you do have, make sure the program that is being used to display the animation has the maximum amount of RAM allocated. To do this, select the application and choose File/Get Info in the Finder. Allocate all your system's spare RAM to the program and make sure that it is the only one running.

If you create a Director Projector file to display your animation this file acts like a program; allocate it the needed RAM. In a perfect world you should allocate enough RAM to run the projector and the single largest animation file in the projector package.

If you plan on continuous animation display, hard disk speed comes into play. In cases where accelerated compression/decompression boards are capable of pumping out images fast enough for full-screen display, a hard drive capable of keeping up with the pace may also be needed. Usually this requires a disk array that is actually two hard drives working in tandem to alternately pour out the data as needed. When creating a kiosk or a training animation with continuous real-time video footage, you may want to consider a disk array solution to assure smooth playback.

You also may want to experiment with different compression settings to see if you can improve your output, but in most cases using the Animation compressor in the QuickTime Compression Settings dialog box will give you the best results.

Outputting animation files on the computer screen is a trade-off. Small screens play animations smoother. Higher screen resolution, 16- or 32-bit, looks great, but will choke on a larger screen. Without hardware assistance, you pay the price for these premium features until more powerful Macs make tiny animation windows history.

CD-ROM OUTPUT

Special considerations need to be made if you are outputting for CD-ROM playback, they include:

- Small windows, usually 320x240 pixels or 240x180 pixels.
- Use Cinepak compression.
- Data rate 200k/sec for double speed drives, 90/k for single speed.
- Quality setting medium.
- Frame rate 15 FPS for larger windows and 24 FPS for smaller windows.

PREPARING OUTPUT FOR DIGITAL DISPLAY

With unassisted digital display, it is quality vs. quantity. The factors that play off each other are image quality, image size and frame playback rate. Large window sizes necessitate slower frame rates and lower image quality. For smooth, good-looking images, you must make a smaller window. The Compression Settings dialog box (below) shows the standard QuickTime options available.

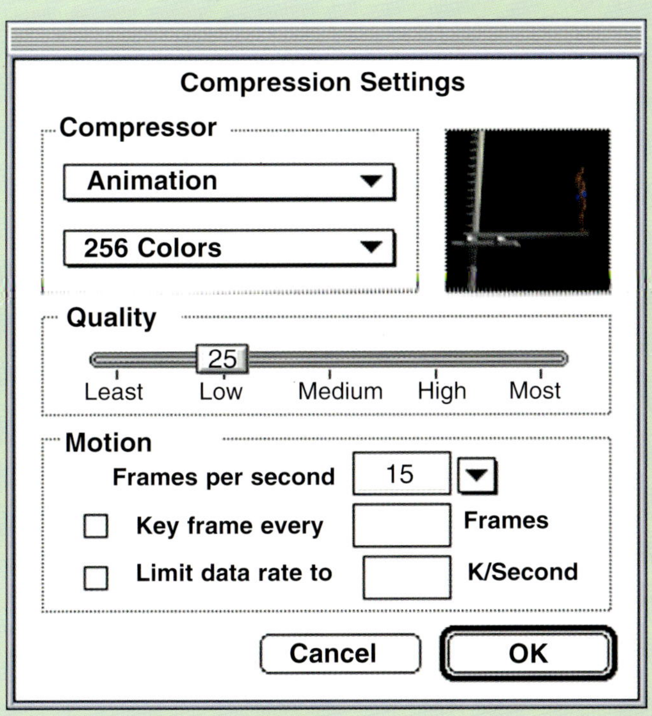

LOW-END MACINTOSH PLAYBACK

Lower-end Macs with 68020 and 68030 processors may only be able to handle a 240x180 window with medium-quality images played back in 256 colors at 15 frames a second.

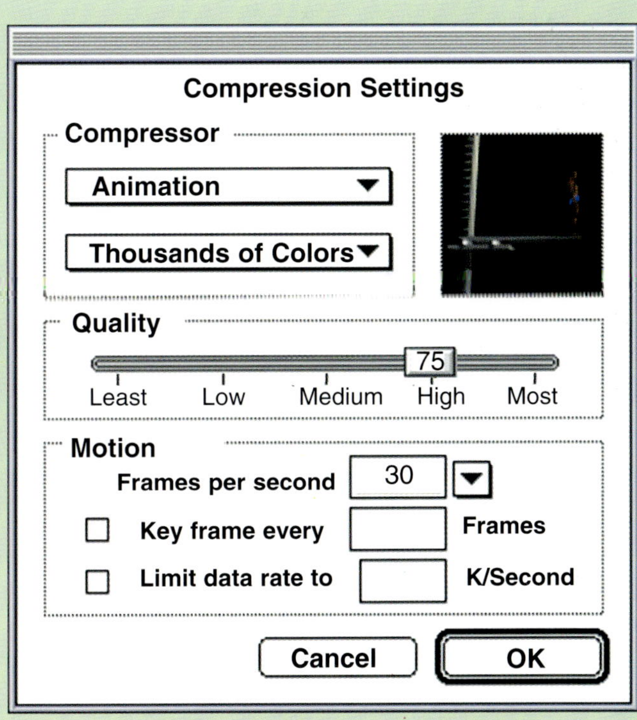

HIGH-END MACINTOSH PLAYBACK

PowerPC and Quadra Macs can handle a 320x240 window in thousands of colors with medium-high quality at 24 frames per second.

VIDEO ANALOG ANIMATION OUTPUT

To many animators a computer is simply the means to justify the end. The artist needs an animation for a project and the computer helps her produce it. Staying in the computer world is not paramount or even desired. The end product is the bottom line and that bottom line often means video.

The problem is that the computer world and the video world have very little in common. They both may be capable of displaying images, but there the similarity ends. One major difference is the video signal each produces. Another difference is that the computer has a much harder time keeping up with the amount of information smooth video playback requires. A couple of hardware solutions exist to help bridge that gap.

VIDEO CONVERSION

To get your computer to output a signal that is compatible for video, either purchase a computer with a built-in video output board, buy an output board or attach an encoder to your computer's monitor output that converts the scan rate. The reason for doing this is that the scan rates of your computer output is incompatible with the video world. To start with, computer displays are *non-interlaced*. This means every line is refreshed sequentially, from top to bottom. Video signals are *interlaced*, where all the odd lines are drawn, top to bottom, and then the even lines are drawn, top to bottom.

This interlacing difference not only affects compatibility, but also the appearance of your image on the video screen. A single pixel-wide horizontal line may look like a sharp hairline on your computer monitor, but on a video display it flickers because of the interlaced screen refresh. The image of that line is refreshed only every other pass, causing the flicker. The flicker problem occurs in grainy textures and backgrounds that have small, pixel-size contrasting elements and it can be very annoying. Solutions include applying a blur filter effect to the problematic line or buying hardware that vendors tout produces flicker-free images. The hardware sellers will tell you that they use some proprietary image-convolution technology to achieve this, but the result is a slight blur to help remove the flicker.

You should design horizontal elements with odd-numbered (other than one) pixel widths. If you normally place an 8-point box around an area, use a 7- or 9-point box instead. This keeps the top and bottom lines from disappearing and skipping scan passes at the same time–which reduces flicker.

There are three main contenders for quality video output. More expensive, but the best of the lot, is the Video Explorer lineup. NuVista Plus and VideoVision rank next as a close tie. VideoVision also inputs video and sound and has an upgrade path to its Studio and Telecast models which offer real-time playback.

REAL-TIME RECORDING

Two dominant methods are used to get your animations recorded to video tape. The first is real-time recording where a hardware compression/decompression (CODEC) board force-feeds your digital data into the video realm. These boards are required because your unassisted computer cannot possibly maintain the data flow rate to display 30 frames (or 60 fields) of full-screen video. Using accelerated, dedicated boards, a high-end Mac (Quadra or PowerPC) can keep up with the demand–just barely.

Add-on systems such as VideoVision Studio and Telecast, Media 100 and Media Composer rely on hardware to both convert your images to an acceptable scan rate and handle the compression/decompression.

The biggest drawback to real-time recording is the need for image compression. To get your image to play back in 24-bit color, full size at 30 FPS, some compression is needed. While the VideoVision Studio output suffers the most in this concern, other systems such as Media 100 and Media

VIDEO VS. COMPUTER IMAGE DISPLAY

Two factors separate video from computer displays. First, video signals are interlaced, writing every other line to the screen. Secondly the scan rates are different. Both of these can be corrected by using a video encoder.

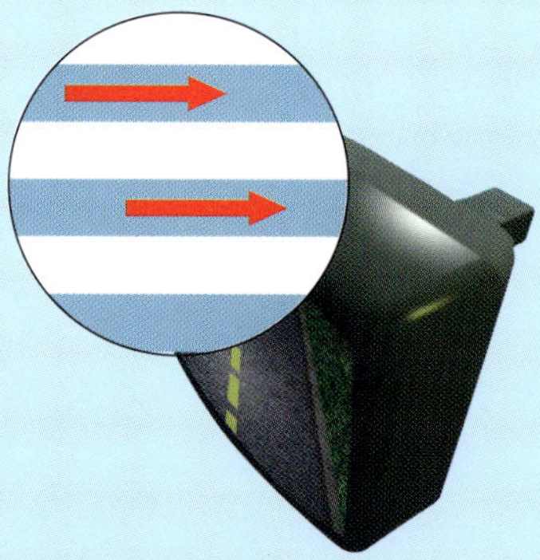

Interlaced display

The odd lines are written to the screen, top to bottom, and then the even lines, top to bottom, and then the process is repeated.

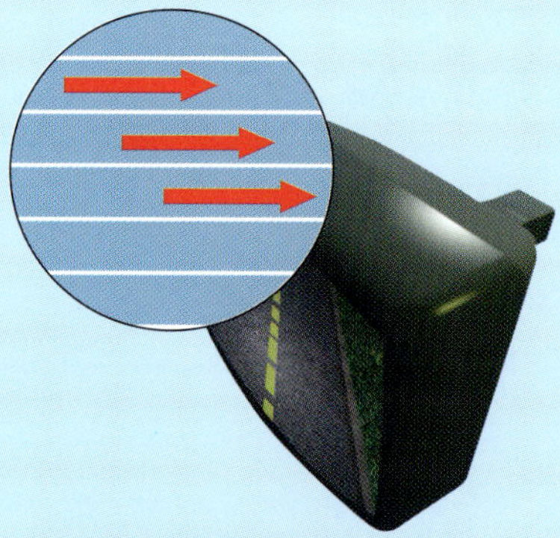

Non-interlaced display

On computer monitors the display is written one line at a time, in order, from top to bottom and then repeated, once for each frame.

FIELD RENDERING

Programs such as Premiere and After Effects support field rendering. This is where an image may have 30 frames, but 60 fields. A field is one of those alternating lines in an interlaced display, so there are two fields present on the screen at any time. With field rendering, each field can have a slightly different image, enabling smoother playback. With no field rendering the same image is in both the odd and even field at the same time.

Composer offer much better output–at a much steeper price.

Since compression takes place as the final step before playback (editing or render output) most systems require that you use the hardware compressor to save the final file. This means if you display your edited animation file with a VideoVision Studio, you need to use VideoVision's CODEC which appears inside the QuickTime options box. You cannot create the QuickTime file on a machine without the CODEC and send it for playback on a different computer for playback. Media 100 and Media Composer promise real-time CODEC conversion which will convert a software CODEC to their hardware CODEC for real-time playback.

Keep in mind that real-time playback capability is a relatively new accomplishment and new hardware and software compression techniques being developed will aid consumer-level output dramatically.

When the animation file is played, the boards output the video signal through standard video connections. Look for an S-video connection for the highest quality signal; use a composite connection as an also-ran, use-it-if-you-have-to option. Higher-end systems like VideoExplorer offer modules that can output RGB to professional recording decks.

FRAME RECORDING

The second solution for recording animation to tape is frame recording. Since computers cannot keep up with the massive amount of data video puts forth–this approach makes the video wait for the computer.

Frame recording records a single frame of an animation at a time, one-by-one. Since the computer is not being asked to spew forth images, you do not need a high-end Mac to handle frame recording. You will need a professional-quality frame-accurate tape deck, a device controller board and a video output source. The frame-accurate tape deck is needed because your computer is going to be telling the tape deck which frame to record, one at a time. This means an investment in a high-quality tape deck, but not necessarily an expensive one.

For industrial quality recordings you can use a Hi8 deck such as the Sony EVO-9850. This machine also contains a built-in controller so all you have to do is purchase a

SETUP FOR REALTIME AND FRAME RECORDING

In a perfect world, you would be able to play your animation at full size, best quality, full speed, and 24-bit color on your Macintosh and hit the record button on your VCR to capture the output. But this is a less-than-perfect world. Even the highest-end Mac chokes on displaying these files. To record your animations, you will need some help.

Real-time recording animations

Hardware compression boards can output the images at a much faster pace than your computer can handle them. This system uses dedicated processors that do nothing but accelerate image compression and decompression. In many configurations (like the one below), the boards process the images in tandem.

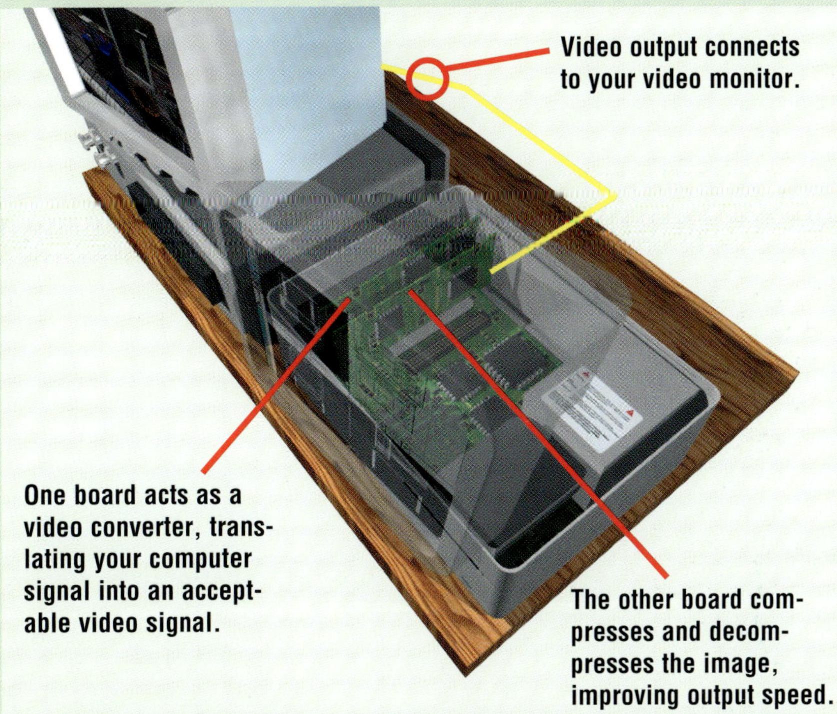

Frame recording animations

The computer uses two separate boards, one to control the tape deck and one to convert the signal. The device control board follows software commands to lay the animation down one frame at a time.

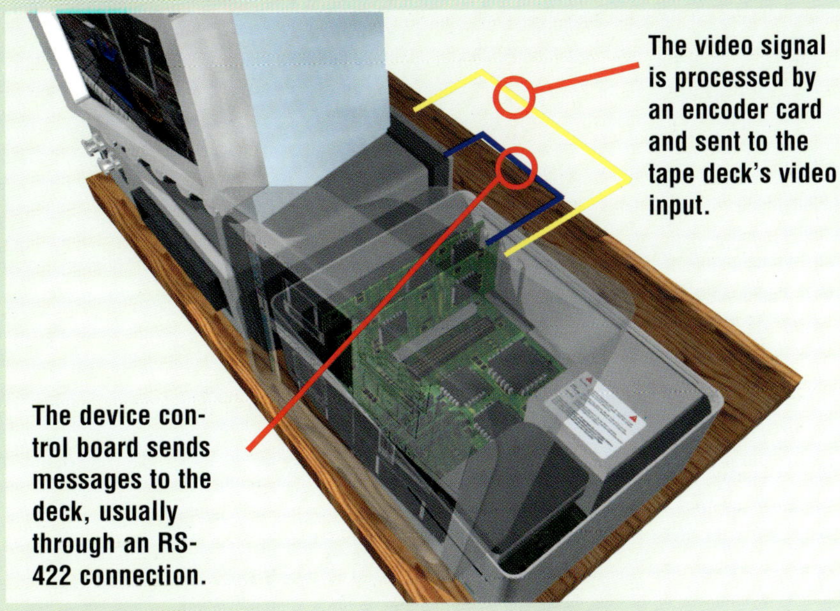

software controller such as the DiaQuest Animaq. Beta decks are the high-end route. Costs have come down recently, so a beta deck can be purchased for less than $10,000. The key is to look for serial ports that match your hardware device control output, such as RS-232 or RS-422.

The device controller acts as an intermediary between your computer and your recording deck. The software tells your device controller that it has displayed a new frame, and the device controller tells the tape deck which frame of the tape to record. Popular device controllers include models from Diaquest, Advanced Digital Imaging, BDC Associates, McQ Productions, V.A.S. Group and Videomedia. Hardware and software support is always changing, so if you already have a recording deck, make sure the device driver you are interested in supports it. Some device drivers include software drivers for programs such as Director and Premiere.

Multiple-pass software is available to help keep down on the wear and tear on the recording deck. This software also speeds up the process of frame recording. Programs like QuickPass by Diaquest record sequential but spaced frames, say frames 1, 15, 30, 45 and 60 in one pass, leaving gaps on the tape between the frames. On the next pass frames 2, 16, 31, 46, 61 are recorded.

Frame recording allows perfect-quality, perfect-speed playback and is still considered the mainstay of most animation companies. As real-time quality increases, frame recording will most likely take a back seat. But if you require picture-perfect frames with no loss to compression as well as perfect playback with absolutely no skips or jerks, frame recording is a very reliable option.

No matter which device control or deck chosen, you still need to convert the computer image into a video image. This requires a video board such as the NuVista Plus or VideoVision. You can use an AV Mac's built-in video output, but in most circles this output is considered industrial quality.

Service Bureau Output

If you want to record your QuickTime or Director file to tape, but you do not have the budget to buy all the equipment, you might want to send your work to a post-production house. Look in your yellow pages for "Video Production Services" or "Video Tape Duplicating and Transfer Services." Ask the service bureau if they have the equipment for putting Macintosh files down to tape. VideoTroupe in New Hampshire offers professional quality output with quick turnaround. You will spend a few hundred dollars an hour, but if you do not need constant access to video equipment, it might be worth it. This also brings up the possibility of saving your file to an 8mm Exabyte tape drive using Elastic Reality's Abekas driver, and giving the digital tape file to a bureau that has the proper equipment to output the file to video. Since the output is digital, and it can be recorded to D1 digital tape, the result is the best possible video output. It also may cost an arm and a leg.

VIDEO OUTPUT OPTIONS

The variables may be seemingly endless, but some possible output solutions are shown (below) that can be followed to get your animations recorded to videotape.

SOURCE	CONTROL/COMPRESSION	OUTPUT
Director movie with imported PICS. Score is scripted with commands included with the Diaqest Xobjects and shared cast files that ship with Director.	DiaQuest control board receives commands from the scripts and controls a Beta SP deck, recording real-time transitions and frame recording as needed.	Video signal sent out from the Macintosh is encoded via a NuVista Plus board and routed to the S-Video input of the Beta SP deck that records the image.
QuickTime movie is exported and imported into After Effects. The resulting movie is saved using VideoVision Studio hardware CODEC.	The movie is compressed using a medium-high quality setting and is played back using Radius' Video playback software included with VideoVision.	The resulting playback can be viewed via the hardware's composite video breakout box connection. This signal is routed to a consumer VCR and recorded.
QuickTime movie is imported into Premiere. The resulting movie is saved using the None software compressor with the highest setting for lossless images.	The movie is opened using DQAnimaq with QuickPass. The software controls multiple pass frame recorded playback to a frame-accurate recording deck.	The video signal is routed from the Mac via a Video Explorer encoder card, and into the recording decks input.
QuickTime movie is imported into Premiere. The resulting file is saved in digital format to Xbyte tape using Elastic Reality's Abekas Driver.	The tape is then delivered to a local post-production shop with the proper hardware or is sent to a video output service bureau.	The video is mastered to a high-end tape deck. The final master can be the end product or edited together with the rest of a production.

STANDARD WINDOW SIZES

Window sizes, whether for analog or digital output, usually are based around a 4:3 ratio. That means that if the window size is 400 points wide, it will be 300 points tall. The guidelines shown below are printed sideways so the window sizes could be shown at full size. A computer screen is drawn in pixels (72 pixels equal one inch). This results in a standard screen size of approximately 8.89" wide by 6.67" deep.

SCREEN SIZES FOR VIDEO AND DIGITAL OUTPUT

Although setting screen sizes for animations is a very fluid process–usually involving typing in numbers for width and height–there are standards for some formats. Video requires specific sizes to conform to broadcast standards, and the graphic and title safe zones must be considered. Digital output is more free-form, relying on the power of the machine that displays the animation as well as other variables such as RAM, video speed and image quality.

640 x 480

This is the NTSC video standard. Although the entire area will not be visible, it is important to consider the entire screen. If a white area is left in the non-viewable area in an animation with a dark background, a slight halo may be visible. Extending your background to fill up the area will solve the problem.

595 x 395

This is the graphic safe area, indicating the viewable area of a video screen. Professional level monitors will allow you to underscan, or allow you to see the full viewable screen. Your final product, however, should be contained in this smaller area.

550 x 395

This is the title safe area. Although titles that extend beyond this line but do not quite reach the graphic safe line will be visible, the final product will be more professional if you keep text within this range.

320 x 240

This is a standard QuickTime window size for digital display. At 50% of a full screen size, the images are large enough to be useful for displaying information, but not so big it chokes the computer when playing back.

240 x 180

This would be considered the standard small QuickTime window, often seen in encyclopedias and informational CDs.

ADJUSTING QUICKTIME OUTPUT

Whether your final output is digital or analog, it is likely you will be dealing with QuickTime somewhere in the process.

QuickTime, a system extension, allows you to move animation files painlessly between your rendering software and your editing program. When used this way, you should maintain the highest quality by setting the None Compressor option set to None and sliding the Quality slider to the Most setting.

QuickTime includes a handful of software CODECs, each serving a particular purpose. If you are using a hardware CODEC, you will have the option to select that device in the same Compressor pop-up menu.

You can also adjust the frame rate, which defines the maximum number of frames that can be displayed in a second. Note that this does not mean your computer will necessarily play back this many frames–it will do its best to achieve this rate, if possible.

Among the Animation, Cinepak and None Compressor settings most often chosen by animators, only Cinepak offers the key frame option in the Compression Settings dialog box. The key frame is a frame by which differences in successive frames are determined for higher compression purposes. The number entered into the key frame box should equal one key frame per second, so if your animation has 30 FPS, set the key frame to 30.

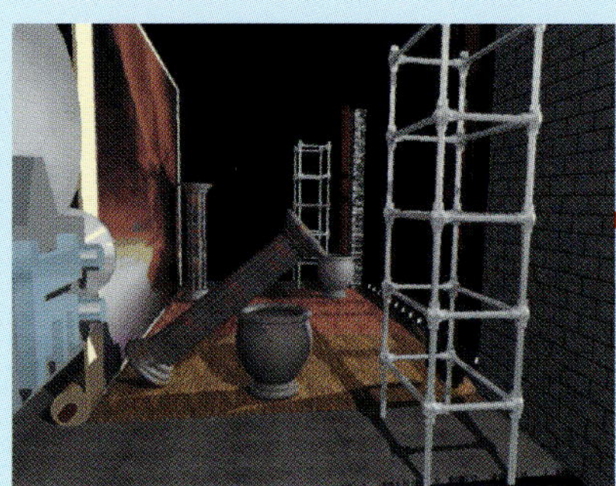

Highest-quality setting/same as original

Medium-quality setting

Low-quality setting

COMPRESSION SETTINGS

The series of images (left) show the different compression settings using the Cinepak compressor. While taking longer to compress, it is better suited for CD-ROM playback.

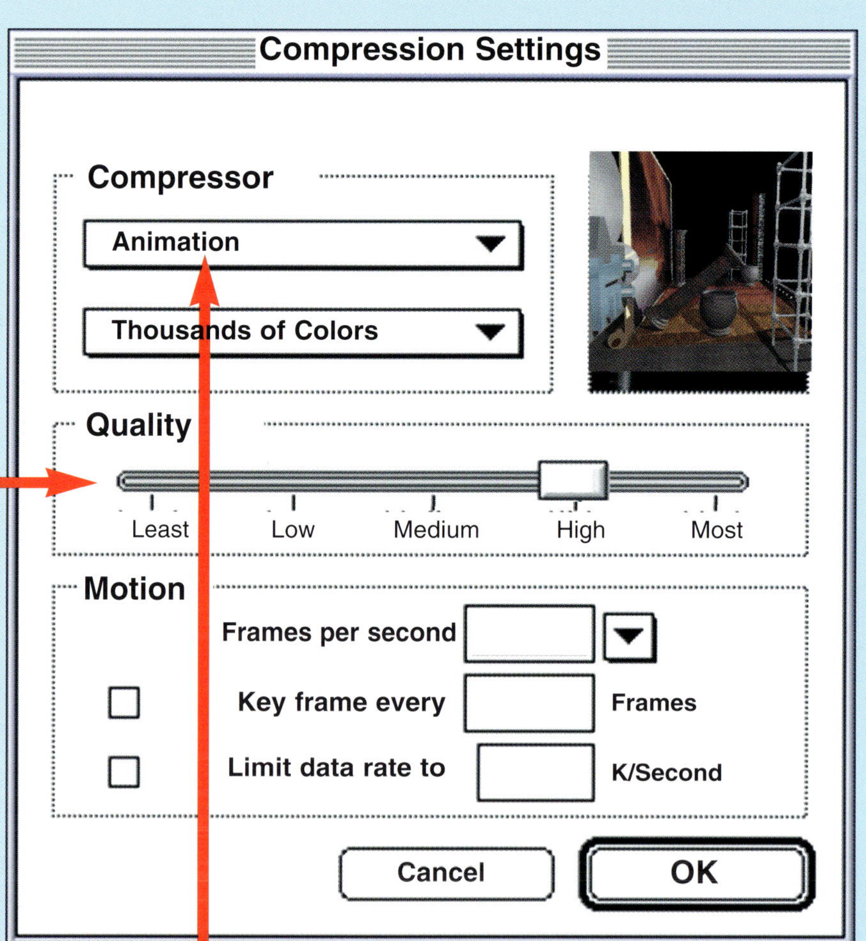

Six compressors ship with QuickTime and can be found in the Compressor pop-up menu. **Animation:** best general-use compressor for projects that are all digital in nature, such as animations. **Cinepak:** higher compression ratios make this desirable for CD-ROM playback. **Graphics:** designed for good 8-bit image playback but low compression. **None:** no compression applied, use when rendering file is to go into an editing program. **Photo:** uses JPEG compression standard for still images; great compression, but too slow for real-time playback. **Video:** the second choice for animation compression; good quality for hard disk playback but slow from a CD-ROM. If you are using a hardware CODEC, such as VideoVision Studio, the compressor for the device would also appear in this pop up menu and would be the selection of choice.

APPLYING SOUND TO ANIMATIONS

The addition of sound to an animation adds the final polish to a project. A sensory transformation occurs when you take an animation and give it a simple music sound track. How you add sound to your animation depends on whether you go the digital or analog route with the project.

At the moment, VIDI's PresenterPro is the only modeling software package that supports attaching audio clips to your models. All other programs require post-production sound editing.

To add sound to a digital file, you must have a digitized sound track. Sound can be digitized by using the microphone built in to most Macs, adding sound digitizing hardware or finding a pre-digitized audio source.

Pre-digitized sounds abound in the Mac world. Local and national bulletin boards have available an extensive collection of sound files. Commercially-produced CD-ROMs are also available from most catalog software retailers like Mac Warehouse, MacPlace and Educorp. The sound files from these sources range from Saturday morning cartoon "Boing!" and "Bong!" to classical music scores.

Digitizing your own audio is necessary if you are narrating your animation. To do this, use a sound editing software like SoundEdit. If you are working in Director, the program has built-in sound-handling options available as a menu selection.

EDITING SOUNDS

Seldom will a pre-existing soundtrack suit your needs completely and rarely will a digitized narration be flawless. This is where editing comes in. While several quality sound products are available for the Mac, SoundEdit by Macromedia is probably the best overall package. The SoundEdit 16 package ships with a CD-ROM filled with sounds and music and is well worth the price for the CD alone.

With SoundEdit you can clean up background hiss and quickly add unusual effects like Echo just as painlessly as you would apply a filter in Photoshop. To do this, select the area you want to affect and choose an effect from the Filter menu. Noise, Envelope, Fade-in and Fade-out filters make editing sounds a snap.

The interface is easy to use and the cut-and-paste metaphor you have grown used to on a Mac can be applied to the sound wave diagram. The software works with your Mac's built-in microphone or a version of Sound-Edit can be purchased with digitizing hardware.

With SoundEdit you can record narration on one track, bring in a digitized music score on another and mix the two together. It is a simple matter to select a portion of the music track and bring the audio level down during the narration and then ramp the volume up once the voice-over is complete.

The sound file can be saved as SoundEdit, QuickTime and SND (a standard sound format) files and imported into programs such as Premiere, After Effects and Director.

Bringing sound into analog animations on videotape is both simple and complicated. It is simple, because almost any sound you can play from a stereo can be patched into a quality consumer video cassette deck or a professional video-editing system. On the other hand, to get the same control over sound mixing that you can get in the digital world takes a lot of specialized audio equipment. Since you can do it on your Mac, you can use a program like SoundEdit to prepare the soundtrack and play it back on the Mac. Some Macs offer better sound output than others, and if you have invested in a VideoVision board, you can take advantage of the break-out box which has sound output connections.

USING SOUNDEDIT TO TWEAK YOUR SOUNDTRACK

SoundEdit is an easy-to-use program that can painlessly take narrations made using the Mac's built-in microphone and mix them with music sound tracks.

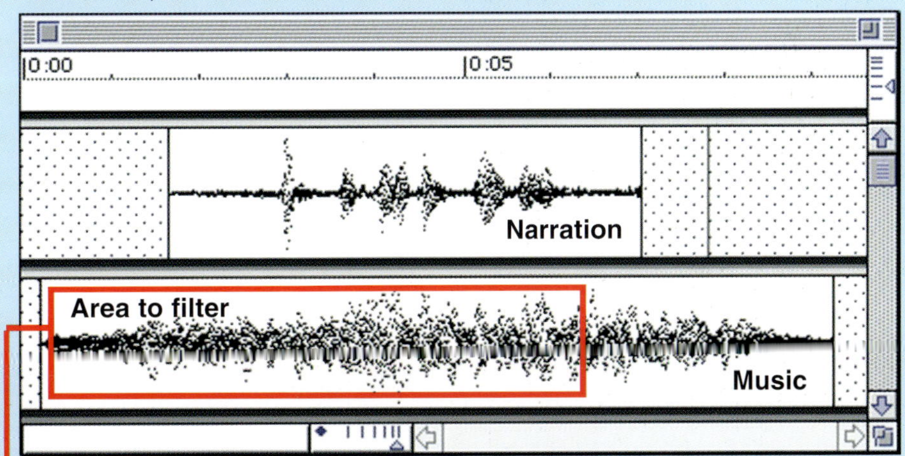

Using cut-and-paste manipulation, the user can easily edit the soundwave. Sound track A can be positioned by dragging the soundwave with a mouse.

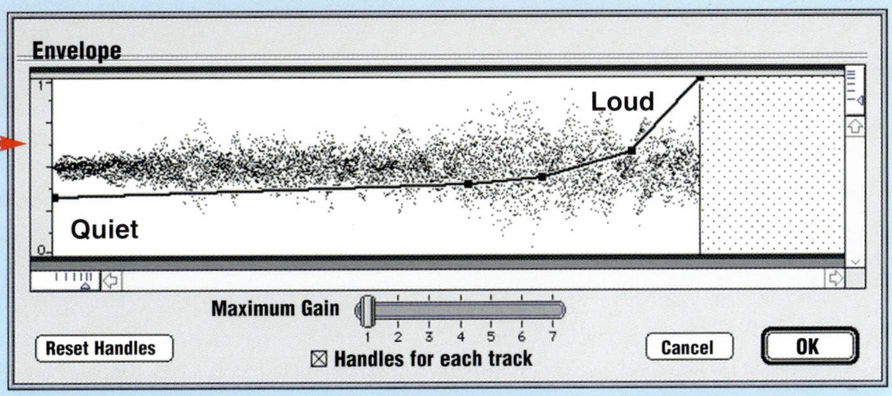

The Envelope filter allows the user to adjust the volume of a selected portion of a soundwave–in this case making the first part quiet and then ramping up the volume.

PREPARING IMAGES FOR PRINT

Even if your work is destined for low-resolution video output, some of your work may be needed at higher resolutions for promotional print reproduction. A way to achieve this is to reproduce a single frame smaller than the original, full screen size to boost the resolution. A 640 x 480 frame at 72 dpi screen resolution can become a 320 x 240 pixels image at 144 dpi. While this might not be high resolution, it gives a good representation of your work. At this resolution you can see the pixels will be observable. If you reduced the image to 160 x 120 pixels, the image becomes 288 dpi, leaving you a small but well defined image.

By comparison, most the images in this book are 300 dpi. Magazine quality is usually 220 dpi and images for newsprint are often reproduced at 160 dpi.

Yet, postage-sized images seldom are satisfactory and the only way to get larger, high quality images is to re-render them at the desired resolution. This adjustment is usually set in the render setup options box. Printed graphics are less forgiving than video images, so use the highest possible anti-aliasing setting you can handle. Images with high anti-aliasing are much crisper and more realistic than ones created with lower settings.

If you are reproducing for print a model done in a video animation, you may want to consider changing the lighting of the scene. Video graphics are illuminated by a TV screen and look dark in the print world. To change the lighting before you re-render the image, increase the magnitude of the lights in the scene. If you are running a frame that you have already rendered, you can adjust the image in Photoshop by tweaking the "Curves" function.

If your original model cannot be re-rendered and you need it larger than the resolution will allow, resize the image in Photoshop and manually clean up the results. Photoshop does an admirable job of interpolating pixels when they are enlarged, but the resulting image may be fuzzy. Selectively using the Sharpen filter and redrawing some edges may clean up the image adequately.

Images for video are normally RGB (Red, Green, Blue) files that will need to be converted to CMYK (Cyan, Magenta, Yellow and Black) for printing. You will notice when you change the images mode from RGB to CMYK that the image seems to flatten out. Many of the colors in RGB cannot be translated to CMYK, but do not be too concerned. After dot gain and ink saturation, much of the life will re-turn to the image.

Images destined for output on Postscript imagesetters should be converted to CMYK and saved as EPS files. If you want to float your 3D object image against a background in a page layout, create a path that silhouettes your image in Photoshop and save the path. In the EPS Options dialog box you will see a pop-up menu to choose a clipping path. Choose the path name that you created earlier. This will cleanly outline the image so that when output on a PostScript imagesetter only the portion within the path prints.

USING ANIMATION FILES FOR PRINT PURPOSES

To get a high-quality, 288 dpi print image, a video frame or a full-sized 13" computer monitor image needs to be reduced by 25 percent. Although the image is small, the quality is good.

This 160x120 pixel, 25 percent reduction creates a 288 dpi image.

The image (above) was reduced by 50 percent, creating a 144 dpi image. While acceptable for presentation purposes, the resolution is not very high. The portion of the image to (left) is from a full sized 72 dpi image.

UNDERSTANDING THE VIDEO SIGNAL

When you purchase video output equipment, you want to make sure that one of the board's features is its ability to synchronize with other equipment. This is usually called Genlock. Genlockable hardware allows your video output board to lock onto the synchronization rate of another device, making sure the scan rate pulses happen at exactly the same time, and assuring the best quality possible. In a professional video studio, the device that your video board locks onto is a black burst generator that emits a signal to define vertical and horizontal pulse rates. All of the other equipment–video cameras and tape decks–also hook up to the black burst generator.

To understand why this is important, it is vital to know a little about how a video image is created in the first place. While most of the following information may be more than most animators need to know, having a basic foundation in the workings of the video world helps clarify subjects such as field rendering and video signal conversion. While different video output products may offer a variety of features, most of them follow the basic principles outlined here.

To display an image onto a TV screen, an electron beam is scanned across a phosphor screen. In order to accurately reproduce an image, the scanning must be done in an organized way. In the television receiver, the scanning is done by the electron beam moving in horizontal lines across the screen. At the same time, the electron beam gradually moves down the screen. When the beam reaches the bottom of the screen, the beam is sent back to the top. A complete picture has 525 horizontal lines and the horizontal lines are scanned alternately.

HORIZONTAL SYNC

For accurate reproduction, the video output card and the television receiver must be synchronized to scan the same part of the screen at the same time. At the end of each horizontal line, the beam must return to the left side of the screen. This is called "horizontal retrace." Coordination of the horizontal retrace is handled by the horizontal sync pulse.

VERTICAL SYNC

At the bottom of the screen, when 262.5 horizontal lines have been scanned, it is time for the beam to return to the top of the screen. The start of the vertical retrace is signalled by the vertical sync pulse which is different in width than the horizontal sync pulses. Since the vertical retrace takes much longer than the horizontal retrace, a longer vertical synchronizing interval is employed.

SYSTEM TIMING

It is important that all video signals arrive at the video switcher in synchronization. This means that the scanning sequence of every source must start and stay in time. Without this, the picture on the television receiver or monitor will roll, jump, tear and/or have incorrect colors when the source video signals are combined. Video frame synchronizers can control timing by delaying one output signal so it can match another signal.

THE VIDEO SIGNAL, LINE FOR LINE

Where a line of a video signal starts and stops is regulated by synchronized pulses in each scan line of video. Understanding how these pulses work will help the animator understand the importance of equipment synchronization.

Look at a single video line in a TV screen. In the example (right) there is a hot spot in the middle of the screen. The change of light for that single line is measured in the electrical voltage. The higher the voltage, the brighter the image.

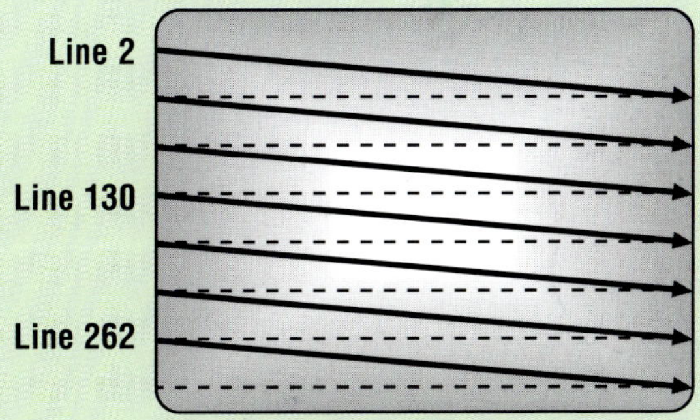

The chart (right) shows the voltage range for line 130 of the screen (above).

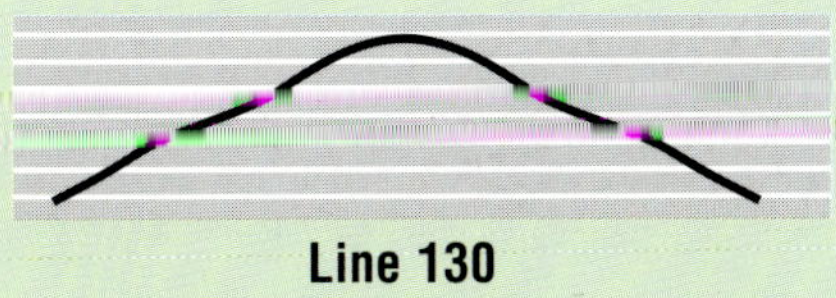

The TV screen knows the line is finished by a horizontal sync pulse which then sends the scanning gun to line 132.

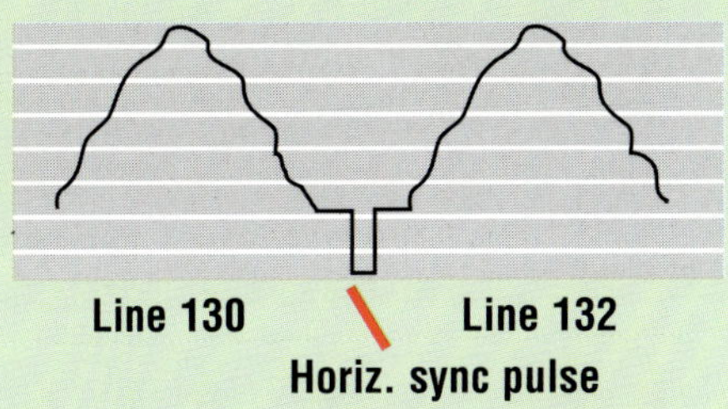

When every line of the screen has been drawn, a vertical sync pulse is sent which kicks the scanning gun back up to the top of the screen again.

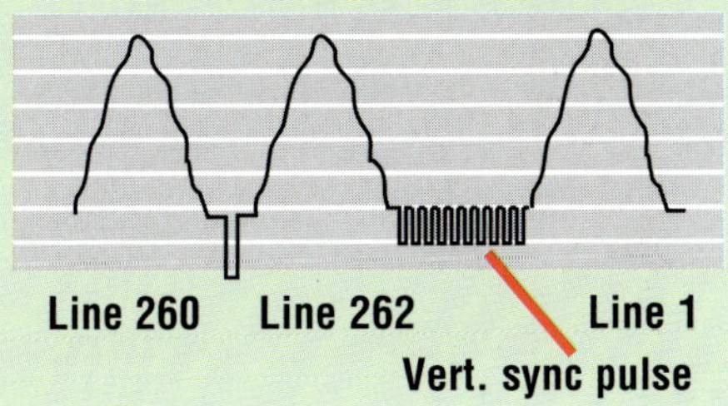

HOW MACS FIT INTO THE BROADCAST ENVIRONMENT

The simplified diagram shows a Macintosh equipped with a video output board wired into a video post-production system scenario.

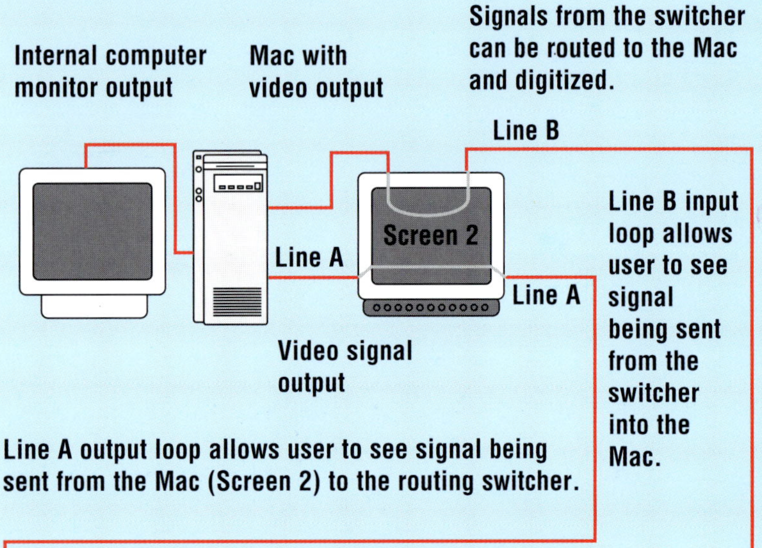

FOLLOWING A SIGNAL

When the final Macintosh image is ready, it is displayed to Screen 2–a video output board that generates a transcoded video signal. The signal is displayed on a monitor as it is sent through a cable to the switching router. At the switching router, the signal can be directed to any number of output devices–tape, monitors or even directly to a satellite. If it is an animation, the output can be placed on tape for playback during a broadcast. If it is a still frame, it can be placed in a still store, where it will be held until it is called up for use in a production.

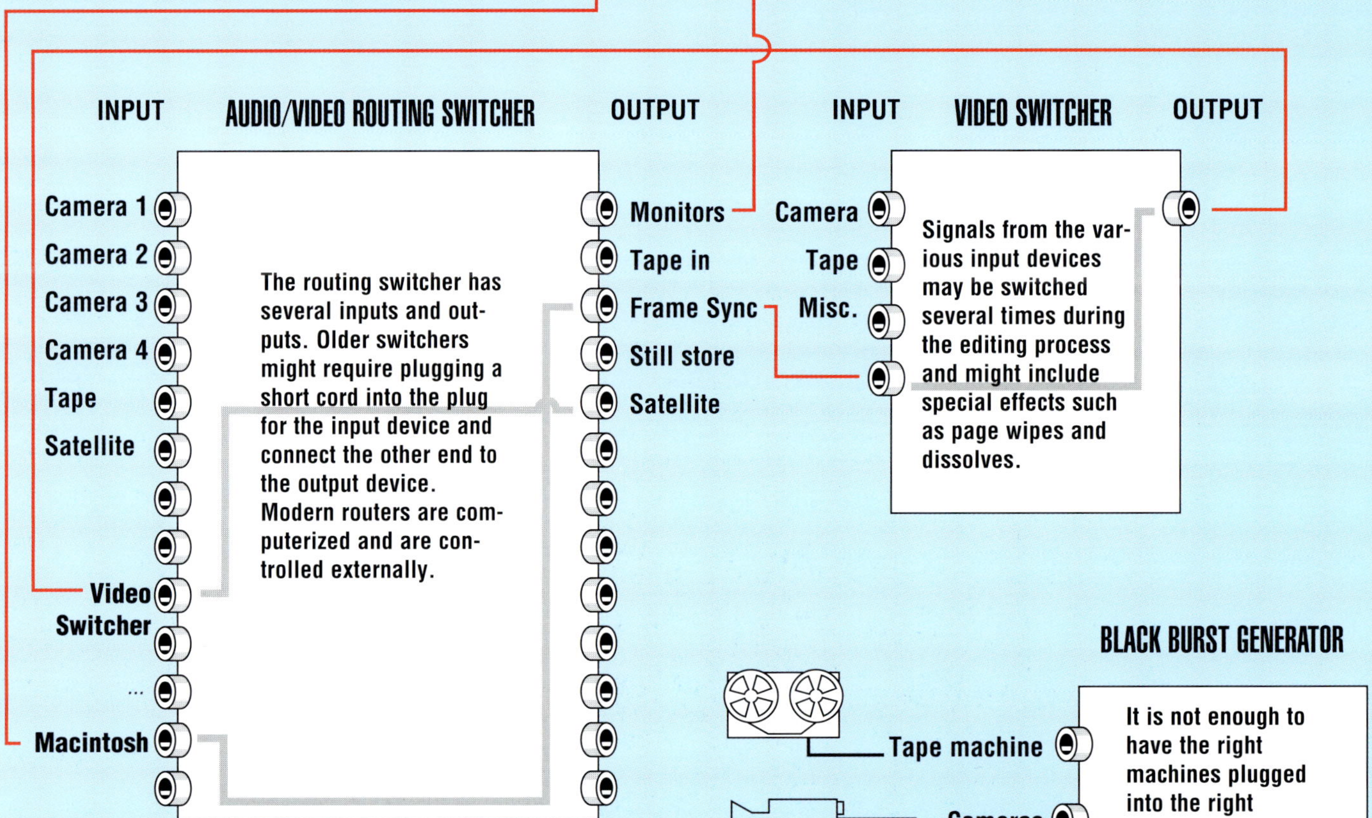

To record animations in a video studio, the output from the Mac could be real-time, taking advantage of hardware acceleration via compression/decompression boards or a video deck controller could be patched into a tape deck that then has the video signal routed to it via the audio/video routing switcher.

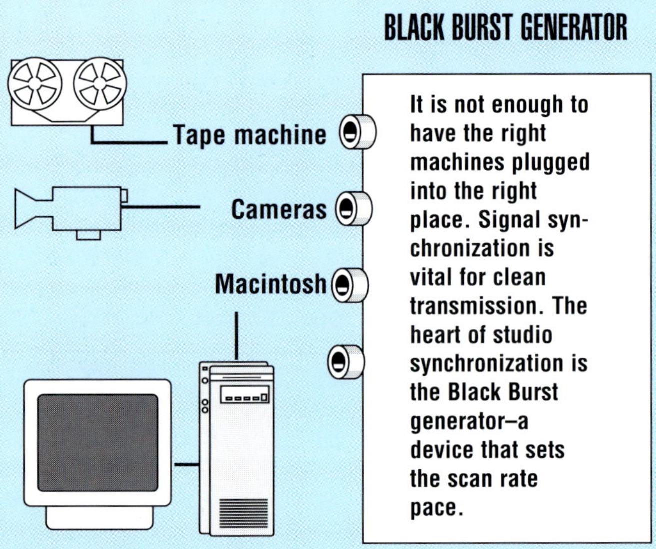

BACK-OF-THE-BOOK STUFF

APPENDIX A: Texture Maps

Detailed texture maps are the key to photo-realistic images. The images on this page can be scanned and used as environment maps in your own models. Scan them as grayscale images at 300 dpi. Resize them to 4 or 5 inches at 72 dpi, then use Photoshop's Despeckle filter to remove any trace of the print halftone pattern.

These images may also serve as guides for making texture maps. The "garbage-in, garbage-out" adage applies directly to texture map resolution. If you are rendering for animations at 72 dpi, make sure your texture map is never larger than the original source file or it will result in a blurry model.

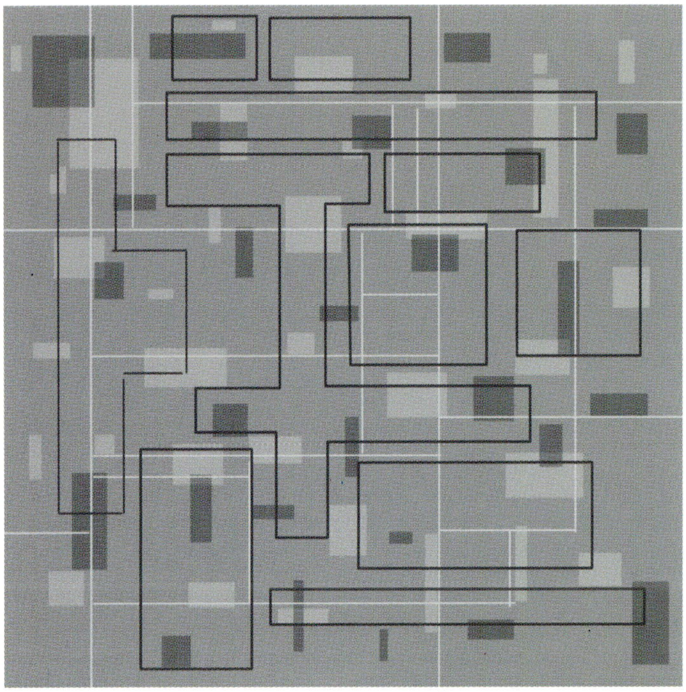

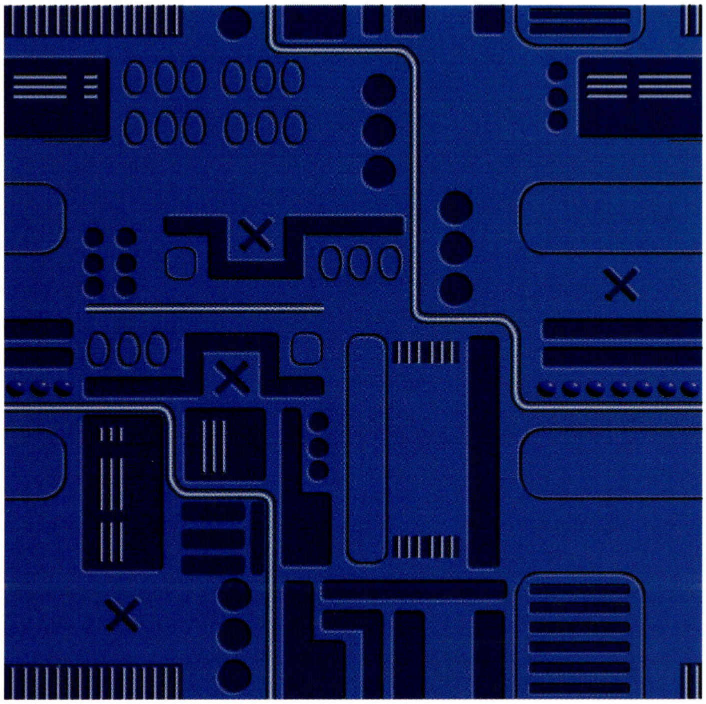

This tiled aircraft texture can be built in a photoediting program by drawing a series of dark and light colored blocks on a gray background and by finishing the texture with dark and light lines and box outlines.

Machine-type textures, such as spacecraft skins and boilerplate maps, are easy to create and can add incredible detail to a model with minimal work. The key is to construct them so patterns that run off on one side continue on the opposite side, making a texture map that tiles.

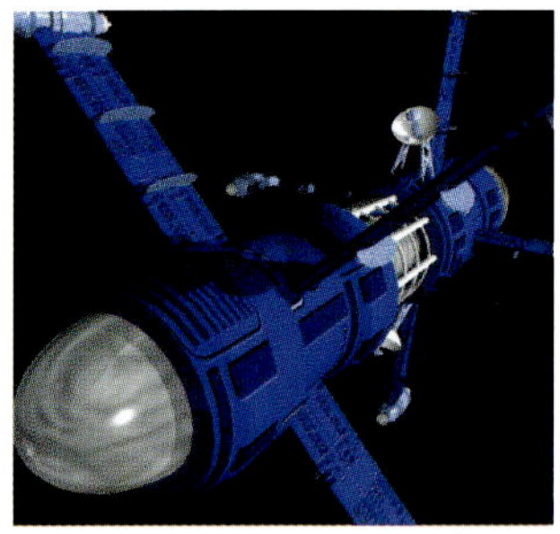

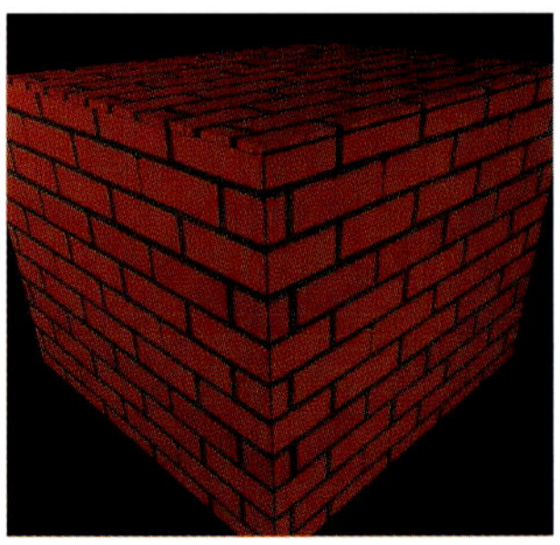

Creating a brick design that tiles exactly is the key to making this pattern work. The eye quickly sees a mistake when a repeated pattern, like a brick wall, does not line up brick for brick.

This world map, made from a mosaic of NASA satellite images, can turn a sphere into a globe using a spherical wrap. To add dimension, convert a copy of the color scanned file to a grayscale image and bump up the contrast. The mountains and the edges of the continents give a feeling of depth.

This texture demonstrates how you can use your 3D modeling program to build your own detailed texture (see page 68). The secret is in using even lighting that keeps hotspots and dark shaded areas from destroying the pattern.

Wood texture maps are one of the most useful image files for animators. Wood textures are difficult to create but easy to obtain. You can take a photo of a sheet of plywood and scan the photo (or have it digitized as a Photo CD) or you can rely on the many texture libraries that are commercially available.

APPENDIX B: Environment Maps

Environment maps–the etheral images that are everywhere, but nowhere–are only seen in reflections. The environment map gives reflective surfaces a feeling that they exist in an environment rather than in the computer world.

The images on this page can be scanned and used as environment maps for models. Scan them as grayscale images at 300 dpi, but resize them to 4 or 5 inches at 72 dpi. Use Photoshop's Despeckle filter and/or blur to remove any trace of the print dot pattern.

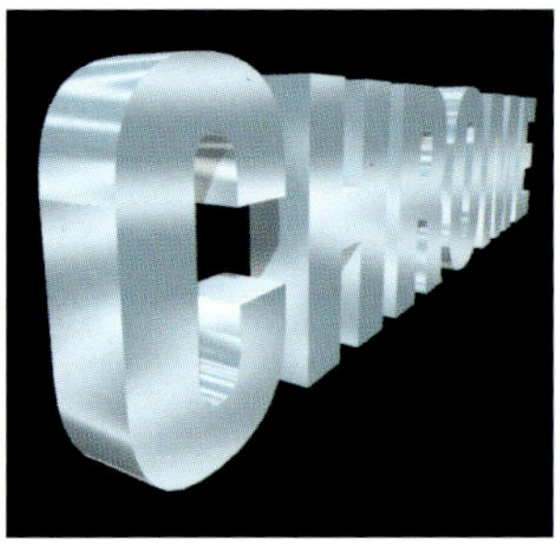

This chrome pattern reflects well on flat and slightly curved surfaces, but may get noisy on round objects such as spheres. This pattern can be made in a paint program by using a white airbrush on a gray background. Using a blur filter helps diffuse the edges.

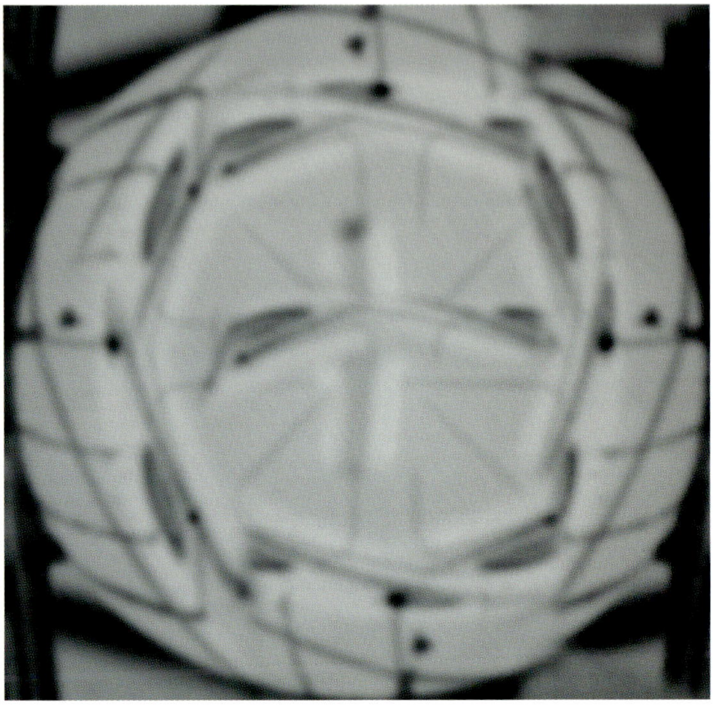

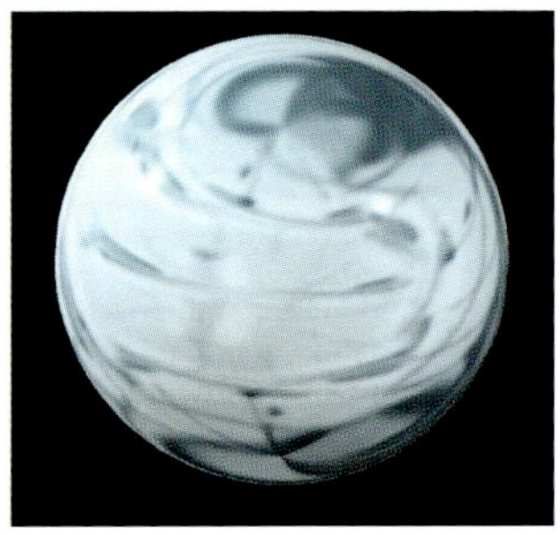

Believe it or not–this image was constructed by scanning a photo of a sailboat deck! To create this pattern, the image was saved as grayscale. Then Photoshop's Spherize filter was applied and the image was mirrored vertically. A good way to make a generic environment map is to take a photo of an empty room and spherize it.

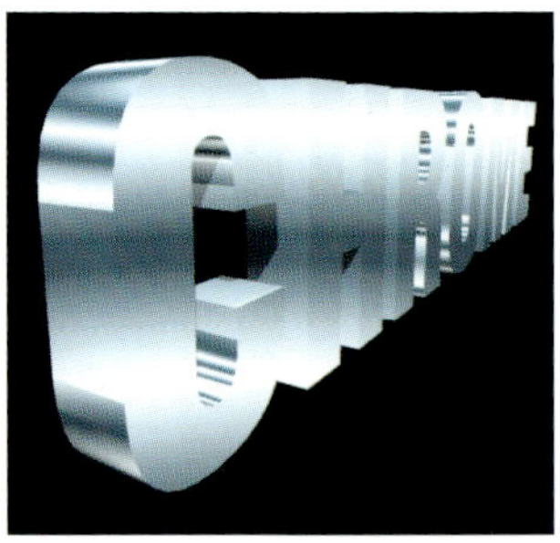

A striped chrome environment map gives a more mechanical, defined chrome-like feel. The higher the contrast between the whites and the blacks, as well as the higher the reflection is (50 to 70%), the more defined and sharp the chrome is. A softer chrome can be achieved by lowering the contrast of the environment map in a photoediting program and reducing the amount of reflection in the surface color.

Entire panoramas can become environment maps which help reinforce your model's setting. You can use the panorama as an unmodified photo or you can create a spherized, fish-eye image in a photoediting program.

A photograph, like this cloud image, makes a great environment map for aircraft scenes where a slight reflection on an airplane's windows gives a distinctive feel that the plane is flying up into the clouds.

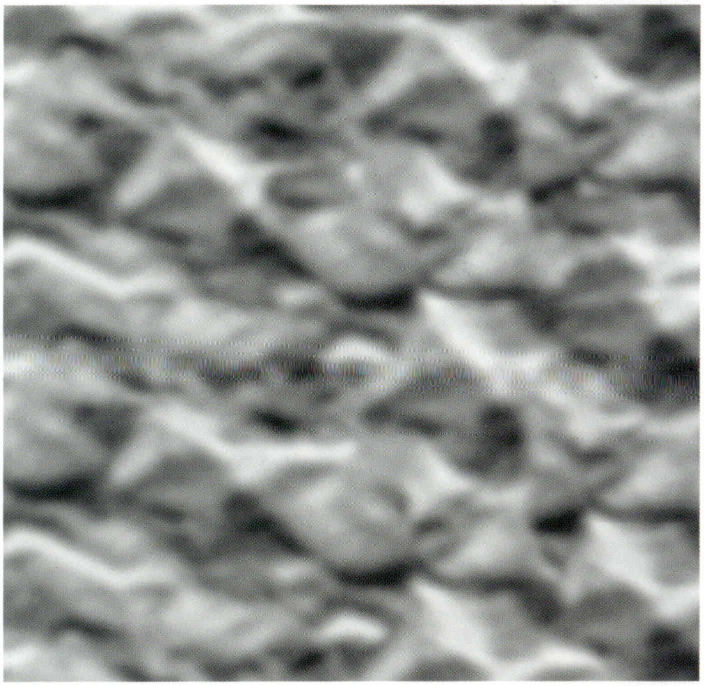

Space scenes benefit from star backgrounds and space environments. One way to create brilliant stars in an image-editing program is to make a white, pointed, four-sided star and then lightly apply Photoshop's Airbrush tool to the center to give it a luminescent glow.

For a good chrome-type environment crinkle up some aluminum foil and scan it, or photograph the foil and have it digitized with a scanner or Photo CD.

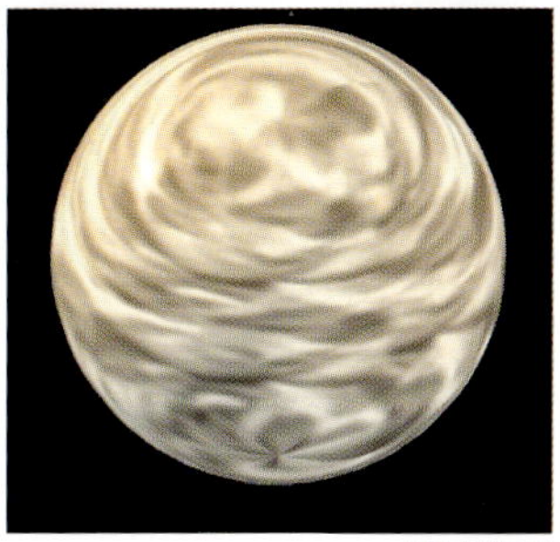

APPENDIX C: Hunting Textures

The world is full of textures and finding them can be a rewarding challenge. Several companies, such as Form and Function, Specular, Pixar and Corel, sell pre-packaged texture collections that make the job easy. Also on the market are products such as Alien Skin, TextureScape and Paint Alchemy that make the creation of textures a snap. The real challenge, however, is finding textures already out there, just waiting to be used. The key to getting them requires an adventurous spirit and a modem.

On-line services offer the first hunting grounds. CompuServe, for instance, stores images in several areas in its Graphics forum, including one just for animators, where many solid resources can be found. America Online has a 3D special interest group (Keyword: 3D sig) consisting of texture files. In some cases, users can even download program-specific procedural maps.

The real thrill comes when you dive into the Internet. Thousands of resources are available from all over the world. But keep in mind the property rights of the images. Many image postings on the Internet include text files that describe how they can be used. Some corporations may frown on you for using their images while other files, like U.S. Geological Survey materials may be in the public domain.

When "surfing the net" you can go through either general searches–using Veronica, Archie or Gopher software for items such as "models" or "textures"–or you can just poke around at different FTP (file transfer protocol) sites. When at a military or educational site, you can usually find file directories called "graphics" or "images." These may provide source files for creating image maps or backgrounds. If you are selling the animations you are creating, be respectful of the rights of the individuals and companies that posted the files.

HAPPY HUNTING IN CYBERSPACE

Looking for image files on the Internet can be done in two ways. The first route is knowing exactly where you want to go. For instance, if you want to go to NASA's Jet Propulsion Laboratory to look around for space-related images, the FTP site would be FTP.JPL.NASA.GOV. Once there, you could browse through their image files. The second method is to search by using programs like Archie, Gopher or Veronica which give you a list of FTP sites that might contain files of interest to you. The images below are the result of a search for space images in two FTP sites.

A quick trip through the NASA's JPL FTP site resulted in the download of these images. These images can serve as image files for backgrounds or as inspirations for model building.

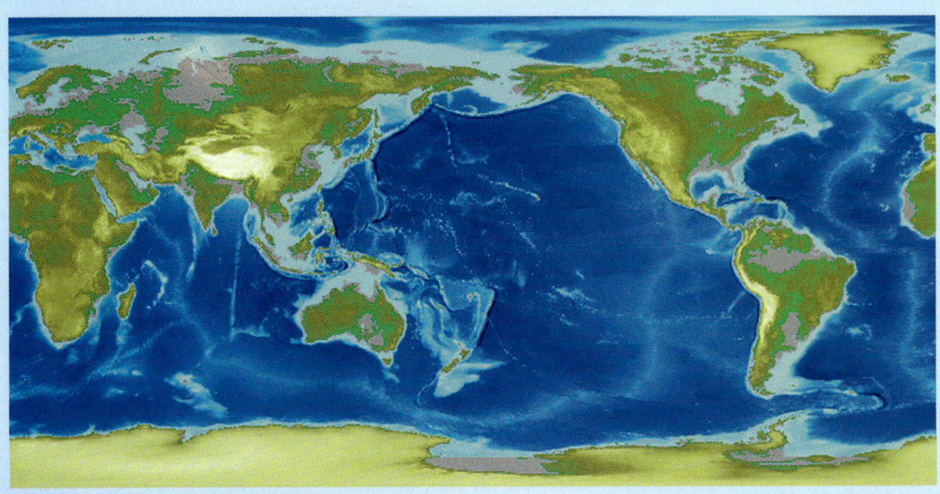

This topographical map of the Earth was created by the U.S. Geological Survey (USGS) and is in the public domain. It is found at the FTP site: WUARCHIVE.WUSTL.EDU
The path to get to the file–like opening folders inside folders on the Macintosh–is: GRAPHICS/GRAPHICS/OBJECTS/EARTH IMAGES/TOPOGRAPHY.

This file could be saved as a PICT file and mapped using a spherical map to a ball, creating an instant globe. The file was small, but would suffice for most animation purposes.

APPENDIX D: Artists

Many thanks to the generous artists listed below for their help. The works of these artists are highlighted on pages 15-28.

Kevin Abbott
kwabbott@aol.com

Peta Allen
2331 Janin Way
Solvang, CA 93463

Bill Baker
9314 South Whitt Drive
Manassas Park, VA 22111

Chris Bernardi
Boise, ID 83706
absynthe@aol.com

Ken Bryan
332 Fifth St. N.E.
Apt. 4
Atlanta, GA 30308

Chuck Carter
801-673-7425
CMCARTER@aol.com

Keith Carter
2416 K Street NW
Suite 606
Washington, DC 20037
(202) 467-6829

Randy A. Cates
President
Computer Animation & Design
PO Box 802
Londonderry, NH 03053
(603) 437-3759

Greg Chambers
3D/sine
7925 W. Washington Blvd.
River Forest, IL
smouthbass@aol.com

John Findley
500 Stanyan St., 105
San Francisco, CA 94117
sweaz@aol.com

Don Foley
dbfoley@aol.com

Joseph Kelter
Bad Cat Design
3006 Aquetong Road
New Hope, PA 18938
Kelter@aol.com
CIS: 76436,3454

Tim Landry
Dream Quest Images
2635 Park Center Drive
Simi Valley, CA 93065
(805) 581-2671
(310) 558-4051
FAX (805) 583-4673

Bryan Leister
Alexandria, VA
BryanL4695@aol.com

Will Morse
421 New Haven Ave., Apt. E
Milford, CT 06460

David Teich
Mind of the Machine
41 Tamara Drive
Roosevelt, NJ 08555
Telephone (609) 448-5000
FAX (609) 443-3228
daveteich@aol.com

A parting note from the authors:

We have tried our best to be accurate and timely, but the winds of the 3D world keep shifting. The software information was accurate as of June 1995. If you would like to make a comment about the current version of this book or suggestions for future revisions, please e-mail us at dbfoley@aol.com.

APPENDIX E: Hardware & Software Companies

The following is an alphabetical listing of software and hardware companies mentioned in this book. The products are grouped by their parent companies. If you are familiar with the product, but not the company, you can cross-reference by using the index.

Acuris
931 Hamilton Ave.
Menlo Park, CA 94025
Telephone: 415-329-1920
FAX: 415-329-1928

Products:
–Adobe Illustrator
–Adobe Photoshop
–Adobe Premiere
–Adobe After Effects
–Dimensions
–FreeHand
Adobe Systems, Inc.
1585 Charleston Road
PO Box 7900
Mountain View, CA 94039-7900
Telephone: 415-961-4400
1-800-447-3577
FAX: 415-961-3769

Product:
–Sketch!
Alias Research Inc.
Attn.: Sketch!
315 N. State St.
Orem, UT 84057
Telephone: 416-362-9181
1-800-447-2542
International telephone number:
801-223-6000
FAX: 801-223-6065

Product:
–SuperCard
Allegiant Technologies, Inc.
6496 Weathers Place
Suite 100
San Diego, CA 92121
Telephone: 619-587-0500
FAX: 619-587-1314
Internet: allegiant@aol.com

Product:
–Abekas Driver
–Elastic Reality
Elastic Reality, Inc.
925 Stewart St.
Madison, WI 53713
Telephone: 608-273-6585
FAX: 608-271-1988

Product:
–form•Z
auto-des-sys
2011 Riverside Drive
Columbus, OH 43221
Telephone: 614-488-8838
FAX: 614-488-0848

Product:
–Avid VideoShop
–Media Composer
–Media SuitePro
Avid Technologies
Tewksbury, MA
Telephone: 508-640-6789
FAX: 508-640-1366

Product:
–Apple Media Kit
–HyperCard
–MacDraw
Claris
5201 Patrick Henry Drive
Santa Clara, CA 95052
Telephone: 408-727-8227
FAX: 408-987-7440

Corel Corporation
PO Box 3595
Salinas, CA 93912-3595
Telephone: 613-728-0826
1-800-77COREL
International telephone number: 613-728-3733
FAX: 408-644-2000

Product:
–Canvas
Deneba Software
7400 S.W. 87th Ave.
Miami, FL 33173
Telephone: 305-596-5644

Diaquest Inc.
1440 San Pablo Ave.
Berkeley, CA 94702
Telephone: 510-526-7167
FAX: 510-526-7073

Product:
–Electric Image Animation System (EIAS)
Electric Image Inc.
117 E. Colorado Blvd.
Suite 300
Pasadena, CA 91105
Telephone: 818-577-1627
FAX: 818-577-2426

Product:
–DeBabelizer
Equilibrium Technologies
475 Gate Five Road
Suite 225
Sausalito, CA 94965
Telephone: 415-332-4343
1-800-524-8651
FAX: 415-332-4433

Product:
–Wraptures and Wrapture Reels
Form and Function
1595 Seventeenth Ave.
San Francisco, CA 94122
Telephone: 415-664-4010
FAX: 415-664-4030

Product:
–Color Studio
–Painter
Fractal Designs Inc.
335 Spreckles Drive
Suite F
Aptos, CA 95003
Telephone: 408-688-8800
FAX: 408-688-8836

Product:
–Morph
Gryphon Software Corporation
7220 Trade St.
San Diego, CA 92121
Telephone: 619-536-8815
FAX: 619-536-8932
AppleLink: GRYPHON
AOL: GryphonSW
Internet: gryphonSW@aol.com

Product:
–Animation Master
Hash Inc.
2800 E. Evergreen Blvd.
Vancouver, WA 98661
Telephone: 360-750-0042
FAX: 360-750-0451

Product:
–Kai's Power Tools
–KPT Bryce
–KPT Vector Effects
H.S.C. Software Inc.
6303 Carpinteria Ave.
Carpinteria, CA 93013
Telephone: 805-566-6200
FAX: 805-566-6385

Product:
–CyberMesh
Knoll Software
PO Box 6887
San Rafael, CA 94903
Telephone: 415-453-2471
FAX: 415-499-9322

Products:
–Director
–Swivel 3D Professional
–MacroMedia 3D
–MacroModel
MacroMedia
600 Townsend St.
Suite 408
San Francisco, CA 94103
Telephone: 415-252-2000
FAX: 415-626-0554

Product:
–Tree Professional
Onyx Computing
10 Avon St.
Cambridge, MA 02138
Telephone: 617-876-3876
FAX: 617-868-8033
Internet: onyxtree@world.std.com
AppleLink: BBX 1991

Products:
–Pixar 128
–Showplace/MacRenderMan
–Typestry 2
Pixar Inc.
1001 W. Cutting Blvd.
Richmond, CA 94804
Telephone: 510-236-4000
1-800-888 9856
FAX: 510-236-0388

Product:
–PixelPaint Pro
Pixel Resources, Inc.
PO Box 921848
Norcross, GA 30092
Telephone: 404-449-4947
1-800-851-1427
AOL: PXLHelp
AppleLink: D0911
FAX: 404-449-3789

Product:
–VideoVision Studio
Radius
215 Moffett Park Drive
Sunnyvale, CA 94089-1374
Telephone: 408-541-6100
FAX: 408-541-6150

Product:
– JAG II
– Ray Dream Designer
Ray Dream, Inc.
1804 N. Shoreline Blvd.
Mountain View, CA 94039
Telephone: 415-960-0768
FAX: 415-960-1198

Products:
–BackBurner
–Infini-D
–Specular Collage
–Replicas
–TextureScape
Specular International
479 West Street
Amhurst, MA 01002
Telephone: 413-253-3100
1-800-433-7732
FAX: 413-253-0540

Products:
–Render Pro
–Vision 3D
–StrataVirtual
–StudioPro
Strata, Inc.
2 West St. George Blvd.
Suite 2100
St. George, UT 84770
Telephone: 801-628-5218
1-800-787-2823
FAX: 801-628-9756

Product:
–NuVista+
TrueVision/Raster Ops
7340 Shadeland Station
Indianapolis, IN 46256-3925
Telephone: 317-577-8788
1-800-SAY-COLOR (729-2656)
FAX: 317-576-7700

Products:
–MetaFlo
–MovieFlo
–PixelPutty
–PixelPutty Solo
The Valis Group
PO Box 831
Tiburon, CA 94920-0831
Telephone: 415-435-5404
FAX: 415-435-9862

Product:
–Viewpoint
Viewpoint DataLabs International
625 South State St.
Orem, UT 84058
Telephone: 801-229-3000
FAX: 801-229-3300

Product:
–Alien Skin
–Virtus VR
–Virtus WalkThrough Pro
Virtus
118 Mackenan Drive
Cary, NC 27511
Telephone: 919-467-9700
FAX: 919-460-4530

Product:
–Presenter Professionals
Visual Information Development, Inc. (VIDI)
136 W. Olive Ave.
Monrovia, CA 91016
Telephone: 818-358-3936
FAX: 818-358-4766

Product:
–Terrazzo
–Paint Alchemy
Xaos Tools Inc.
600 Townsend St.
Suite 270 East
San Francisco, CA 94103
Telephone: 415-487-7000
FAX: 415-558-9886

Products:
–Shade
–YARC Boards
YARC Systems Corp.
975 Business Center Circle
Newbury Park, CA 91320
Telephone: 805-499-9444
FAX: 805-499-4048

Mail Order Catalogs:
MacMall
2645 Maricopa St.
Torrance, CA 90503-5144
Telephone: 1-800-222-2808
FAX: 310-222-5800

Mac'sPlace
100 Financial Drive
Kalispell, MT 59901
Telephone: 406-758-8000
FAX: 406-758-8080

MacWarehouse
PO Box 3013
1720 Oak St.
Lakewood, NJ 08701-3013
Telephone: 1-800-255-6227
FAX: 908-905-9279

Additional companies mentioned, not strictly software/hardware:

America Online
8619 Westwood Center Drive
Vienna, VA 22182-2285
Telephone: 703-448-8700
1-800-827-6364
FAX: 703-883-1509

CompuServe
5000 Arlington Centre Blvd.
Columbus, OH 43220
Telephone: 614-457-8600
1-800-848-8990
FAX: 614-457-0348

VideoTroupe
PO Box 67
Windham, NH 03087
Telephone: 603-893-4554
FAX: 603-893-9717

GLOSSARY

alias: an attribute of computer generated images which causes jagged, stair-stepped edges.

alpha channel: a channel, in addition to the red, green and blue channels, that contains masking and transparency information.

straight alpha channel: incorporates a separate (fourth) channel to handle transparency and masking information.

pre-multiplied alpha channel: changes the value in each of the three (R,G,B) channels without adding a fourth channel.

anti-aliasing: program process required to remove the stair-stepped or jagged edges created when one object ends and another begins. Can be accomplished by blending the image edges together or super-sampling them to get rid of the hard, jagged edge.

averaging: an anti-alias method.

backgrounds: tangible and precise images used to enhance or give meaning to a scene.

bezier curves: graphical tools that allow users to precisely edit paths by adjusting the tangent of an arc, usually by clicking and dragging on handles.

boolean operations: take objects and use the information from one object to add to or subtract from another object, resulting in a single new shape. The subtractive process is not so much a carving out as it is a molding–where one shape defines or redefines another. When joining two objects, the result allows the two shapes to share a seamless texture map.

central processing unit (CPU): the little chip that runs the machine or the main box into which you plug in monitors, keyboard, CD-ROM and so forth.

color depth: can be measured by the amount of information per pixel.

RGB files: Red, Green, Blue–usually used in video.

CMYK files: Cyan, Magenta, Yellow and Black–usually used in print.

CPU: *see* central processing unit

depth setting: *see* recursion

dithering option: allows normally smooth graduated tones to simulate the graduation by using dots for tonal change instead of the banding.

Drawing Exchange Format or File (DXF): image import and export format developed by AutoDesk and used by most modeling programs.

ease-in: accelerates movement slowly or naturally by adding more frames at the beginning of the sequence.

ease-out: decelerates movement slowly or naturally by adding more frames at the end of a sequence.

effects switcher: performs transitional effects–like dissolves–as the video from one deck switches to the other deck.

encapsulated postscript (EPS): image import/export format for saving images created in a drawing program.

event mark or events: changes that take place on the timeline. *See* also key frames.

environments: influence everything which reflects light in your scene so that the objects with some degree of reflectivity will give the feeling that the images are within an environment.

extruded shape: depth given to a 2D form to create a 3D shape.

field render: this process writes a frame for each odd and even layer of a video signal (for example, an image has 30 frames but 60 fields). The result is the smoothest possible animation.

floating-point processors (FPU): computation power that allows artists to create 3D artwork and animations on the computer. (also known as math processors or math chips)

frame: a single image

frame recording: records a single frame of an animation at a time, one by one, to videotape. Allows for perfect quality and speed playback.

frame resolution : number of dots per inch (dpi) used in a single line of the image. Standards for:
NTSC and computer screen resolution–72dpi
newsprint–160dpi
magazines–220dpi
books–300dpi

Gouraud shading: rendering algorithm; fast shading mode that allows smooth rendering and accurate lighting, but usually does not support texture maps or shadows.

graphic safe: for video or TV, the area within the NTSC (640 pixels x 480 pixels) window that incorporates the cropping from all sides (usually a half inch on all sides).

horizontal retrace: at the end of each horizontal line, the beam must return to the left side of the scene. Coordination of the horizontal retrace is handled by the horizontal sync pulse.

images: video images are normally RGB (Red, Green, Blue) files. Print images are usually CMYK (Cyan, Magenta, Yellow and Black) files.

image imports/exports: handled by several formats, including QuickTime, PICT (PICT2), PICS, EPS, and DXF

image map: usually a PICT file applied to a model surface.

in-betweening or tweening: computer calculation of an object's position between two points over a number of frames.

ink effects: influence how texture maps and layers are superimposed on other layers.

interlaced: video signals screen refresh or draw all odd lines, from top to bottom, then the even lines, top to bottom. *See also* non-interlaced.

jaggies: very definite stair-stepped transitions between objects in the 3D world. *See also* alias.

key frames: reference points in the timeline where an event occurs.

linear event mark: an object travels in a direct path between event marks with no spline control.

lingo scripts: Macromedia Director's native scripting code that gives the user interactive control over what a movie is doing.

linking: physically connects one object with another. Links can pivot freely or be constrained. The relationship between objects is commonly referred to as child and parent. The child can move independent of the parent. When a parent moves, all child objects move.

mapping techniques: cubical, cylindrical, spherical, straight, and wrap.

metaballs: merge spherical shapes to create organic objects.

motion path: path which represents an object's actions. Allows for accurate editing and instant feedback on an object's position.

non-interlaced: computer display where every line is refreshed sequentially, from top to bottom.

nonlinear: the smoothness in which an object enters and leaves an event mark. Can be controlled by a spline control.

NuBus cards: internally mounted cards provide self-contained improvement, such as acceleration, or provide a link for external devices, such as video cards.

numbered PICTS: a series of PICT files numbered sequentially.

orthographic mode: three viewing windows showing working area for the top, front and side.

Phong shading: rendering algorithm.

PICS: image import and export format. This is a file format that contains all the PICT frames of an animation. PICS does not allow compression methods like QuickTime, but keeps the quality of the image intact. Most animation programs and utilities support the PICS format.

PICT (PICT2): image import and export format.

pixelation: where the eye can detect individual pixels which make the image.

primitives: elementary shapes that can be used when creating models.

procedural or volumetric maps and surfaces: computer-generated surface and color treatment that rely on mathematical algorithms rather than importing an image from an external file.

QuickTime: image import and export format. Apple's system extension combines video, sound and still image compression into a single package.

ramp: an audio term relating to sound volume.

ramp up: increase in sound.

ramp down: decrease in sound.

Random Access Memory (RAM): loaded into your RAM at any given time is the program you are using, your system program, extensions and control devices and your project data.

ray tracing: rendering algorithm that allows for reflections and transparencies.

real-time recording: relies on hardware compression/decompression boards that send the video signal through the computer fast enough to display 30 full-sized frames a second.

real-time playback: ability to re-play an animation at the normal speed usually requires some type of acceleration for full screen images.

recursion or depth setting:

for reflections: number of times a reflection will bounce back and forth.

for transparencies: it determines how many transparent objects you can look through before clear objects are no longer transparent.

reflection maps: reflection of objects can be controlled to make them slightly reflective or mirror-like.

rendering: computer takes the information the user has given it and converts it into the final image.

RIB format: a MacRenderMan format that can be used to transport files.

SCSI devices: system expansion that allows seven devices to be daisy-chained.

singular viewing plane or single world view: a single plane which allows the user to change quickly from top, bottom, front, side or a variable angle. The user moves around the model (changing views) via menu selection, navigational arrows, mouse manipulation or a virtual trackball. This system's advantage is that it allows the viewer to work with a single, large window.

skinned objects: tool for creating irregular shapes by wrapping a skin over "ribs" to form a solid object. The ribs are usually a series of 2D shapes that have been edited to form an underlying structure.

spline control or curve: allows the motion at peak points to be smooth instead of sharply defined.

super-sampling: involves rendering a file several times larger than the size of the final image. Information from the larger image is used to better define the edges for the smaller, final image.

swept objects: tools for creating irregular shapes by taking the geometry of one shape–circle–and make it follow the geometry of another form–curved line. The result is a linear, but irregular shape.

synchronize: for accurate reproduction, the video output card and the television receiver must be synchronized to scan the same part of the scene at the same time.

three-space: allows a modeler to view, simultaneously, a scene from three distinct viewing planes. This provides useful and immediate feedback on perceiving exactly what is going on from each vantage point.

tiled textures: small swatches of images, usually in PICT format that, when replicated side by side to cover an object, make a single seamless texture.

timeline: reflects the different actions of objects over time.

tweening: *see* in-betweening.

visual retention: information transmitted from your eye to your brain in a manner that accounts for the transitions from one image to the next.

volumetric maps and surfaces: *see* procedural or volumetric maps and surfaces.

window size: video standards for NTSC require sizes that work out to be close to 640 pixels wide by 480 pixels deep. This is also the same size for a 13" computer screen. With the 640x480 window size set, a good portion of the edges of the animation will be chopped off–around 1/2 inch on all sides. Area within the non-chopped region is called graphic safe, and must be planned for while the model and animation are being constructed.

z-axis: gives depth in the 3D world. Allows the object to move closer to you or farther away. Additional rotation possible.

INDEX

Author's Note: Software and products are listed here with a cross reference to the parent company's name. (The companies listed had ownership as of 5/95.)

U

V

W

X

Y

Z

INDEX OF CHARTS